the
total look

Hairdressing and Beauty Industry Authority/Macmillan Series

Hairdressing Training Board/Macmillan Series
Series Standing Order ISBN 0–333–69338–8

You can receive future titles in this series as they are published by placing a standing order. Please contact your bookseller or, in case of difficulty, write to us at the address below with your name and address, the title of the series and the ISBN quoted above.

Customer Services Department, Macmillan Distribution Ltd
Houndmills, Basingstoke, Hampshire RG21 6XS, England

the
total look

the style guide for hair and make-up

professionals

Ian Mistlin

First published 2000 by
MACMILLAN PRESS LTD
Houndmills, Basingstoke, Hampshire RG21 6XS
and London
Companies and representatives throughout the world

ISBN 0-333-69948-3 paperback

A catalogue record for this book is available from the British Library.

This book is printed on paper suitable for recycling and made from fully managed and sustained forest sources.

10 9 8 7 6 5 4 3 2 1
09 08 07 06 05 04 03 02 01 00

Printed in Hong Kong

contents

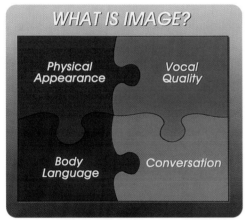

Ian Mistlin

1

appearance and image matters

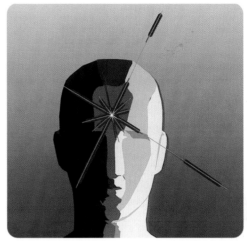

Ian Mistlin

2

enhancing your role

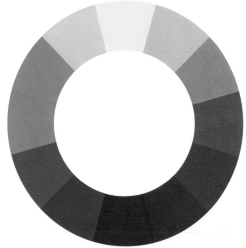

James Darrell

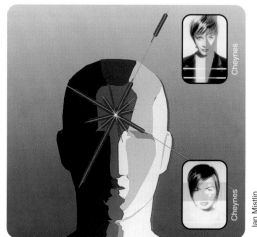

Cheynes
Cheynes
Ian Mistlin

products courtesy of Screenface

6
contributing to creating a total look

7
developing your photographic imagery

8
it's a wrap

foreword

If you've ever seen the popular television series Star Trek Voyager™ then you'll know that the star ship and its crew were set adrift in the delta quadrant some 70,000 light years away from Earth. At warp 10 it would take them 70 years to return home to Earth. Yet each episode has the crew of Voyager zig zagging its way home, pausing only to look at some new planet or learn from a new race of people.

This book by Ian Mistlin is like that voyage home. Not just in a straight line A to B, but taking the opportunity to learn from different ideas and exploring other concepts that might be quite alien. Like the series, this is about science exploration; the science is the way you learn and the route you choose and the exploration is what you achieve in your voyage.

This is an outstanding book. Start your voyage now!

Alan Goldsbro
Chief Executive
Hairdressing and Beauty Industry Authority

introduction

Have you noticed how some people have the ability to successfully style their hair, experiment with make-up, mix and match colours, chose flattering clothes, wear eye-catching accessories and always look great, whereas others never quite get it right?

For a lucky few this natural talent is a true gift, however, for many individuals it doesn't come easily. Think of the men and women you know … think of well-known celebrities … think of the stars of stage and screen. Make up two lists marked 'stylish' and 'unstylish'. Those people with style appeal have one characteristic in common: confidence. Style reflects self-confidence. The confidence to express individuality in clothes, hairstyle and make-up, poise and presence; in fact every aspect of personal presentation.

It is important at this stage to define the difference between style and fashion. Fashion very much reflects current trends. Trends that often start on the street, in the clubs, on the catwalks around the world, trends that are worn by dedicated followers, often regardless of suitability, that eventually find their way into our shops and boutiques.

In contrast stylish people creatively adapt beauty and fashion trends to enhance their physique, suit their personality and lifestyle. They have the confidence to know that what makes them different can make them special. They understand how to integrate the elements of style, colour, make-up, hair, clothes and accessories to compose and create a successful total look.

However, for those persons with little or no idea about appearance matters, what is the answer? Where should they go for help? Who best to see?

If you are a hairdresser, a make-up person, a beauty therapist, a sales person or a colour and image consultant working on the front-line and cutting edge of beauty and fashion you all share something in common.

…you are all advisers, designers, and artists.

Customers or clients seek your particular speciality, your knowledge, skills or products; and most importantly want your professional advice, guidance and reassurance on how they can improve their looks and appearance.

We are talking about relationship building, the relationship between you and your customers or clients. Success will depend on:

- whether you can come up with solutions to meet their requirements or needs
- your ability to make them feel good about their decisions and about themselves
- your level of confidence
- your knowledge and skills

How would you like to enhance your ability as an adviser, add power and depth to your consultations, presentations or sales?

Are you hungry for knowledge and eager to learn new skills that will help you to meet the needs and requirements of present and future customers or clients?

Do you admit to having gaps in your knowledge, gaps that leave you rather exposed and weakened in what are highly competitive industries, and during changing times?

How would you like new work directions that will give new dimensions to your services and vitality to your career?

Do you feel that your talents remain untapped and do you wish to awaken your creative potential?

How many of you fear failure, erect work barriers, avoid experimentation or shy away from certain services and get stuck in a rut?

Are you training for a specific career qualification or attending a starter course that will add to your knowledge and skills repertoire?

Do you realise that your future success depends on a better understanding of foundation theory yet your questions remain unanswered?

If you share these beliefs and desires and want to make positive changes and progress, this book is for you.

For everyone in search of style enlightenment *The Total Look* is for you. It is a guide for hair and make-up professionals written with the client in mind. It is intended for those of you who seek to:

- expand beauty and style knowledge
- complement consultation skills with a better understanding of the client
- develop expertise as a designer
- compose flattering looks
- increase skills repertoire
- improve craftsmanship and artistry
- create stronger imagery

structure of the book

The book is divided into eight parts. Each part covers an essential stage in contributing to the 'make-over' of a client or model.

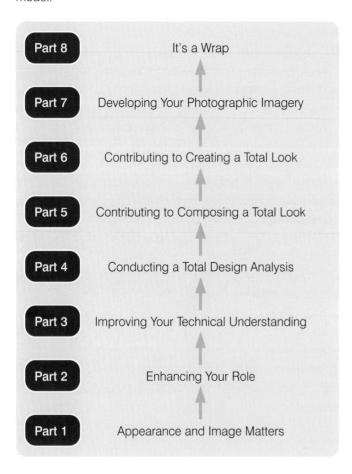

Part 8	It's a Wrap
Part 7	Developing Your Photographic Imagery
Part 6	Contributing to Creating a Total Look
Part 5	Contributing to Composing a Total Look
Part 4	Conducting a Total Design Analysis
Part 3	Improving Your Technical Understanding
Part 2	Enhancing Your Role
Part 1	Appearance and Image Matters

Think of all the stages in terms of a giant sandwich made up of different layers. The layers represent knowledge, skills and attitude. These three components are vital ingredients associated with a specific task or service. They are essential for producing a positive performance and achieving good results.

Knowledge provides the fundamental *understanding* and the foundation to support your design and styling services; **skills** describes your *ability* to perform; and **attitude** describes your *willingness* to perform. Attitude is the component that 'glues' everything together.

Parts 1–4 are concerned with assimilating knowledge and learning 'how to'. Parts 5–7 develops 'doing skills'. The book concludes with Part 8, 'It's a Wrap', a portfolio of images and insights.

a journey plan

Knowledge alone is not sufficient, neither is skill. To be competent in *conducting*, *composing*, *creating* and *developing* you will need to be able to gather, draw on, link and mix and match different categories of knowledge, information, data, images and skills into an orderly form. In effect, you control the process and stages.

Consider the stages in terms of a 'journey'. To help you successfully complete this journey I have drawn up a 'journey plan'. It illustrates what route to take in order to compose and create. The journey plan also illustrates the parties involved and the key intermediary stage of **total design analysis** when clients' needs must be identified and instructions taken.

Each party contributes essential things as ingredients to the relationship.

You bring to the relationship yourself, that is your personality, your knowledge and skills.

The *client* brings to the relationship themselves, a host of image issues, possible requirements and unmet needs.

You also supply the props or elements of style which you will use to compose or create. These are your resources.

The *client* supplies the canvas or media that you will work on and in addition the materials that you will work with.

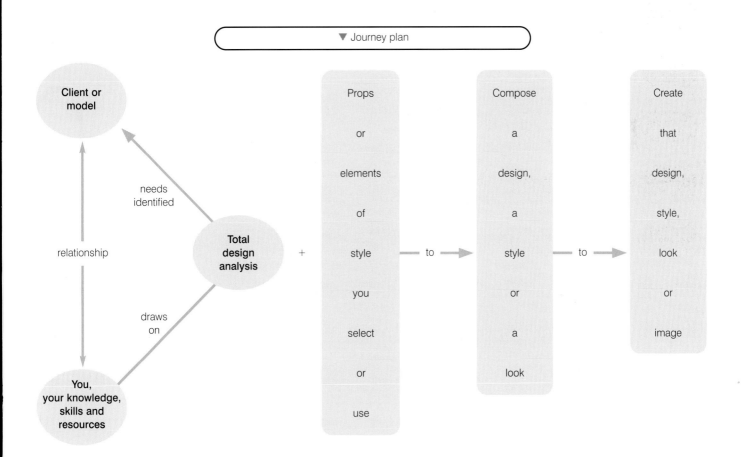

▼ Journey plan

■ signposting the journey

The range of ingredients are summarised on the linkage plan. The object of the plan is to flag up key areas of knowledge, skills and issues that you will need to:

- ■ draw on
- ■ match
- ■ analyse
- ■ link
- ■ select
- ■ apply
- ■ use

Use this plan to mark out links to help you complete your style challenges and journeys.

Join me on this style adventure and challenge. Add to your repertoire. Open up exciting new career opportunities. Explore new horizons. Add vitality to your work and in the process help your customers to maximise their style potential.

Good luck and have fun!

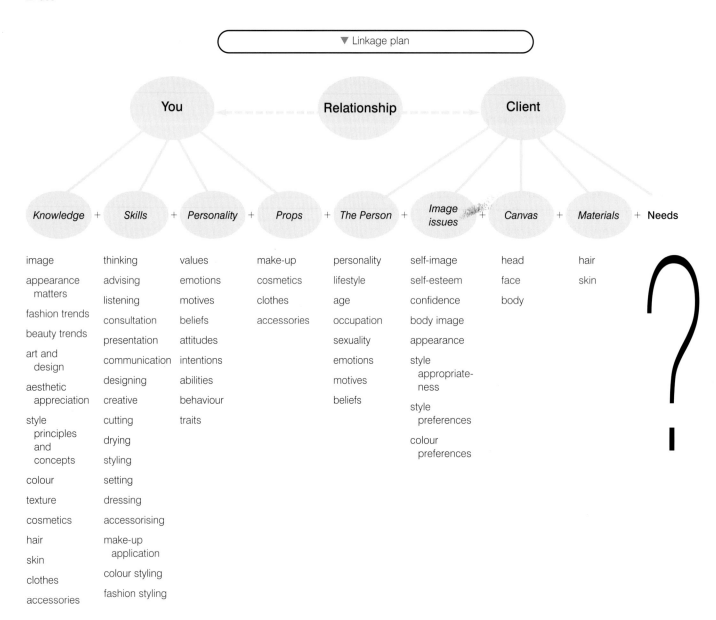

▼ Linkage plan

You ---- Relationship ---- Client

Knowledge +	Skills +	Personality +	Props +	The Person +	Image issues +	Canvas +	Materials +	Needs
image	thinking	values	make-up	personality	self-image	head	hair	
appearance matters	advising	emotions	cosmetics	lifestyle	self-esteem	face	skin	
fashion trends	listening	motives	clothes	age	confidence	body		
beauty trends	consultation	beliefs	accessories	occupation	body image			
art and design	presentation	attitudes		sexuality	appearance			
aesthetic appreciation	communication	intentions		emotions	style appropriate-ness			
style principles and concepts	designing	abilities		motives	style preferences			
colour	creative	behaviour		beliefs	colour preferences			
texture	cutting	traits						
cosmetics	drying							
hair	styling							
skin	setting							
clothes	dressing							
accessories	accessorising							
	make-up application							
	colour styling							
	fashion styling							

?

about the author

Ian Mistlin launched his hairdressing career with the Vidal Sassoon organisation in the early seventies where he soon established himself as one of their top designers.

In 1976 he was promoted to manager of their Sloane Street salon. It was there that he first developed his business and management skills.

Change is what Ian sought after fourteen successful years with the Vidal Sassoon organisation. Trading his management hat for artistic goals, from the mid-eighties Ian worked as a hair and make-up session stylist represented by top London agencies. His editorial work has been featured in countless beauty and fashion magazines. In addition he has worked on prestigious advertising shoots and fashion shows at home and abroad.

From this pedigree background, Ian established an image consultancy in the late eighties, offering clients personal style guidance and advice. Consultations were supported by one-to-one hair and make-up services.

Driven by the desire to gain a deeper insight into image and impression management, Ian began to research personal development, self-esteem and self-presentation issues. It was from this period on that Ian Mistlin diversified into writing educational books.

His first book *How to win clients and interpret their need* was published in 1994. *The Total Look* is his second book.

Ian's writing draws upon his wide knowledge, his wealth of experience and a unique blend of expertise, which give his books a refreshingly new direction and real hands-on authority.

It is as an authority and a desire to help others develop which now forms the foundations to Ian Mistlin Associates, a management and learning consultancy specialising in the hair and beauty industry.

acknowledgements

I wish to extend my appreciation to the many individuals for their help and support.

First I thank the team at my publishers who have contributed to the book from conception to birth, in particular Suzannah Tipple, vocational publisher, Isobel Munday, managing editor, and Tessa Hanford, copy editor.

I am most grateful to all the artists and photographers who have contributed imagery and insights. I would like to thank the following: Cheynes; James Darrell; George Ong/Yardley; Charles Worthington; Ozzie Rizzo at Sanrizz; Guy Kremer; D & J Ambrose; Ishoka; Klownz; Staffords; The Natural Hair Company; Andrew Jose; Mark Hill; Julie Bellinger Consultancy; Judy Bennett PR; Hamet Evans PR; Bell Pootinger Good Relations; Ketchum Life and Vidal Sassoon press office for supplying images and press releases; Prescriptives for letting me use their 'colour printing' image; Screenface for letting me have make-up products; Lorraine Nordmann for step-by-step make-up images; and Direct Colour Promotions.

Lastly, but by no means least, many thanks to my wife Glenda for her support and skill in typing the manuscript and preparing graphics.

WHAT IS IMAGE?

Physical Appearance

Vocal Quality

Body Language

Conversation

Jan Mistlin

1 appearance and image matters

This section provides an overview of every-day image and appearance issues that affect how a client looks. These are issues that are essential to your understanding of clients and their style preferences.

---

appearance is important

the total image

common hair and make-up stereotypes

appearance is important

Appearance matters in society today. Much has to do with social acceptability, values, ideals and in Western society, the role and power of the media in delivering daily doses of visual images of beautiful models and seductive advertising campaigns. Supermodels are in constant demand for their ideal faces and bodies. The *ideal body* is not a real person but a powerful collection of mindsets or visual images that describe our perception of the perfect body. These mindsets are a vision of our imagination formed as early as infancy, childhood and adolescence. Such ideals are the product of forever changing beauty and fashion trends. The picture is even more complex because of the different societies, groups and subcultures that interact and often conflict with each other. Each subculture has its own definition of its ideal body and its own beauty and fashion ideals: ideals that manifest themselves as style trends.

◼ making an impression

According to research, we rely heavily on *appearance clues* to find like-minded people that we want to form relationships with. In our daily lives our business and social relationships are initially established by using the power of the *first impression* as a filtering system to sort out all those people with whom we would like to do business, strike up relationships or simply avoid.

It can take as little as 30 seconds to 4 minutes for someone to form a lasting opinion of another person. Often assessments are unfair and permanent. Whether we realise it or not we are all guilty of judging people by their looks, so much so that we rely heavily on a variety of props including:

■ colour
■ cosmetics
■ make-up
■ hair
■ clothes
■ jewellery
■ accessories

We use these props to merchandise and change our bodies into objects of desire, attractiveness and appropriateness.

Our assessments are made up of preconceived visual images or stereotypes, heavily influenced by our cultural roots, emotional experiences, religious belief, historical folklore, superstitions and symbolic associations.

Vidal Sassoon

Take for instance our clothes, their colours, how we wear our hair and make-up. They all convey vital impression clues to others, revealing much about:

■ age
■ lifestyle
■ personality
■ occupation
■ sexuality
■ political and religious beliefs
■ emotions
■ style preferences

Although we rely heavily on the power of attractiveness and first impressions to signal to others what we have to offer, the most convincing signals transmitted are those that are the result of presenting a balanced *total image*.

the total image

Total image is a complicated mixture of different ingredients and influences acting together. Total image is a composition that takes into account physical appearance, body language, vocal quality and conversation. It includes:

- colouring
- gender
- age
- height
- facial expression
- eye contact
- hair and make-up
- build
- clothes and accessories
- posture, movement
- behaviour towards others
- vocal quality, articulation and vocabulary

Ian Mistlin

■ 'inner' and 'outer' beauty

It is a person's visual image that we are instantly aware of. Once interest has been aroused and there is a desire to further the relationship, physical attraction often becomes less important in favour of a person's inner beauty. Furthermore, there is a unique relationship between 'inner beauty', i.e. how a person feels about themselves and the way a person presents themselves to others. I call this 'outer beauty'.

My philosophy to image is based on an 'inside-out' approach. That is, we are only able to successfully present ourselves when our 'inner beauty' and 'outer beauty' are in perfect harmony. This means that the whole person must be considered.

■ definition of image

This leads us to the question whether the word 'image' is used too freely by people in the image consultancy world. It would perhaps be more precise to use the word 'style' on matters concerned with looks.

Similarly, it is wrong to consider any one part of the face or body in isolation. Instead it is important to appreciate the total look and understand how the different elements of style can be integrated successfully to compare a stylish composition.

To advance this discussion we need to ask how image is defined. Image can be taken to represent 'the personality presented to the public by a person', 'the general impression of a person or particular part of them', 'a mental or conceptual picture', or 'the photographic representation of a person or thing'.

■ an image maker

The book takes the view that as a hair and make-up artist you are also an image maker.

When clients or customers seek your image services they do so with one thing in common: they all want to feel good and look their best.

How accomplished you are will largely depend on changing attitudes and habits, increasing confidence and awareness as well as passing on your skills. Every client has potential. However, it is often knowing how to develop this potential, by creatively adapting beauty and fashion trends, to suit the client.

making assumptions

A word of warning. Do not fall into the trap of making danger-ous assumptions. Use the first impression in a measured and controlled manner. Support any assumptions with further investigations and information gathering before making recommendations. They might otherwise prove to be invalid simply because your judgement was cast with prejudices and wrongly conceived impressions that were based on stereotyping.

As an image maker, always consider whether the recommendations you give or the images you create will help your client make a positive impression on others. Such recommendations must be linked to understanding their lifestyle needs.

The following diagrams illustrate some stereotypes, prejudices and symbolic associations that you need to be aware of.

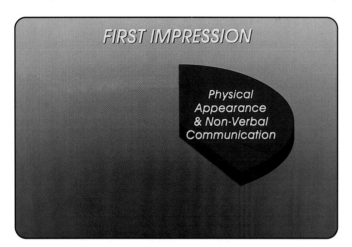

FIRST IMPRESSION

Physical Appearance & Non-Verbal Communication

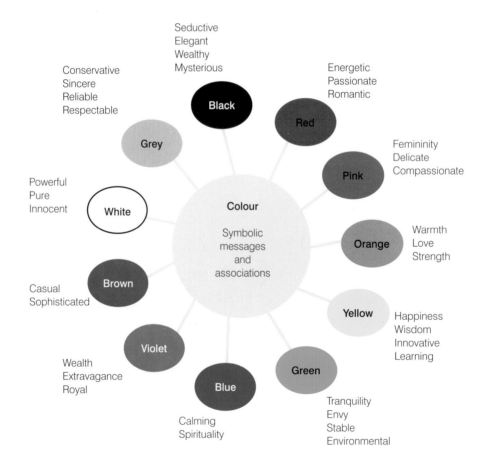

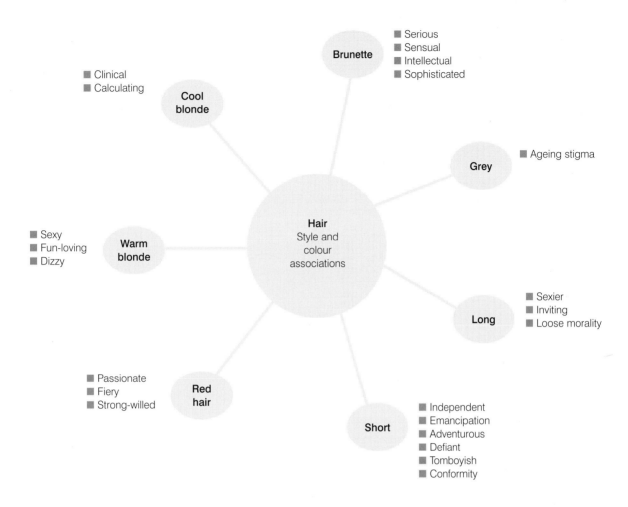

- Brunette
  - Serious
  - Sensual
  - Intellectual
  - Sophisticated
- Cool blonde
  - Clinical
  - Calculating
- Grey
  - Ageing stigma
- Hair
  Style and colour associations
- Warm blonde
  - Sexy
  - Fun-loving
  - Dizzy
- Long
  - Sexier
  - Inviting
  - Loose morality
- Red hair
  - Passionate
  - Fiery
  - Strong-willed
- Short
  - Independent
  - Emancipation
  - Adventurous
  - Defiant
  - Tomboyish
  - Conformity

image and personality

When it comes to personality, you will need to appreciate the impact that your client's personality has on the way they look. It was the eminent psychologist Carl Jung, who put forward the dimensions *'extroversion'* and *'introversion'* to describe personality types. Jung and his followers described each according to certain qualities and preferences. It is important to appreciate that we all have a combination of both extrovert and introvert in us.

In terms of style preferences, the extrovert and introvert exhibit different expressive style behaviour. The essential differences are shown below.

The extrovert	vs.	The introvert
■ actively likes to stimulate others		■ likes a much simpler quieter look
■ makes a fashion statement by wearing dramatic and flamboyant style of clothes and eye-catching style detail		■ attaches little importance to stimulating others or to the wearing of impact clothes or colours ■ prefers more plain, uncluttered and sophisticated look
■ colours worn tend to be medium to deep contrasting or bright energetic colours		■ colours worn are much quieter, softer and less bold
■ bold eye-catching jewellery is often worn		■ jewellery usually is minimal and less eye-catching

common hair and make-up stereotypes

Whilst it is impossible to fit a person neatly into a definite category, particularly as most people have dominant and secondary preferences, I have included a brief description of common hair and make-up stereotypes:

■ *Classic*

Hair is well-groomed, usually long in a ponytail, a chignon or softly styled bob.

Make-up is conservative, natural and soft.

■ *Dramatic*

Hair is often worn long in neat, structured chignons. Geometric or angular cuts are favourites, so too are short, sharp looks.

Make-up is designed to make a statement and accentuate features.

■ *Romantic*

Hair is often worn loose and voluminous either natural or with a perm. Shorter bob lengths are popular and are often layered and textured. Hair up often complements the look. With make-up, the focus is on darker eyes and full, luscious lips, but not overbearing.

■ *Natural*

Hair may be worn loose and casual. Little attention is given to styling and dressing.

Little or no make-up.

■ *Feminine*

Hair is worn long and softly wavy. Hair up is dressed loosely. Popular shoulder lengths are soft bobs.

Make-up is very soft and natural.

■ *Arty*

Hair if long is either worn loose, pulled back off the face or in a type of chignon. Texture is often straight or permed.

Make-up features strong well-defined eyes; nude or tinted lips.

■ *Tomboy*

Uncomplicated hair: short crops or long smooth ponytails.

Make-up is very natural and soft.

2 enhancing your role

Evolving and conceiving images or ideas are essential stages in composing and creating a total look. This section introduces you to the ideal professional. It will help you improve your powers of perception, conception, style interpretation and origination.

2.1 style composers and creators

■ style and design

There are few things that escape some form of style treatment and design influences. From the houses we live, the cars we drive, the books we buy, the clothes and jewellery we wear, the magazines we read, the advertisements we see and even the services we use. Style and design are at the very heart of everyday life. So too are the individuals we call designers, be they architects, interior designers, furniture and fabric designers or designers of clothes, graphics, gardens and gadgets. The world of style brings together a diverse range of talents, hairdressing being no exception.

■ how to define a hairdresser?

The names and titles used by hairdressing personnel can often be confusing. Should they call themselves a hairdresser, a hairstylist, a hair designer, a hair technician or even a hair artist?

dictionary definitions

Various dictionaries describe each as follows:

- A *design* can be described as a plan or scheme to be carried out; a preliminary sketch or scheme.
- A *designer* is a person who provides plans or schemes for a purpose.
- A *style* is somewhat more difficult to describe although in this context a useful working description is *'a noticeable superior quality or manner with regard to appearance'*.
- A *stylist* is a person aiming at achieving a good style; a person who has a high regard for quality of appearance and the *'looks'* of something or somebody.
- A *dresser* is a person known within the theatre as a dresser of actors or actresses. Associated with hair it implies a person who literally dresses hair.
- A *technician* is a person skilled in a practical art or craft.
- An *artist* is a person who makes 'art' a fine craft; a craftsperson, someone who produces something in a skilled manner.

Let me for the moment use *hair professional*, to describe a hairdresser.

■ what is a hair professional?

In many respects the 'hair professional' shares much in common with an architect and structural engineer.

the architect

The architect must be able to turn structural design concepts into reality, through a rigid application of aesthetic principles and technical drawing skills, which evolve into detailed scaled plans. These will form the basis to a set of working, three-dimensional models, material specifications and instructions. Throughout this design process careful consideration would have been given to designing a structure that is aesthetically pleasing and in harmony with its immediate surroundings.

The hair professional must also be an architect of hair structures. They must ensure that their designs are aesthetically planned, paying careful attention to the proportions that enhance head, face and body features. Similarly, they must have a commanding technical knowledge about the materials they work with; none more important than hair. Lastly, but by no means least, they must consider whether the proposed style is in harmony with the client's personal and lifestyle needs.

the interior designer

Let us turn our attention from structural design to interior design. It is the interior designer who is often engaged to provide the finishing touches to a basic room. It is their ability to create 'sets' that are visually pleasing, environmentally friendly, functional and comfortable. This is achieved by first considering the dimensions of a specific area, and then deciding how it can be transformed using colour to visually alter shape and proportions, as well as create a mood; accessories to enhance; furnishing and fabric to give texture appeal: appeal that is both visual and tactile.

the technician

The hair professional must be technically sound and be able to call on an array of technical goodies including colour, treatment products, perming lotions and styling aids.

The technician often adopts a more straightforward approach to hair and is concerned with the importance of technique and technical skills, including cutting, colouring, perming and finishing.

bringing it all together

However, technique is not enough. The missing ingredient is artistic feeling and artistic appreciation. The hair professional must continually search for new style ideas fed by a constant stream of inspiration to produce that spark of creativity to sculpture and finish hair into the desired shape. Success relies on a complex relationship between the client, the elements of design, the material properties of hair, the element of spontaneity, and the mood to craft hair into the most aesthetic form.

Consequently, when I use the words 'hair professional' it is because there is nothing else which describes the qualities that 'complete hairperson' must have. Such a person would need to be a technician, a designer and an artist.

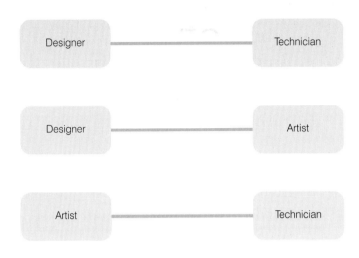

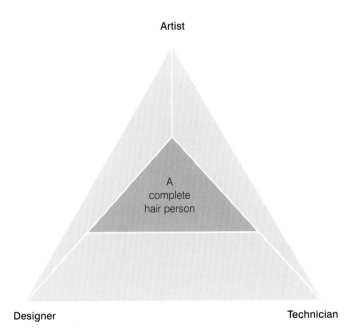

the ideal person ... the ideal balance

In many respects the complete hairperson must be comfortable wearing all three 'hats', sometimes all together, sometimes just two, sometimes separated.

The ideal balance is for the designer and technician; designer and artist; and artist and technician to operate as one.

These pairs can be located at the opposite end of a line as follows:

Questions to consider:

1 Which pairing do you relate better to?
2 Where do you sit most comfortably along these lines?
3 Are you more technically minded with a strong technical bias towards generating a design?
4 Does your style work have a strong design presence in terms of aesthetic suitability?
5 Do your style recommendations favour a more artistic solution and less of a technical input?
6 Are the practical dimensions of your style work more expressive and less technical in favour of a creative and artistic approach to styling?
7 Would you say your artistic and technical qualities and skills are equally balanced?
8 Can you move freely in either direction and take on all three roles depending on the stage in the styling process?

other professionals

the fashion designer

Returning to the adventures of different designers and on the question of cut, texture and colour appeal. No person is more conscious of these technical properties than the fashion designer whose work often starts from rough sketches of style ideas before transferring them onto cloth. This is, of course, an oversimplication of the overall process, where stages include fabric selection, pattern design, cutting, tailoring and finishing before a first sample is ready. In terms of pattern design, every garment, even at the drawing board stage, has to be correctly proportioned, structured and sized.

the beauty therapist

When it comes to body style, it is the beauty therapist who draws together science and art into designing treatments to help present, protect and perfect our desire for facial and body beauty. Such treatments reflect the need to improve skin texture, tone and muscle fitness through a combination of cosmetic and massage therapy. There are many factors that contribute to the fitness and appearance of the skin. The beauty therapist must be aware of the importance of ensuring that the client's physical and emotional elements are in harmony and that the skin's delicate pH balance is maintained. Consequently, the right choice of products is essential. Careful consideration must be given to the task in question as well as their suitability for the client's skin texture. You may ask where does art come in?

Let's not forget that a skilful massage is an art and a most beneficial part of the beauty process. Besides preparing the skin for further cosmetic therapy a sensitively conducted massage does much to relax the body and mind, remove stress and store inner tranquillity.

the make-up artist

The make-up artist and beauty stylist must also possess artistic and technical mastery to create and make faces beautiful using suitable cosmetics, colours and techniques. Make-up can do more than simply add colour. If correctly selected and applied, it can be used to improve skin texture, even out skin tones, enhance eyes, visually alter facial features and proportions as well as improve facial interest, attractiveness and style appeal.

the fashion stylist

It is often the fashion stylist who is responsible for sourcing and getting the clothes and accessories to be worn by a model on a photographic assignment; contributing to the overall look.

an image consultant

An image consultant is the name given to professionals who provide advice on appearance matters and personal presentation.

■ the role of an adviser

An adviser is a person who offers advice, help or guidance in a professional capacity. They are sought by others because of their specialist knowledge and skills. Individuals who operate in this capacity are frequently referred to as 'consultants'.

Increasingly, people in specialised jobs find themselves being advisers or consultants for some of the time. People in this role find themselves having to influence other people or advise them on a possible course of action. It is a role that requires excellent diagnostic, consultation and interpersonal skills.

I take the view that a professional hair person must also wear the hat of an adviser or consultant. Technical expertise and artistry is not enough. Clients today want objective advice, information and guidance. They want to be informed about the latest beauty and fashion trends or which products to use. Clients want to be advised on how they can look their best, how to manage and care for their hair. You must have the knowledge to offer this. You must be willing and able to extend your knowledge and skills into other areas of beauty and fashion.

Similarly in the world of image consultancy, the professional style consultant must have the knowledge and skills to offer technical advice on colour, hair, skin, fashion accessories, fabrics and cosmetics. In addition they must have an eye for detail and a flair for fashion styling.

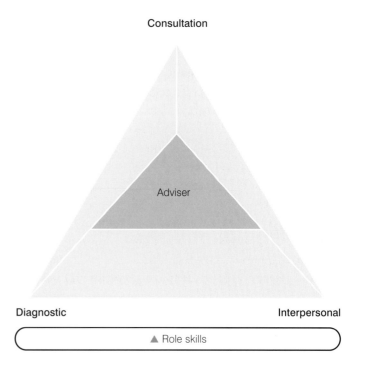

2.2 developing your creativity and creative thinking

▣ what is creativity?

Creativity, along with its partner innovation will be fundamental to future success. Creativity is associated with the generalising ideas. It is also the starting point for successful innovation.

Creativity is best explained as a mind process which takes us away from left-brain logic into the world of imaginative thinking, the outcome of which being flashes of insight, new ideas, new concepts, new mental images.

> 66 99
>
> *Creativity is a marvellous capacity to grasp two mutually distinct realities without going beyond the field of your expedience and to draw from their juxtaposition.*
>
> (Preface to Max Ernst Exhibition, 1920)

At the moment of insight creativity may well be the result of both sides of the brain working together, so that a new pattern of beliefs emerges.

The creativity of an artist, writer, painter or musician is taken for granted. The creativity of the scientist, chemist and mathematician is also recognised. In management and business, the running of a company needs a creative-thinking approach. Survival, vitality and growth depend upon that spark of creativity. Research of a new product design, packaging the product and marketing it, requires bringing together a wealth of creative talents. The story doesn't end there: in order to make the product, there is a need to consider manufacturing strategy, that is how to produce it cost effectively, ensuring that the quality is maintained. The future of the product relies on a team effort to pool together creative and technical expertise.

Those success stories in hairdressing are no different to those in the manufacturing industry. In your case the products you manufacture are heads of beautiful and stylish hair, stunning make-ups and exciting total looks.

It is accepted for artists to develop their creativity and creative skills; however, how many of you would appreciate the need to improve your creative thinking in order to develop your skills?

▣ innovation

Innovation is the process that enables imaginative thinking to become a reality. According to the DTI, "innovation is the successful exploitation of new ideas".

Innovation is something that all designers need in abundance. Innovation lies behind many of today's outstanding design stories and achievements. It is the process of solving needs in new ways or finding solution to old problems. For designers to be innovative they must continually search for new ideas. They must create ideas and then develop and present the idea for others to produce or make. Similarly, what separates one 'make' from another is the innovation associated with 'producing' the goods. Both require a creative style of thinking.

To be successful, you will need to be highly innovative in order to conceive technically sound and aesthetically suitable compositions prior to creating them.

creativity	innovation	product or service
ideas	development	produce/deliver

▣ .the need for vision

We talk about the need for vision but what do we really mean? Taken quite literally it implies that we need to improve the manner in which we 'see' or conceive something. We need to capture in our mind a picture of what we are hoping to achieve and keep sight of it.

People who are visionary are said to be *intuitive*. Such people make successful artists, inventors, writers and business men or women. They are able to bring past experience, information, knowledge, images and sources of ideas together in a way which gives rise to flashes of insight and subsequent inspiration from the unconscious mind. It is the moment of discovery – when new ideas, new concepts and compositions are born.

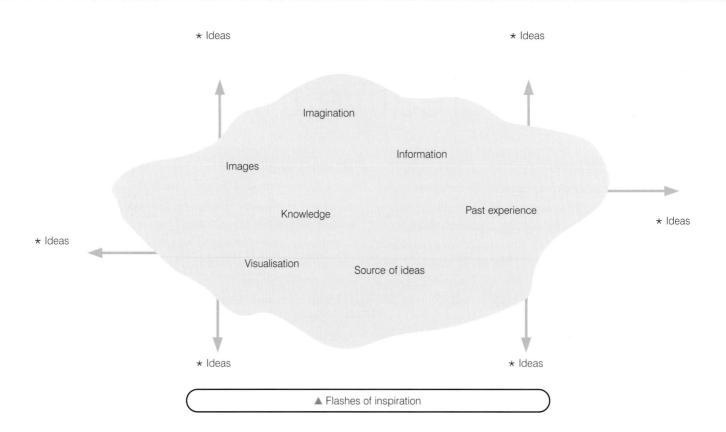

★ Ideas   ★ Ideas

Imagination

Information

Images

Knowledge

Past experience

★ Ideas

★ Ideas

Visualisation

Source of ideas

★ Ideas   ★ Ideas

▲ Flashes of inspiration

brain activity

Research indicates that intuition is a specific form of intelligence associated with right-brain activity. The right side of the brain processes information without us being aware of verbal reasoning processes. This right-brain thinking has been described as more visual, pattern manipulating and intuitive, and therefore superficially like *creative thinking*.

This is in contrast to the left-brain activity or thinking which has been described as more linear, logical, verbal and sequential (step by step).

Left-brain thinking	Right-brain thinking
Linear thinking	Whole thinking
Logic	Visualisation
Verbal	Imagination
Detail	Intuition
Sequence	Recognition

However, although the two halves each provide a specialised function, they are connected by bundles of nerve fibres, and ideally should work in harmony, with neither side dominant over the other.

■ what is creative thinking?

> 66 99
> *Creative thinking is the relating of things or ideas which were previously unrelated.*
>
> Anon

From birth we have the ability to use our brains in ways that most of us 'forget' as we grow into adults.

As mentioned earlier, the brain is divided into two halves. In early childhood we had no difficulty reaching into either and moving freely between them; however, during our development negative conditioning has encouraged us to become left-brain dominant.

Throughout our early years the right half dominated, assimilating the world around us, translating events and outcomes, visualising and letting our imagination run wild. However, as we grew older, the various forces in our lives such as parents, teachers to some extent and society in general, discouraged us from 'day-dreaming' and irrationality but rewarded us for being alert and responsive.

Consequently, we soon discovered it paid to use our analytical left-brain 'mode'. The result, our imagination and creativity became stifled by mental barriers, suppressing our creative thinking and skills.

As you will discover later, to deal with practical design problems you will need to be able to switch between both analytical and creative modes.

Analytical thinking	Creative thinking
Logical	Imaginative
Predictable	Unpredictable
Convergent	Divergent
Vertical	Lateral

the creative process

Creativity is a thinking process. It is basically a problem-solving process made up of the following cycle of stages.

stage 1: preparation

Creative thinking is thought provoking. It requires you to feed your mind with knowledge, information, images, ideas and other sources of inspiration.

It will also require you to gather information about clients, their problems and needs. This is discussed in depth in Part IV. For those of you who produce photographic imagery your ability to conceive and create ideas is essential. Your success will initially depend on stimulating and triggering the subconscious mind.

stage 2: incubation and evolution

Here the subconscious mind takes over. It is a critical stage where the mind begins to shift, link, match, analyse and evaluate all information into an orderly and meaningful form. It is a stage that requires 'whole thinking'.

using 'whole thinking'

To meet the everyday challenges and needs of your clients you need to be aware that in order to solve their problems, give advice, come up with ideas, you must adopt a versatile method to problem solving.

identifying the problem

First you need to identify the type of problem. Some problems usually only have one answer and rely on an analytical thought process. Other problems require a more imaginative creative approach, giving rise to a number of possibilities. It is a mental challenge that requires you to use logic to focus or converge your ideas and imagination to expand and explore all possibilities. Imagination explores the world of the unpredictable.

A person who thinks creatively is said to be a lateral thinker.

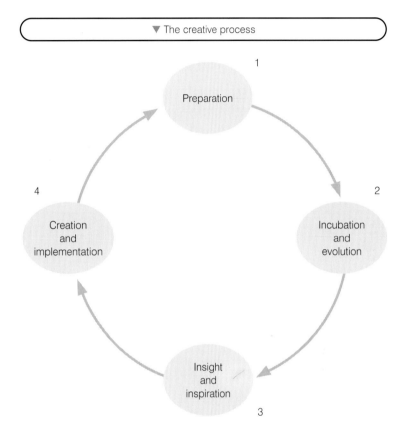

▼ The creative process

1 Preparation

2 Incubation and evolution

3 Insight and inspiration

4 Creation and implementation

finding a solution

In practice, to meet your clients' needs, you should use an inclusive approach, one that calls on both analytical and creative thinking. The analytical thinking gives one solution. Creative thinking follows and this gives rise to a number of ideas which can then be analysed to further solutions.

Your ability to compose and come up with recommendations requires analytical skills during the *consultation* stage to interpret and satisfy such requirements as:

- application
- practicability
- manageability
- versatility
- suitability
- appropriateness

Each demands a solution, resulting in a creative assessment to produce ideas for discussion. The analytical and creative cycle then repeats to narrow the solutions down until you reach a decision, as to the appropriate course of action.

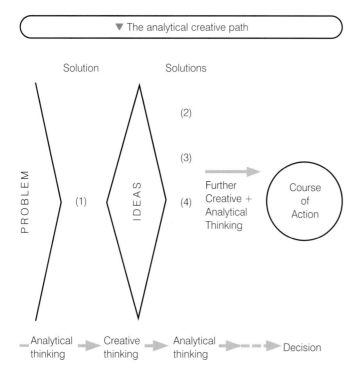

▼ The analytical creative path

producing the result

The practical course of action to produce the *result* requires you to use your *creative skills* by interpreting the course of action.

Throughout the cutting, styling, colouring or perming procedure, it is common to switch into an *analytical* mode to continually reassess your work.

Throughout this process it is also essential to develop and work on your *communication skills* so that good constructive dialogue exists between you and the client.

stage 3: insight and inspiration

This is the moment of discovery – when new ideas, new concepts, new compositions are conceived and born. It is the time of great joy for any artist or even scientist in search of the answer. It was the moment that Archimedes shouted Eureka!

stage 4: creation and implementation

This is the stage when conceived ideas or compositions become reality. It is a time when talent, flair, skill and technique are put to the test.

■ rising to style challenges

Each time a client consults you or you undertake a model assignment you face a style challenge. It will be a challenge of many dimensions that initially requires you to define your goals and then think about what you will have to do to achieve them. This will involve setting design and style objectives. The author Peter Senge in his book *The Fifth Discipline* argues that the gap between where we are now and our vision of where we want to be generates a creative tension. It is that tension which drives us to achieve our vision. However, if the gap is too big then it may be impossible to achieve; and if it is too small there may be insufficient drive. A lack of vision or an inability to 'see' or perceive things may cloud our judgement and block progress.

challenging perceptions

Creativity may also be blocked by false perceptions or perceptions you think are real. Perception is an information-gathering process. It is a mind process which draws upon our capacity to examine our ideas about our external world, e.g. perception of people and beliefs about things, situations and occasions. It also includes our internal world, or self-image, e.g. perceptions about what we are like and beliefs about our abilities. You are probably asking why is there a need for this. The answer is relatively simple: to bring about change. Changing self-perceptions can improve creativity. Such adjustment can overcome incorrect assumptions and break out of negative mindsets. In practice it is more complex.

Since it is our 'vision' of our inner and outer worlds which inevitably shapes much of what we do; if we can change our perceptions, we may be able to change our behaviour, which may be hampering our self-development, and thus preventing the development of our full potential. To develop true potential your mind must be consciously 'set up' that means recognising and removing all negative barriers or blocks.

recognising and removing mental barriers and blocks
developmental blocks

Cultural blocks are caused by attitudes in society, parental influences and other peers telling you from an early age what was right and what was wrong. What your strengths and weaknesses were. What is possible and what is not. These all contribute towards you erecting an artificial barrier in your mind as to your capabilities, thus imposing restrictions on developing or improving greater creative skills.

emotional blocks

The fear of appearing stupid, showing yourself up, making mistakes or the fear of failure, present a negative barrier.

ego

There is nothing wrong about seeking recognition; it can bring about tremendous self-satisfaction. However, self-doubt over self-glory can inhibit you from moving forward onto other challenges. Recognising and eliminating your cultural blocks will help you greatly to improve and develop your creative powers. Work on learning to love yourself for who and what you are. Developing and improving your self-esteem is vital.

Recognise and eliminate any emotional block in your mind about your competence. Don't be too hard on yourself. No wild or imaginative ideas will be produced if you have self-doubt about your skills. It is better to have tried and failed than never to have tried. There has to be a first for everything – you will soon get better the more experienced you become. As you begin to improve, your skills, your confidence, will grow.

The stage is now set for your creative quests and conquests.

2.3 exploring art, style and design

■ appreciating beauty and art

Beauty fascinates us. We are all stimulated and attracted by beautiful things whether it be a work of art such as a painting, a sculpture, an exquisite piece of jewellery, a room interior, a garden landscape, a piece of music or a person's facial features. We all have our opinions as to what we consider to be pleasurable and beautiful.

Beauty is then so many things. On the question of looks, it is often said that beauty is in the eye of the beholder. Everyone has the potential to look more attractive, elegant, smart, stylish, well groomed, youthful, glowing and radiant. Such are the words we commonly use in our everyday language to describe aspects of what we consider beautiful in relation to style matters. What is important is that every client or customer has a chance to fulfil this potential with your help. Successful styling will centre on you having an artistic or aesthetic appreciation of beauty and art forms.

■ the link between art, style and design

Beauty is art: the art of creation. Beautifying is the art of making. Successful styling is an art. It is about developing your skills as a composer and creator, as you turn conceptual style ideas into reality. This must be supported by an underlying sense of creativity and technical supremacy to craft hair into the most suitable forms, dress hair into wondrous creations, decorate faces using carefully chosen make-up, style bodies in the most flattering of garments and outfits, accessorise with selective items of jewellery. It is essential to create looks that are aesthetically pleasing, sensibly planned to suit a person's age, lifestyle and personality; technically correct and brilliantly executed to ensure a perfect finish.

It is impossible to talk about style without considering its partner, design. Similarly, it is impossible to design something without understanding art. Art, style and design are inseparable.

What's more they are linked together by a common language of words and images that describe the 'elements of design'.

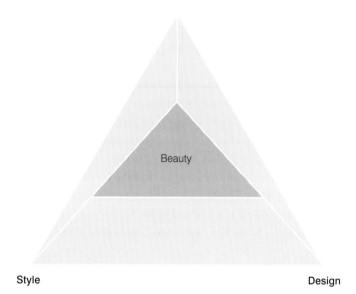

■ the elements of design

Whether on a drawing board, computer or in the mind, a style starts life as an arrangement of mental or visual images. Therefore we need a language to convey information about what we plan, see and register. Our visual and mental appreciation of such design arrangements is based on the *design pattern* of what we see, whether it be a structure like a bridge; an object like a terracotta pot, an article of clothing, a piece of cloth, a haircut; an item of jewellery. Just about everything around us has some form of design pattern.

gain inspiration

Draw inspiration from the great artists in history; artists like Rembrandt, Modiglian, Monet, Fragonard, Renoir, Van Gogh, Picasso, to name but a few. Visit galleries and observe how they applied the elements of art – *line*, *space*, *shape*, *proportion*, *scale*, *texture* and *colour* – to their figurative and still life work. They were masters of seeing the way that bodies and objects were 'designed' and how the different elements interrelated as they recreated the composition with such realism and likeness of expression. They also had the ability to remember intricate design detail and recreate paintings from memory.

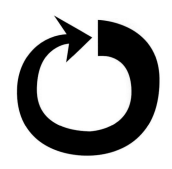

■ the elements of art

lines

In terms of artwork, lines can be used to create the outline of, say, an object, a still life composition or a figurative drawing. The outline describes the shape of the object or figure. The area contained by lines is called its space.

Lines give things a sense of movement and direction. A line can be defined as a trace of a moving point which can move in straight lines, curves or a combination of both. The more multi-directional a line the more movement. The space between two lines meeting at a point forms an angle.

There are four basic line directions. They are:

1 horizontal

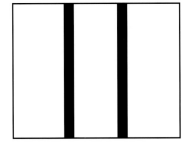

2 vertical

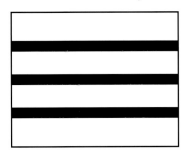

3 diagonal

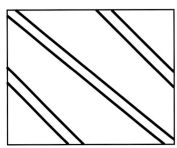

4 curved

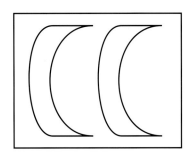

Lines have certain optical properties which can be used to create different style illusions. The more fluid or flowing a line, the softer the effect.

line association

Lines may also affect emotions. We associate the four basic line directions: horizontal, vertical, diagonal and curved with certain qualities, which in turn can be linked to different human states. For example:

- A *horizontal* line is said to be relaxing and peaceful and is associated with a state of calmness or a period of restfulness.
- A *vertical* line is said to signify strength and is associated with a state of alertness.
- A *diagonal* line is said to be associated with action and linked to a state of restlessness.
- A *curved* or *oval* line is associated with gracefulness.

converging and diverging lines

When diagonal lines come towards each other they are said to converge.

When lines converge they focus attention towards the point where they meet.

As diagonal lines spread apart they are said to diverge.

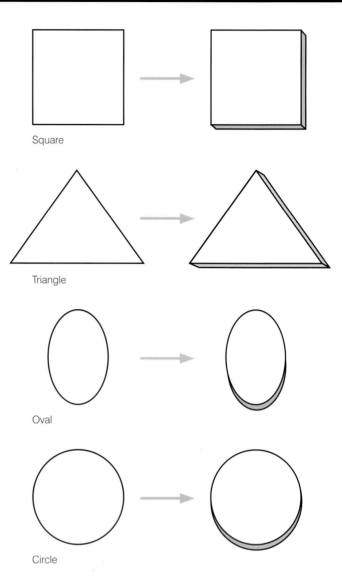

Square

Triangle

Oval

Circle

When lines diverge they will focus the eye outwards.

shape, form and space

This describes an area contained by a definite *outline*. *Shape* is something which has *form* or figure; that something can be said to occupy a certain *space* relative to its environment. For example a ball relative to a table or a haircut relative to a person's head.

Shape can be two or three dimensional. Two-dimensional shapes include:

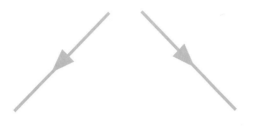

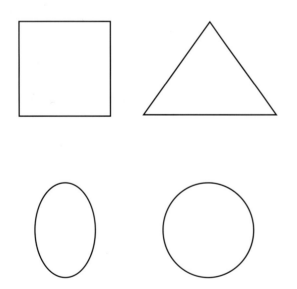

When these objects are given a third dimension, that is depth, then the following are obtained:

Shapes can be considered as being regular or irregular.

regular shapes

Regular shapes are thought of as being more predictable and include geometric and symmetrical shapes. Regular shapes occur naturally, but are more commonly man-made. Interestingly, people in the West are said to favour regular shapes and predictable patterns, compared to people from the East who seem to prefer irregular shapes and patterns.

irregular shapes

Irregular shapes do not have lines of symmetry and are said to be asymmetrical. Irregular shapes are considered more interesting to look at and are more commonly found in nature.

contour

Associated with shape is the word *contour* which is used to describe the outline of something.

For example the contour of the vase is made up of curvy and straight lines.

The leaf has curvy contours and curvy lines.

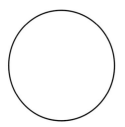

A circle has a round contour.

The mug has straight and curved contours.

colour

Colour is an integral part of everyday life. We see it, register it, explore it from an early age, work with it and apply it, perhaps without really understanding what colour is.

What would our world be like without colour? Spare a few moments to look around you and absorb this amazing dimension. Appreciate the tremendous variations of different colours as well as the spectacular array of different colour relationships. Nature is a rich source of colour. It has provided artists since ancient times with a basic palette of coloured pigments to paint with. In addition, it has inspired and fascinated poets, philosophers and scientists throughout history by its power to heighten emotions. Much has been written about the psychology of colour. For years philosophers, psychologists and doctors have investigated colour in an attempt to understand why we react differently to colours and to explain the link between colour selection, the psycho and personality.

Our response to colour is complex and heavily influenced by the symbolic message associated with different colours. For an observer of people and bodies much can be inferred from the colours that people wear. For a wearer colour can be used to signal appropriateness not to mention enhance personal presentation and appearance.

It is with the aesthetic use and application of colour in relation to appearance that I will be focusing, and in particular, make-up and hair colouring.

The face will be your canvas, colour your medium and make-up your material. Think of hair colour as make-up for the hair. This is where the world of art and science come together.

To further your understanding of colour as an art medium you will need to explore the scientific properties of colour and appreciate what colour is. This is discussed further in Part 3, Section 3.1, but for now let me say that colour is light energy. In fact, it is made up of different wavelengths of light which are absorbed and reflected from the surface of objects.

The great artists had an 'eye' for colour. They understood the properties of light and colour. Artists such as Leonardo da Vinci, Caravaggio and Rembrandt were pioneers in the effect of chiaroscuro, the Italian for 'bright-dark'. They were masters of using contrasts of light and shade to spotlight, add impact and interest to their paintings.

As make-up artists you can be masters of colour to create shape, shade, space and expression to the face, give harmony or add contrast.

Similarly as hair stylists the world of colour can be used to give definition and added dimensions to your design creations.

texture

Texture, like colour, is all around us. We live in a world of different textures which we learn to distinguish. Our eyes tell us whether a surface is shiny or matt. Our sense of touch gives us information about the feel of something. For example, whether it feels smooth or rough. Associated with texture is our ability to judge whether a material is light or heavy. Being able to experience and judge texture is said to be linked to having 'an eye for texture and an excellent *tactile memory*'.

tactile memory

What is meant by tactile memory? To help explain this consider the following senses that humans have, and rely on, to register and remember information about the environment that they live in.

Of the senses:

- 85% of what a person remembers comes through seeing
- 11% of what a person remembers comes through hearing
- 4% of what a person remembers comes through touch, smell and taste

In our early informative years we rely both on touch and sight to explore different surfaces. The older we get the more tuned our eyesight gets as recognizing different textures and

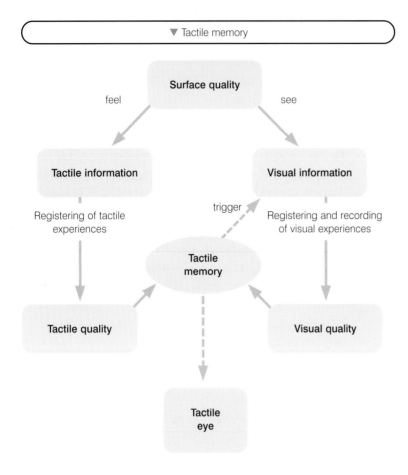

▼ Tactile memory

Surface quality

feel — Tactile information

see — Visual information

Registering of tactile experiences

Registering and recording of visual experiences

trigger

Tactile memory

Tactile quality

Visual quality

Tactile eye

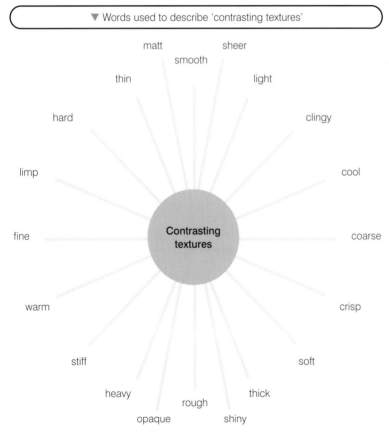

▼ Words used to describe 'contrasting textures'

Contrasting textures

matt, sheer, smooth, thin, light, hard, clingy, limp, cool, fine, coarse, warm, crisp, stiff, soft, heavy, thick, rough, opaque, shiny, shiny

similarly our sense of touch becomes more and more sensitive to how something feels. Our textural experiences are registered and recorded; experiences that we later rely on and need to recall. At this time we no longer need to touch every surface to know how it feels because we have built up what is called tactile memory. This is triggered by what we see and in turn triggers our power of recall to associate how a particular surface feels without the need to touch it.

what is surface quality?

The surface quality of a material like hair, skin or clothing fabric can be described in terms of different contrasting qualities.

These are the words that designers and artists use. In this book I will be mainly focusing on texture in relation to skin and hair.

properties associated with textural quality

There are a number of properties associated with texture that you need to consider. They are the effect that texture has on the colour of a surface and the effect that texture has on the weight.

textured qualities and the colour of a surface

The colour quality of a surface, that is how bright it appears, will depend on the nature of the texture. For example, a smooth surface appears strong due to its light-reflecting properties, whereas a textured surface appears more matt due to its absorptive properties. Some surfaces of a more transparent nature both reflect, absorb light and allow light to pass through.

textured qualities and weight

There are two kinds of textural weight: tactile weight and visual weight.

Tactile weight refers to how heavy a material or fabric feels relative to others. We rely on tactile memory to help evaluate the differences between materials and fibres.

Visual weight refers to those materials, fabrics and even hair that look lighter or heavier than they feel because of their colour or print properties. For instance warm, dark and bright colours tend to look dense or heavy. Cool, light and dull colours look visually lighter.

Both kinds of weight can be expressed as relatively lightweight, medium weight or heavyweight.

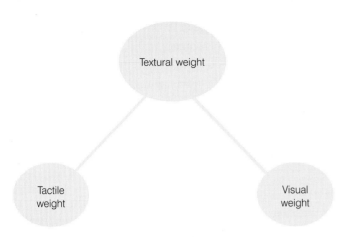

the language of design

Just about everything around us has some form of design pattern. In fact, even our faces and bodies have a unique design pattern or profile which can be described by using the words line, shape, texture, colour, composition, to convey precise information about specific visual qualities.

As you get more familiar with the world of art and the language of design you will begin to appreciate that the same words can also be used to convey specific information about the visual appearance of a hair design or style and even a make-up look. You will need to use these words quite freely and confidently when you talk to clients about a particular cut or look. Similarly, if you are asked by a magazine to produce style comments to accompany some of your photographic work, this language will be essential.

Hence, from an art perspective, faces and bodies and the world of design and style are linked by a common language, that is by the same words or components.

Designing is the process of combining these components in different ways to compose and create new forms or effects.

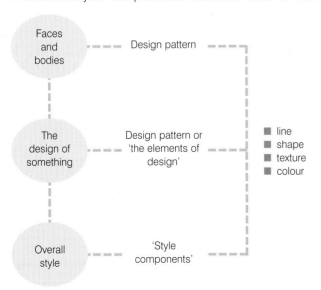

Let us now look more closely at these patterns, elements and components in relation to:

- the face and body
- hair design and styling
- make-up design and styling
- clothes, accessories and fashion styling

the design pattern of the face

We are fascinated by faces. We are attracted to them, we respond to them. But what is there about facial beauty that stimulates our interest? How do we judge faces and what aspects about the face do we consider? Beauty in women is said to be based on:

- large eyes
- small nose
- full lips
- a small chin
- high cheekbones
- a delicate jaw
- a smooth unblemished skin
- clear colouring

Such characteristics not only describe the qualities that we use to rate attractiveness but also describe the overall composition of the face and facial features in terms of shape, line, texture and colour. As you become more used to studying faces you will notice that everyone's face has a unique design pattern, which must be assessed before advancing your design services.

shape in hair design

Undoubtedly *shape* is a vital consideration in hair design and an important component of a style. But what do we mean by shape in relation to hair design and how can you work with it to change *dimension*? In effect, I have already given you the answer. A haircut or style on a head exists in three dimensions. Imagine it contained within a cube. That is it has the dimensions of height, width and depth.

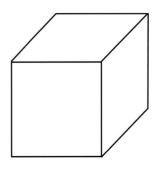

hair design in three dimensions

We talk about the *height* of a style. This describes the distance or *depth* of the hair from the top of the scalp. Points of depth when joined together produce an outline or outlying shape.

Synonymous with height is *length*. The length of someone's hair or the length of a style describes the distance or point at which the hair falls to rest as measured from the top of the scalp. Points of length when joined together form:

■ the external line or *perimeter* of cut or style or

■ the internal line of the cut

Width describes the horizontal dimensions of a haircut or style, that is the dimension from side to side.

Depth as well as describing the dimension from the top of the style to the scalp also refers to the dimensions from front to back.

When visualising, analysing or creating a style or cut it must be considered and viewed as a three-dimensional structure. Furthermore, when it comes to deciding on a style to suit a client's head, face or body dimensions, you will need to ensure that you choose or control these dimensions carefully. Associated with the dimensions, height, width and depth are the terms 'bulk', 'weight' and 'volume'.

bulk, weight and volume

Bulk is used to express the size or thickness of something. We often say that a person is bulky. In hair design a designer may say that a cut looks too bulky. This expresses the need to remove bulkiness or thickness from a particular region.

To be more precise the words 'volume' and 'weight' can be and are used in this context. Hair designers talk in terms of 'the volume of a look', 'there is too much weight', and 'the need to remove weight'.

The use of these terms can be best explained by referring again to a cube and its dimensions: height, width and depth.

By multiplying the height, width and depth the volume of the cube is calculated. It is an expression of the three-dimensional space it occupies.

Volume in hair design expresses the space that a cut or style occupies.

Weight is a term used to express the physical heaviness of something. The weight of an object can be measured and expressed in terms of specific units.

Hair designers frequently use this term when describing, creating or checking haircuts. Whilst no measuring device is involved, the skilled designer is able to spot weight simply by looking. Consequently, it would be more precise to use the words 'visual weight'.

working with shapes

For style and design purposes it is the outline or silhouette of a shape we must consider. In terms of facial and body shape I will be working with the following geometric silhouettes:

■ rectangle

■ triangle

■ inverted triangle

■ hourglass

■ oval

■ figure eight

■ circle

Much of your style and design work is concerned with working with shapes and combination of shapes, be they the contour of a garment or outfit, the shape of an earring, hair ornament and haircut in relation to face or body contours. The important question is, ask yourself whether or not the shapes relate to one another in terms of linear characteristics. If shapes have things in common they can be said to be of the same family, which is the basis of a successful combination.

Combining shapes of different families creates visual problems. For instance, a 'square peg in a round hole'.

The combination of shapes introduces the important *principle of repetition*.

■ style lines in hair design

The *line* of a cut or style is the direction or directions in which the hair falls or is positioned. Hence line gives *direction* to a style. Variations of line create *movement*.

The line of a cut or style is important as it visually directs the eye of a viewer along the direction in which the hair is cut, styled, dressed or coloured. Hence the direction and movement all contribute to the visual image of a look. Lines that follow through or flow smoothly throughout a look give a softer effect to that style. Broken lines of movement look harder and give a style impact. Texture, wave and curl are examples of how movement can be used in hair design to create softness.

The four basic style lines that can be incorporated into your designs are *vertical*, *horizontal*, *diagonal* and *curved*.

vertical lines in hair design

Whilst it is impossible to cut a vertical line in hair, vertical line detail can be introduced by varying the height of a style as viewed from the top of the scalp, and the length of a style.

Cheynes

▲ Example of the use of curl to create interior style lines

Vidal Sassoon

▲ Example of a cut that has broken lines of movement

Ian Mistlin

▲ Example of interior lines of a cut

Vidal Sassoon

▲ Examples of a cut with strong exterior perimeter

horizontal lines in hair design

Examples of external horizontal lines are a square fringe or the square lines of a bob, when viewed from the back or side.

diagonal lines in hair design

The use of diagonal lines in hair design is common. Consider the angle of a diagonal line in the form of a side fringe that sweeps across the head from one side to the other.

A diagonal fringe is a very useful way of introducing asymmetry into a very round face or as a way of reducing the area of an extra high forehead.

curved lines in hair design

External curved lines can be used, in haircutting, to add softness to a classic one-length cut, and make it less angular. For example, an Isadora, page-boy or halo type cut.

The cuts rely on a curved line to produce a soft flowing external line to cut.

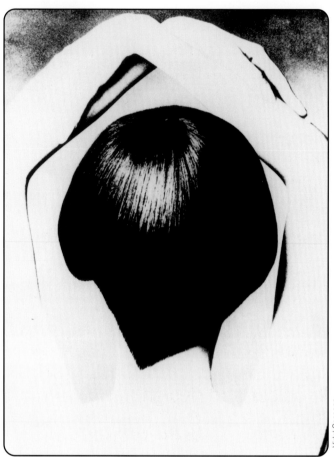

Vidal Sassoon

Curved lines can also be formed by styling and dressing hair into various forms.

■ style lines in make-up design

Style lines formed on the face tend to be more softly curved as they follow the contours of the face and features.

The most dramatic use of line on the face is in relation to the eye and lips. Here make-up is used to enhance, emphasise or even correct natural shape.

For instance in eye design the correct placement and application of eyeshadow colour is essential in order to correctly proportion, contour and control shape, size and most importantly the proportion of the eyelid to brow.

Careful blending of eyeshadows is essential in order to avoid creating harsh demarcation or dividing lines between colour and skin, or between two colours.

The correct use of eyeliner is also essential in order to define the eye. Applied to the eyelid at the lash base consideration and care must go to deciding on how thin, thick and even the line is. Thin lines are more delicate and subtle. Thick lines are dominant and confident style trends may well dictate which is used. An uneven line is associated with a wobbly hand!

Vidal Sassoon

Curved lines can also be incorporated internally into your hair designs by using round graduation cutting technique to build up 'weight' on a particular region of the head.

Similarly lip liner and lip colour can be used to give lips suitable line treatment.

> ☑ **tip**

line treatment and concepts to consider

- Be aware of the optical properties of lines.

- Be aware of the relationship between the interior line movement and the exterior line detail in your designs so that both are in harmony.

- Be aware of the relationship between line, balance and proportion. All cuts and styles rely on definite line for balance.

- Be aware of the relationship between the lines of a cut or style and the lines that make up a person's face shape.

- Be aware of a person's facial features and the direction of lines that describe the shape of their eyes, nose, eyebrows, mouth.

■ colour and design

The great artists and their 'eye' for colour must have been founded on their knowledge about colour pigments, the properties of colour, the dimensions of colour, colour relationships and a colour memory that enabled them to work so creatively with colour and reproduce so realistically the beauty of nature and the beauty of the human body. Although colour in the human body is not as diverse as that found in nature, it is nevertheless also organised in harmonious patterns. These great masters appreciated and identified this, as they captured the natural beauty of skin, hair and eyes so well on canvas, giving their paintings the dimensions of mood, personality and life.

Choosing colours that go well together does not come easily to everyone. Many people over the years, lose the 'eye' for colour. As children, we readily explore colour, but as we get older we develop prejudices; we erect barriers so, consequently, we cannot be totally objective about dressing with colour or proficient in selecting suitable make-up. However, once a person understands the physical relationship between colours it will give them tremendous style-awareness and the advantage to use colour more creatively. No longer will the client stand and stare with uncertainty deciding on whether certain colours go successfully together.

Similarly, imagine how much wiser you will be when you are advising, selecting and applying make-up to enhance a person's skin tones and facial features; evaluating your present make-up box; contemplating changing a client's hair colour; and co-ordinating a selection of fashion garments or accessories if in the first instance you recognise a person's unique *colour pattern*; and know how to choose colours that enhance it. Success will depend on understanding the simple rules of colour harmony and colour relationships. For instance why certain colour shades when worn next to the face play such amazing effects on the skin and face colour or why certain colours worn as eye make-up intensify eye colour.

colour suitability … making colour work

Colour suitability will depend on taking four factors into consideration. These are skin, hair, eye colour and the colour relationships thus formed between the worn or applied colours.

The relationship between colours will depend on their relative positions around the colour wheel (see section on colour combinations). It is important to note that a person can wear almost every colour on the colour wheel as long as it is the *best hue, value and intensity for them*. These are the dimension colours that artists use. *Hue* describes the name of a colour as well as family name. *Value* is the lightness or darkness of a colour. *Intensity* describes the strength of a colour.

By firstly considering the suitability of colour worn next to, near or on the face, you will soon begin to appreciate the importance of the face as the focal point to a person's body. When colours are in harmony with a person's natural colouring, they will look aesthetically more attractive and pleasing to others, People's response will altogether be more positive.

the 'wrong' colours

Wearing the 'wrong' colours can play amazing tricks on the skin tones and eye colour, completely altering a person's facial style by:

- making them look tired and haggard
- making them look older
- casting shadows
- emphasising facial lines, wrinkles and blemishes
- creating a greyness or pasty complexion
- making the face appear fuller and shorter
- dulling the eyes

Wearing the wrong colours can certainly affect a person's personal presentation. Often it will appear that the colour is wearing them rather than the other way around.

the 'right' colours

In comparison, the 'right' colours can:

- enhance a person's natural colouring
- make them look younger
- lift their features

- make their skin look clearer and healthier
- accentuate the colour of their eyes
- help make their eyes seem larger and brighter
- add sparkle to the eyes
- make the face appear more defined

Similarly, when it comes to make-up design, although you may not be applying 'paint to canvas' in the true sense, the face is your canvas. The relationship between colours that you select is especially important if you want to use colours that enhance your client's features and bring out the natural beauty of their eyes. The same can also be applied to hair colouring.

why do certain colours flatter?

To understand this, we will be examining the relationship between colours and the *colour combination* formed between the colour pigment complexes in skin, hair and eye colours. This will be influenced by five relationships. They are:

1 The *degree of warmth or coolness* of a colour applied or worn in relation to the degree of warmth or coolness of the client's skin tones, eye tones and hair colour.

2 The *degree of lightness or darkness* of a colour applied or worn in relation to the client's overall *depth* of colour or with respect to separate colour *values* of their skin, eyes and hair.

3 The *degree of purity or softness* of a colour applied or worn in relation to the overall colour *intensity* or *chroma*.

4 The *degree of contrast* that the clients exhibits. Contrast refers to the differences, if any, between colour values, i.e. hair vs. skin, clothes vs. skin, make-up vs. skin.

5 The *degree of selective reflection* that occurs when colours that are worn are reflected back onto the skin and the effect it creates. Similarly, the effect can also occur on the face due to changes in hair colour.

These relationships are now briefly explained.

the significance of warm and cool

The importance of this will become clearer as we proceed in our study of colour. For now, let me say that the best clothing, make-up and hair colours for your customer or client will depend on your understanding of colour temperature and your ability to evaluate the degree of warmth or coolness in the skin tones, eyes or hair. The term used by colour consultants and make-up companies to express this is *undertone*.

getting the depth of colour right

Getting the depth of colour right is essential both as hair colourists, make-up artists and fashion stylists. That means judging how light or dark a client's hair and skin is and then prescribing, applying or choosing colours that are of equal or similar colour value.

the need for purity or softness

Some clients will look better wearing brilliant or bright colours as opposed to soft or muted colours. Purity of a colour describes its degree of saturation. It is a direct measure of how much grey is in a colour. This being the case soft or muted colours are 'greyed'. Chroma is a term used by colour analysts.

the importance of contrast

Applied to a person's colouring, contrast can exist between skin, hair and eye values. The level of contrast will influence which colour values look best on your customer or client.

Their 'level of contrast' can be described as low, medium or high and should be repeated in the value of their clothing, make-up or hair colouring.

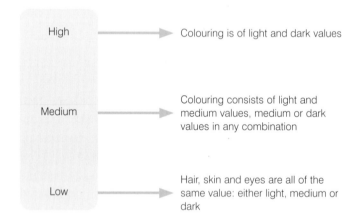

High	Colouring is of light and dark values
Medium	Colouring consists of light and medium values, medium or dark values in any combination
Low	Hair, skin and eyes are all of the same value: either light, medium or dark

the degree of selective reflection

All colours selectively absorb and transmit certain wavelengths of light. These give us our perception of colour (see colour mixing and primary colours). Depending on the colour, how close to the face it is worn and light conditions, certain wavelengths will be transmitted and reflected back onto the skin. It is on the face that colour mixing of these selectively reflected colour wavelengths occurs and together with skin pigments combine to affect a person's natural tones. Consequently, a person will look more attractive if there is a balance and harmony between the hue, value and intensity of colours on their face or body.

As designers, artists and advisers, you need to appreciate colour and know how to work effectively with it, both creatively and technically. The starting point must be a basic understanding of colour before you can truly fulfil your role.

texture and design

On the question and use of texture the great artists clearly identified and recognised the importance of surface quality. Their classical figurative paintings portraying the female figure in all its forms: nude, semi nude and clothed, illustrate with brilliance the textural properties of skin and hair. They also provide us with perfect examples to appreciate the draping properties of fabrics on the body and the importance of choosing fabrics that successfully interact with the body's textural qualities. Their skill to capture surface quality so aesthetically and in such fine detail can be said to be linked to having a highly developed 'eye' for texture and an excellent tactile memory.

Texture is a key design element and must be fully appreciated when designing. Similarly, it is a fundamental style component and quality which contributes to a person's total look. But what does 'texture' mean to different designers and artists? When we talk about the texture of hair, the texture of skin, the texture of a make-up product, the texture of a hairstyle or make-up look or even the texture of a fabric, what do we mean? Similarly, how as advisers, designers and artists can you improve, create and work with texture?

If you are a fashion or image adviser you will need to have a detailed knowledge and understanding of texture.

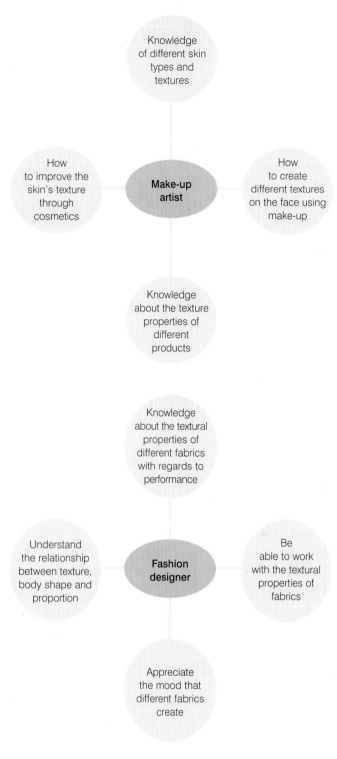

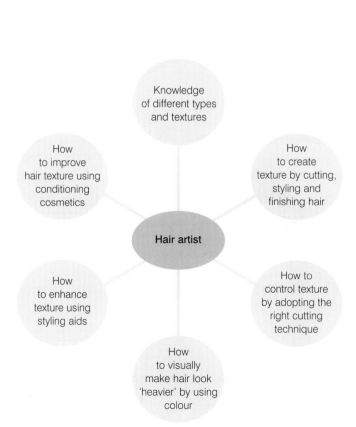

style principles and concepts

So far my discussion on design has been focused on the individual elements. However, you need to consider the composition of your work, that is how these elements can be combined into your conceptual images and creations so that they complement each other to produce a design that looks right or is pleasing to the eye. For example:

- a haircut in relation to the contours of the head and face
- an outfit of clothing in relation to body contours
- make-up in relation to a person's natural colouring
- hair colour that harmonises with a person's natural colouring
- fabrics in relation to facial textures
- jewellery in relation to facial contours

The aim is to be sure that each element not only complements its localised area but in addition complements the total composition. In this way you do not treat any particular area/part of the body in isolation but consider the whole picture.

The principles and concepts are the ways in which design elements may be used to control a design. This is the key to successful designing.

The principles and concepts that I will be applying are:

- repetition
- rhythm
- harmony
- contrast
- proportion
- balance
- diversion and emphasis
- line illusions
- the perception of scale

repetition

Repetition as the word suggests, involves the principle of repeating related lines, angles, curves, textures and colours, so as to create a harmonious effect. This will be of particular relevance as you advise on what:

- is the best shape or silhouette of outfits/garments to wear
- fabrics suit a client's body type
- is the most suitable style detail to go for
- colours look best
- jewellery to wear
- is the most compatible cut or style to suit a client's face shape

The answers to these questions focus on the need to create harmony by:

- repeating a person's body shape in the silhouette of an outfit or garment
- repeating the body line, i.e. the line of the garment. For example on straight bodies use straight lines, on curved bodies use curved lines
- matching fabric types to body types. For example, straight bodies use crisp, taut fabrics, curvy bodies use more fluid fabrics
- relating style detail in clothing to 'lines in the face'
- relating style line and detail of a cut to that of the client's face, i.e. soft facial features to a soft style
- relating colour of clothing to natural colouring

Repetition is a principle of movement that links common features in a design. It creates unity.

However, it is important at this stage to also be aware that repeating a shape will emphasise it, which may not be aesthetically suitable. In which case you will need to consider rebalancing aspects of the head, face and body.

rhythm

Like repetition rhythm is a principle of movement. Rhythm occurs when a number of design elements are arranged into an ordered and predictable pattern, which the eye can follow. Just as the ear responds to audio beat; the eye responds to visual beat. The visual beat of lines can be fluid or staccato. Shapes can take on a rhythm depending on how regularly they are repeated; so too can colour changes within a design. Any pause or interruption brought about by sudden changes of pattern upsets or destroys rhythm.

rhythm in hair design

Applied to hair design here are some examples.

◀ Smooth, fluid external lines of a hair cut.

Vidal Sassoon

◀ Dramatic and exciting lines of a jagged fringe.

Vidal Sassoon

◀ Abrupt rhythm and shape created by the textural properties of a cut or style.

◀ Change of rhythm created by use of colour.

rhythm in fashion design

In fashion and clothing design rhythm is linked to the structural and decorative components of a garment.

harmony

Harmony occurs when one or more aspects of a design are alike. Hence there is a degree of repetition and consistency. Colour and colour harmonies is the subject of much discussion in this book in relation to make-up design and styling colour of clothes.

harmony in hair design

Within hair design repeated rounded lines create harmony. The mixing of curved and straight creates unrest.

In relation to a hair design or style, total harmony is said to exist if the structural design, detail and finish is aesthetically pleasing, appropriate and functional taking into consideration the person, their physique and features; colouring, age, gender, lifestyle and personality (see Part IV conducting a total design analysis).

harmony in make-up design

In make-up design harmony can be achieved by the combining and linking of monochromatic colours. For example light brown, medium brown and dark brown. The medium brown is used to soften the transition.

harmony in fashion design

With regards to the total look and fashion styling for make-overs, clothes and accessories need to harmonise with the physical characteristics of the model.

However, variety is the spice of life. A degree of variety can add contrast and interest to a design. For example in the use

of line, shape, texture, pattern, tone of colour within a garment. Although too much variety can create too much contrast and confusion.

contrast

Contrast is about combining opposites or totally unrelated features that have nothing in common. Minimal and well-placed contrast can help lift a design.

contrast in hair and make-up design

In make-up and hair design contrast has wide application particularly with the use of colour contrasts, contrast of texture, contrast of shape and contrast of space.

proportion

Proportion can be described as the relation of one part to another or to the whole. It can also be described as the correct relation in size, distance, amount or ratio between one thing or another. Proportion is a comparing process as the viewer seeks to judge similarities or differences that are perceived as pleasing to the eye.

proportion in hair design

In hair design you must concern yourself with the proportion of a design or style in relation to the proportions of the body, head and face. This will mean taking into consideration relative proportions of length and width. Visual illusions associated with line and scale also need to be considered.

Texture must be considered with respect to its effect on bulk, size and space occupied by a design or style. This in proportion to overall face and body proportions is also critical. Colour proportions can also affect a hair design particularly if horizontal contrasts of colour are introduced.

proportion in make-up design

Proportion in make-up design is determined by considering the proportions of the face and features before applying colour. Colour depending on where and how it is placed is used to visually change proportions. Colour proportions can be varied according to the hue, value and chroma of the colour used. Care must be taken not to create obvious colour demarcations.

Also note that some colours advance or have greater visual power than others. They need to be used in small amounts.

proportion in fashion styling

Proportion in fashion styling is linked to viewing the dressed female body in terms of pleasing segments or proportions. It is based on the aesthetic ratio of 3 : 5 : 8, which expresses zones of the body against an ideal height of 8 heads. The ratio is known as the Golden Mean.

The theory is that variations of height and figure problems can be visually adjusted by combining garments of varying lengths to change proportions.

balance

Balance is a visual quality. It is also known by another name 'visual weight'. Balance is associated with proportion and symmetry.

Symmetry describes 'planning proportions between parts of a whole'. For example, if we take a circle and divide it equally into two halves:

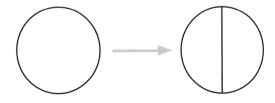

Each half is said to balance symmetrically or is a mirror image of the other.

In terms of pleasing proportions, two equal halves are interpreted by the brain as stable. This is known as formal balance. The opposite is informal balance when there is an asymmetrical relationship between both sides of an axis. For example if we take a rectangle and divide it as follows:

an imbalance exists between the two halves and as a result we do not view this relationship as pleasing.

The differences may be simple variations in design or detail or significantly contrasting and exciting. Hence balance is a comparing process.

balance in hair design

Balance is a visual quality achieved by perfecting your technique and eye for design detail during the cutting, styling and dressing of hair. The aim is to maintain the right distribution of hair around the head and face, so that the symmetry of the design or style is pleasing to overall head, face and body shape, when viewed from different angles, i.e. front, side and rear.

Before a flattering design can be composed or created the proportions of the head, face and body must be observed and assessed with a view to suitable line treatment, shape, texture and finish. Mastery of cutting, styling and dressing techniques will be essential.

Problems of balance can be due to

- uneven one-length cuts
- uneven layering
- incorrect graduation
- wrong positioning of knots, rolls and pleats
- poor dressing out and finishing of hair
- incorrect choice of hair accessory and positioning

balance in make-up design

Similarly in make-up design balance is of key consideration and of prime visual importance. First consideration must be the assessing of the client's overall facial proportions and then the proportions of the facial features. The next stage is to plan how you can use and apply make-up to rebalance or enhance their face shapes and features.

diversion and emphasis

To create a diversion means to distract a person away from something. This principle can be cleverly used in styling to divert the viewer's attention away from some aspect of the client's face or body which may not be their best feature.

The concept is to create a visual diversion that is eye-catching so that an observer looks to a person's assets not at a problem area.

The aim is to emphasise the asset by using the tactic of creating a focal point.

line illusions

Artists have long known about the optical proportions of lines, in particular about the illusions created by horizontal and vertical lines. But how do they work and how do we perceive them?

When we look at a line our eye automatically lengthens it making it appear longer than it really is. As our eye looks in the direction of a line any obstacle or break to the movement changes our perception of length. Consequently, lines can be used to create the illusion of balance or imbalance.

Below are five identical vertical lines. Study them carefully, Which one appears longer and which appears shorter?

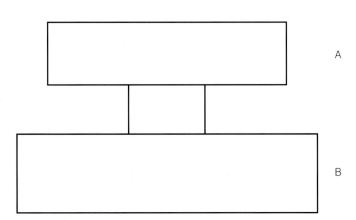

Lines 1, 3 and 5 look the shortest. Line 2 the longest and line 4 in between.

Now consider the diagram below. Are your eyes drawn to rectangle A or B?

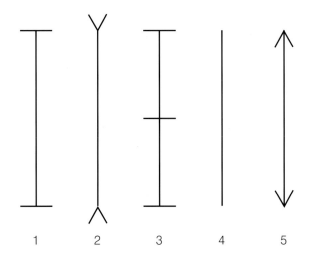

Now turn the book on its side so that the rectangles lie vertical. Which rectangle creates the illusion of being larger?

The answer to both questions is rectangle B. The reason for this is that eyes are always drawn to the broadest horizontal line.

These examples illustrate two important concepts. Vertical lines make one look up and down and create the illusion of length and horizontal lines make one look across and give the illusion of width.

the perception of scale

Compare the following circular illustrations. In all three the centre circles are the same size. However, when surrounded by circles of different sizes an interesting optical illusion happens.

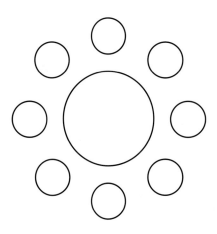

Surrounded by smaller circles, the centre circle appears larger.

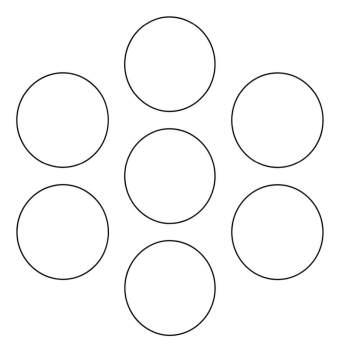

Surrounded by circles of the same size, the size of the centre circle remain the same.

Surrounded by larger circles the centre circle appears smaller.

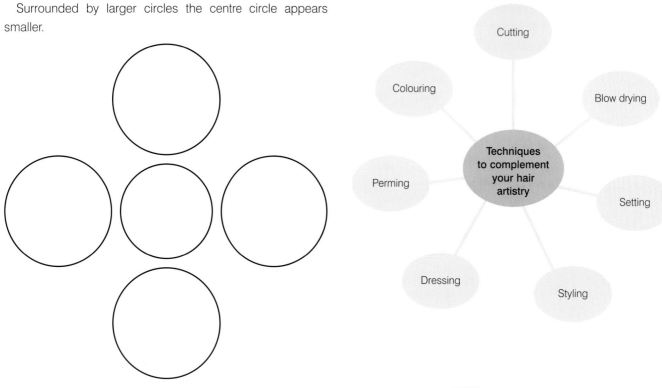

Scale can be defined as the proportion which the representation of one object bears to another.

Use this principle to appreciate the correct overall size of a hairstyle in relationship to your client's head, face and body.

If your client has a small face, a very full big hairstyle can make it look even smaller. Conversely a large person who has a very short, cropped hairstyle will tend to look larger.

Scale also plays an important part of illusion dressing and in accessorising. By adjusting the scale of garments of clothing, a person can appear smaller or taller.

■ technique

Artistry in hair and make-up will also require you to be strong technically. That is, being skilled or have a mastery to perform a particular procedure. The professional hair or make-up artist needs a complete toolkit of techniques to craft hair or paint faces. Especially important is knowing when to use a particular technique or adapt a technique to come up with new styles or creations. In effect technique is a necessity. It provides a firm foundation from which to develop your role and work.

■ summary

As the book develops I will be using these words, principles and concepts to describe the design pattern of the head, face and body and in particular how these words can be used to visually assess bodily contours, colourings and textures.

Elements of design	Elements of style	Style principles and concepts
line	hair	line
shape	make-up	proportion
texture	colour	balance
colour	clothes	symmetry
	accessories	scale
		repetition
		emphasis
		diversion
		harmony
		rhythm

The next step is to apply these style concepts to advise clients or customers on how they can look their best and put together winning compositions by successfully relating and integrating all the elements of design. The object is to achieve flattering proportions, good balance and harmony. Harmony is said to exist when all parts combine so that nothing appears to be out of place. This will be the subject of much discussion throughout the book.

Finally, you will discover how to apply the same concepts in your work, on the shop floor, in your studio or on a photographic shoot as you seek to turn conceptual ideas into creations that work.

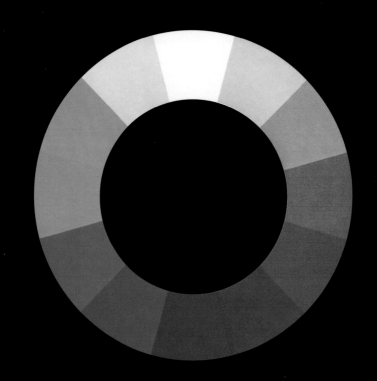

3 improving your technical understanding

Understanding colour theory is essential for all colour work. Learn about the properties, the qualities and language that artists and designers use and discover why people have different hair, skin and eye colours.

3.1 colour

■ the properties of colour

Before the seventeenth century, it was believed that colour existed in objects, irrespective of the light under which they were seen. However, in 1666 Isaac Newton succeeded in demonstrating that light is the source of all colours. In his classic experiment, he split a beam of sunlight into a colour spectrum by passing it at a certain angle through a glass prism. The spectrum formed was made up of a band of colours of different wavelengths of light – red, orange, yellow, green, blue, indigo and violet – each refracted at a different angle. Red light with the longest wavelength and lowest frequency was refracted least; violet light with the shortest wavelength and highest frequency was refracted most.

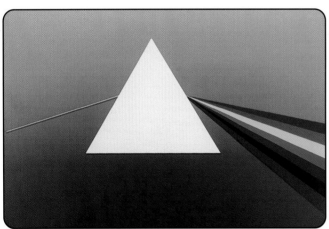

Ian Mistlin

Do you remember doing this experiment at school, or seeing it occur naturally in the form of a rainbow? By using a second prism, Newton directed the band of colours to reform a beam of 'colourless light'. In effect he showed that white light is composed of the colours of the spectrum. Newton's work, titled *Opticks*, laid the foundations of optics as a science, establishing colour theory and proving that light is the source of all colour.

White light is made up of different wavelengths, which vibrate at slightly different speeds or frequency.

spectral colours and wavelengths

Part of spectrum	Wavelength	Shortest/ Longest	Energy
Violet	420 mm	Shortest	
Blue	460 mm		More energised
Green	534 mm		due to greater
Yellow	564 mm		vibrational speed
Red	650 mm	Longest	

spectral colours as they appear in a rainbow

Red Orange Yellow Green Blue Indigo Violet

The order and range of colours are easy to remember through the following rhyme:

> *Richard Of York Gives Battle In Vain*

The first letter of each word corresponds to the name and position of the colour in the spectrum.

seeing colour

Many colour consultants, advisers and educators talk about the need to develop a client's or customer's 'colour eye'. Whilst this refers to the importance of stimulating and changing a person's taste for colour, we need to understand the role the eye plays in 'seeing' colour. A useful analogy is to liken the eye to a camera. Colour waves pass through the eye. The amount of light entering the eye is controlled by the iris. The lens brings the incident light rays to focus on a region called the retina which is equivalent to the 'film'. It is here that sensitive light receptor cells called cones and rods begin the work of deciphering the components of light into electrical impulses. The cones regulate the quality of light received and enable us to see colour, whilst the rods regulate the quantity of light we see, enabling us to see black and white.

The eye has three kinds of cone receptors which react selectively to different regions of the visible spectrum. They are sensitive to red, blue and green.

The electrical impulses from the respective cones are recombined by specialist cells in the retina and relayed to the brain as a brightness signal and two hue signals, one hue describes the amount of red or green. The other describes the amounts of blue or yellow.

surface colour

Why do surfaces reveal different colours when they are struck by the same source of white light?

This phenomenon of sensation of colour was not fully explained until 1900 when the physicist Max Planck proposed that oscillating atoms emit and absorb energy in packets or quanta.

The atom is the fundamental atomic structure of all matter and consists of a positively charged nucleus surrounded by an orbit of negatively charged electrons.

Planck proved that light is composed of quanta which he named photons. It is these photons or packets of energy that are captured by orbiting electrons, causing them to jump to a higher energy orbit, before eventually returning to the original orbit. As the electrons return they release this absorbed energy as a small amount of unmeasurable heat.

When light falls on a coloured object the photons present within the respective wavelengths behave as particles, some of which are absorbed (if they are of a high enough energy to excite the atomic electrons), transmitted and some reflected.

It is these reflected protons – making up a 'mixture' of colour wavelengths – that our visionary mechanism deciphers and registers to create different *colour sensations*.

A red dress looks red because the red surface absorbs nearly all the colour waves except red (namely green and blue) which is scattered and reflected back from the entire surface of the dress to our eyes and registered. The other 'colour waves' have been turned into heat.

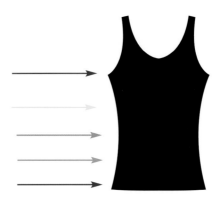

A black top in a matt fabric will absorb nearly all the light that falls on it, reflecting very little; here it appears black.

This effect is called *selective reflection of colour*.

A black surface is the most efficient at absorbing 'sunlight', harnessing the energy and converting it into heat. Hence on a hot day, the darker the colour worn the hotter one feels due to the phenomenon known as black body radiation effect.

A white surface on the other hand scatters and reflects almost all colour waves equally and thus appears white. Consequently, lighter colours or whiter tones appear physically cooler than darker colours or blacker tones which seem physically warmer.

So far, I have only referred to surface colours that are reflected, but as you would expect, the same reasoning can be applied to mixed colour waves. Take for instance a yellow-green leaf.

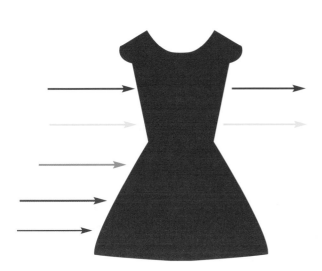

The colour we see is made up of varying proportions of both yellow and green that are reflected from the leaf surface after the other spectral colours have been absorbed. Similarly, a yellow ball in white light will appear yellow. This is because it absorbs the blue light, scattering away red and green waves which appear yellow to our eyes.

The effect of selective reflection is of particular relevance to your work with respect to the impact of light on colour pigments.

Colour pigment molecules are present in practically every naturally occurring object or those artificially created by man. Each pigment's molecular composition is such that it has a 'resonance' or affinity for a particular wavelength or group of wavelengths.

contemporary colour theory

the history of the colour wheels

Our understanding of contemporary colour theory and colour mixing is best discussed by examining the history of the colour wheels and the contributions made by some eminent colour theorists starting with Isaac Newton, then Wolfgang Goethe, Philip Otto Rung, Michel Chevreul, Johannes Itten and Albert Munsell.

Isaac Newton

It was Sir Isaac Newton in 1706 who first linked colours together in the form of a continuous circle. This followed on from his classic experiment in which he separated out the component elements of sunlight to create a spectrum or rainbow. The seven spectral colours were red, yellow, orange, green, blue, indigo and violet, which he represented as follows:

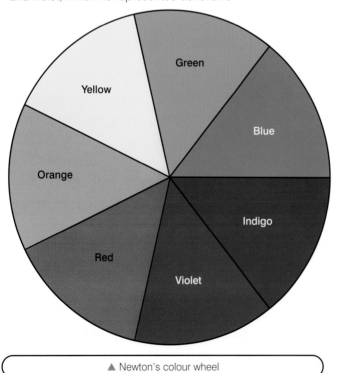

▲ Newton's colour wheel

Wolfgang Goethe

In 1792 the German philosopher, novelist and poet, Goethe, published his version of the colour wheel which depicted only *six* spectral colours. Later is his published work, *The Doctrine of Colours*, Goethe strongly attacked and opposed Newton's discovery, based on his argument that colour was composed of lightness and darkness. That is yellow was the first colour to appear when white was darkened, and blue was the first when black was lightened. Although these ideas were not borne out by physics, Goethe did formulate his wheel around the idea of pairs of colours: yellow and blue; yellow–red (orange) and blue–red (violet); red and green.

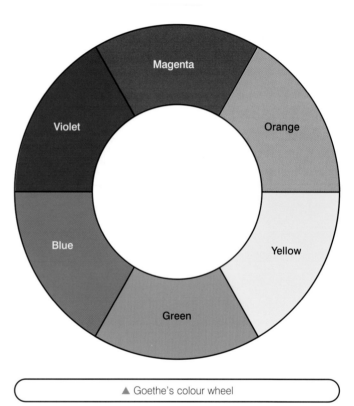

▲ Goethe's colour wheel

Johannes Itten

The Swiss artist, Johannes Itten, who taught at the famous Bauhaus School of Art in Germany in the 1920s, continued the work of Eugene Chevreul (1786–1889). Chevreul was one of the first to investigate colour and it was he who established the relationship between colours. Itten's colour wheel depicts twelve *hues* in a circle. Located in the triangle in the centre are the three *primary* colours: red, yellow and blue, which are pure pigments, and cannot be created by the mixture of other pigments. Alongside each primary, in the form of flat triangles, are the three *secondary* colours, which are derived in theory by the mixing of equal parts of the following:

red + blue	⟶	violet
blue + yellow	⟶	green
red + yellow	⟶	orange

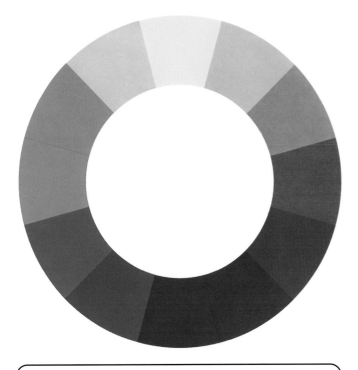

▲ Johannes Itten's colour wheel

Surrounding these triangles are a further twelve divisions of colour, made up of three primaries and three secondaries. Between each primary and secondary are a further six tertiary colours.

These are formed by the theoretical mixing of equal parts of a primary and secondary:

red + orange	⟶	red orange
yellow + green	⟶	yellow green
orange + yellow	⟶	yellow orange
red + violet	⟶	red violet
violet + blue	⟶	violet blue
blue + green	⟶	blue green

Albert Munsell

There is another colour wheel which I would like to introduce at this stage. It is the wheel devised by Albert Munsell and is widely used as the basis of colour matching. His wheel design depicts ten hues.

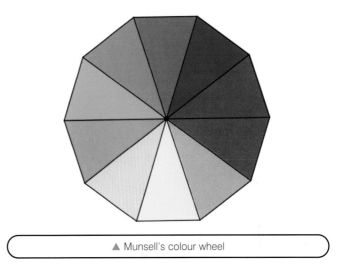

▲ Munsell's colour wheel

colour mixing

In the account on the mixing of colour pigments so far I have overstressed the word 'theory' because in the real world of colour we do not have primary pigments that are pure. There is no such substance as yellow paint which reflects only yellow wavelengths or for that matter a blue paint that is entirely pure. Similarly, from a selection of different 'reds', 'yellows', or 'blues' on the market which one would you use?

colour mixes, tints or tones

Colour mixes, tints or tones can be derived from a 'pure' pigment by the following additions:

- ■ Washing = + water
- ■ Tinting = + white
- ■ Shading = + black
- ■ Warming = + yellow and brown
- ■ Cooling = + blue
- ■ Muting = + complementary colour

A further range of tones can be achieved from hues that are first shaded, warmed, cooled or muted and then lightened, i.e. tinted or washed.

It follows that when a 'pure' pigment A, which has a certain resonance, is mixed with another colour pigment B, the resulting mix is colour tone C which will take on a new resonance contributing to the visual impression of C. This is how new colours are built up.

Try mixing 'pure' yellow and 'pure' blue pigments together:

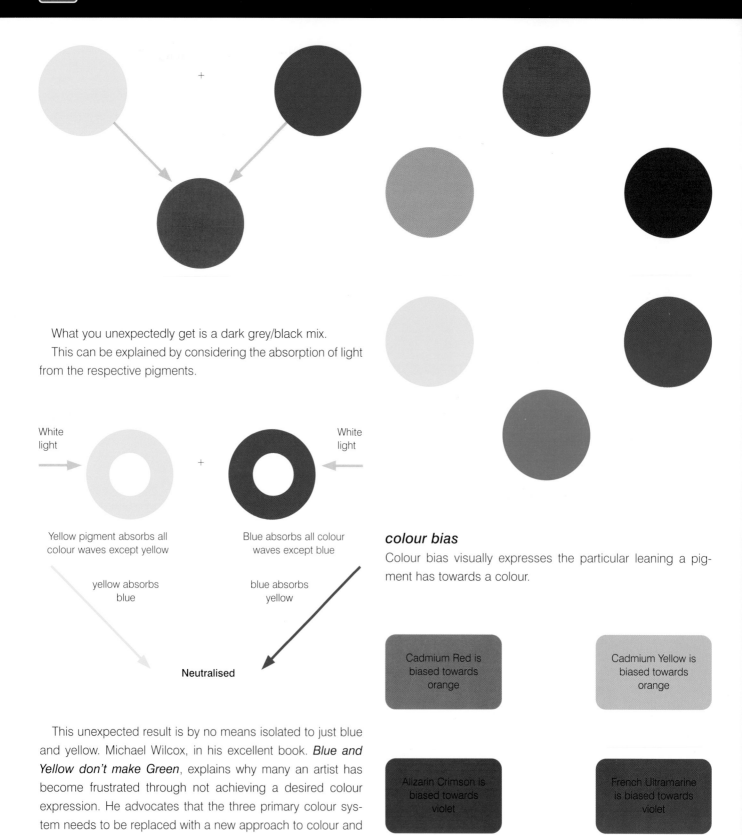

What you unexpectedly get is a dark grey/black mix.

This can be explained by considering the absorption of light from the respective pigments.

White light → Yellow pigment absorbs all colour waves except yellow

+

White light → Blue absorbs all colour waves except blue

yellow absorbs blue

blue absorbs yellow

Neutralised

This unexpected result is by no means isolated to just blue and yellow. Michael Wilcox, in his excellent book. *Blue and Yellow don't make Green*, explains why many an artist has become frustrated through not achieving a desired colour expression. He advocates that the three primary colour system needs to be replaced with a new approach to colour and that we have to change the way that we think about colour.

He recommends that the following six principal colours should be treated equally, if we are to make logical decisions about selecting colours to mix, based on the *colour bias* of each pigment.

colour bias

Colour bias visually expresses the particular leaning a pigment has towards a colour.

Cadmium Red is biased towards orange

Cadmium Yellow is biased towards orange

Alizarin Crimson is biased towards violet

French Ultramarine is biased towards violet

In effect what these examples explain is that pigments are *not pure* but made up of varied amounts of '*colour impurities*'.

For example Cadmium Yellow is made up of yellow, some orange and a small amount of green.

Alizarin Crimson is made up of red, violet and a touch of orange.

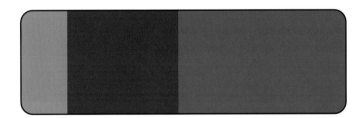

Ultramarine is made up of blue, some violet and a little green.

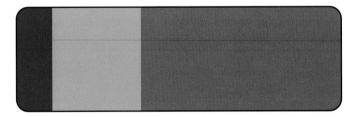

Cadmium Red is made up of red, orange and a small amount of violet.

It is only by taking the entire colour composition and its characteristics into consideration when mixing that consistently good results will be achieved.

Similarly the colour of clothes you wear, the make-up you apply and the hair products you use are made of dyes or pigments in varying proportions, which consequently give us a wealth of shades ranging from neutrals to high fashion colours. It is an important concept to grasp in furthering your understanding of the visual impression or qualities of colour.

■ the dimensions and language of colour

In 1915, the American artist and professor A. H. Munsell set out to devise a standard means of communicating about colour that would meet the needs of artists, scientists, industry and the general public alike. Since then it has been updated continually and is still one of the best systems of classification used today.

His system described the surface colour of a solid in terms of three *dimensions* based on *hue, value* and *chroma*. In his system these three dimensions are measured against an imaginary vertical scale of greys ranging from true black at the bottom and true white at the top.

These three dimensions are represented spatially in the form of a colour tree, with the trunk of the tree corresponding to the value scale and the horizontal axis or branches corresponding to the chroma scale.

The brightness scale runs vertically around the equator. Munsell's ten hues are arranged in sequence with colours of the highest chroma further away from the vertical axis. Consequently hues of lower chroma are found closer to the vertical.

hue

Hue describes the quality by which we distinguish one colour or a colour family from another. It is also the name we use to describe the name of a colour hue, e.g. red.

Colour or *hue family* is the name given to a group of similar pure fully saturated colours, to which no white or black has been added. Technically differences in hue are attributed to the wavelength of light waves reflected that form the surface colour. It is this selective absorption and reflection of light that forms the surface colour of say our hair, skin, make-up and clothes and the way that we perceive colour.

The six basic hue families are the reds, oranges, yellows, greens, blues and violets. You will notice that each family name is represented by a colour pigment which in some way differs from the next by what can be described as a different 'personality'.

value (lightness or darkness)

When you describe a blue as dark or an orange hue as light you are expressing the value of the colour. Munsell in his system used value to describe *the relative lightness or darkness of a hue to another hue*. Or alternatively the degree of harmony or contrast created by combinations of light and dark.

Based on an imaginary vertical 'value scale of greys' ranging from black at the bottom to white at the top, colours of the same lightness as a given grey are assigned the same numerical value and arranged on the same horizontal level.

If we consider the 'pure' pigment hues, you will observe that some hue families have pigments that display a wide range of values from light to medium, medium to dark, whilst others may only exhibit light values.

chroma (intensity or saturation)

Intensity or saturation describes the strength or purity of a colour. The term was originally coined by dyers to describe the strength or purity of a dye as a means of distinguishing it from a greyed colour. Munsel represented intensity on his horizontal *chroma* scale.

It is a scale where the less intense samples will approach grey, while the more intense or *brighter* samples will approach a pure jewel-like colour. As a sample becomes greyer it moves through a series of *shades* and conversely as it moves towards white *tints* are produced.

Shades and tints are *tones* of a hue. Tones can also be described in terms of lightness and brightness which can often add to the confusing use of names to describe colour.

Intensity can also be expressed using the term 'colourfulness' which is a subjective visual sensation in proportion to the total brightness of a hue. *Brightness* when used to describe a light source implies a luminous source and when used to subjectively describe a colour is a synonym for lightness.

Lightness is a relative value (as is brightness), depending on whether you are comparing a colour with black, grey or white.

The brightness of a colour will depend on the light conditions within the environment where the colour is judged. Hence when a colour is observed under different conditions of white light its relative brightness will vary so will its apparent colourfulness, but the saturation or intensity will stay constant.

To explain this, imagine buying a light lemon yellow jumper in a shop, where the internal lighting is not very bright. On walking towards the front windows which are bathed in brilliant bright sunshine, the light lemon yellow colour will appear brighter and more intense, although its lightness remains unchanged since the quality is relative to the surroundings.

Chroma can be altered by mixing a colour with black, white, grey or its complement.

◼ colour temperature

Our understanding of colour temperature which categorises colours as warm or cool is defined as the warmth and coolness of a hue. However, to appreciate this property more clearly we need to introduce into our reasoning the following ideas:

- ◼ psychological temperature
- ◼ relative temperature
- ◼ physical temperature

psychological temperature

As we discussed earlier, many of our emotional responses to colour are made up of complex visual images through our experiences and symbolic meanings.

Red in ancient Egypt was the colour of the sun god Ra. It is the colour of fire, passion and excitement.

Orange in Greek mythology was the colour of Jupiter. For the Chinese and Japanese orange is the colour of love and happiness. It is the colour of sunsets and those rich autumnal shades.

Yellow for the ancient Greeks represented fire and the sun. It is said to be selected by those people who are intelligent.

Hence we associate the reds, oranges and yellows as *warm* hues.

Blue in Greek and Roman mythology was symbolic of the sky gods, Jupiter, Juno and Mercury. Think of the visual images of those deep blue 'cool' waters around the world and the calming effect that blue has on us.

Violet is the colour of Jupiter and has been used to indicate knowledge, nostalgia and old age. Closely associated to violet is purple which is associated with wealth and sensuality. It was a colour favoured by Roman emperors and that worn by Catholic priests. Violets of many shades, including lavender, mauves, lilac, magenta and purple are synthesised from red and predominately, blue.

Green in Greek mythology was the colour of Venus the goddess of love and fertility. It is the colour of growth and hope.

Green is abundant in nature in many forms.

The addition of blue gives cool blue-greens. The addition of red and orange gives ranges of brown-greens.

Hence we associate blues, greens and violets as cooler *hues.*

However, this psychological basis is not sufficient enough to formulate a classification, for as we began to see within these hue families it is too general, especially when we need to consider a wide range of pigments and colours resulting from their mixing.

relative temperature

This is a useful term applied to colours of the same hue family only. Together with our awareness of psychological temperature we can begin to isolate those hues within a family that are:

- cooler getting cool
- warmer getting warm, or
- those that are neither warm nor cool but more balanced

This colour temperature relativity is important to grasp when judging colour based on the psychological composition of cooler.

Green for example can seem warmer or cooler depending on the proportions of yellow (warm) and blue (cool) that go to make up the respective hue.

Violet as we discovered is synthesised from red and blue. Red being psychologically warm and blue being psychologically cool. Hence those violets that are predominately blue are relatively cool compared to a violet with more red, that is warmer.

Oranges as they are composed of red and yellow hues are psychologically warm.

Although white, black and grey are not colours in the true sense we nevertheless need to place them with regard to colour temperature.

White symbolic of the heavenly spheres is the colour of the moon. It is associated with purity, joy and innocence, and frosty, snowy cold wintry weather.

Black is symbolic of death, mourning and grief. The Chinese associate black with the north. It is also associated with wealth and sophistication. Extinct of all colour, black is negative and cold.

Grey is achieved by mixing black and white or by mixing exact pairs of complementary colours – red and green, violet and yellow, blue and orange – which give rise to a neutral grey.

physical temperature

To expand our perception of colour temperature even further, it would be useful if we had a means of expressing the temperature of colour *tones.* That is those resulting from the mixing of hues from different hue families or the addition of white, black, yellow, brown, blue or complementary colours.

The general term used by colour consultants to express the degree of warmth or coolness of a colour tone is *undertone.* To be more scientific, undertone describes the hue, value and chroma levels of a colour.

It is based on the reasoning that warm colours have a yellow base and reflect a golden undertone whilst cool colours have a blue base and reflect blue, ash or greyish undertones.

However, you only have to study a selection of different yellows to see that some appear warmer, whereas other seem cooler, which might seem surprising considering yellow comes from the side of the colour wheel that is considered warmer. Similarly blue can be warmer or cooler but it comes from the side of the colour wheel that is psychologically considered cooler. The same applies to reds.

colour temperature and value

Our understanding of the physical temperature of a colour tone in terms of degree of warmth/coolness is more scientifically explained by considering the relationship between temperature and value.

Take a look at the following colours. Which one appears cooler and which appears warmer?

If you think that the lighter colour looks cooler you are right.

Colours with light values or whiter tones appear physically cooler than colours with darker values or of black tones.

This is because of their respective abilities to absorb light energy and hence heat (refer back to surface colour).

Light colours reflect light or heat, while dark colours absorb light and heat. A white object placed in the sun will absorb only a small percentage of the light rays falling on it, compared to an equivalent black object which absorbs a higher percentage of light energy.

■ visual impressions

Colour is rather like a mixture of family and friends. The simplest analogy is to consider a family tree. Have you ever tried to trace family connections and found out whether particular individuals are closely or distantly related? Starting at the top of the tree there will be those members of the family that are closely related, i.e. brothers and sisters. Their closeness is often highlighted by similar physical characteristics even maybe personality.

With blood relations such as a brother and sister, irrespective of whether they have a lot in common, there is an underlying physical closeness, by virtue of the same parents.

Half brothers and sisters are also related by sharing one of the same parents.

The brothers and sisters can in turn produce offspring that are related, called cousins, and so on.

genetic colour link

Similarly there is an infinite number of related colours that are formed from the same parents and hence share similar characteristics. All of these are 'born' out of the following traditional primary hues or parent colours – red, yellow and blue – which when theoretically mixed give rise to 'offspring' of secondary colours – orange, violet and green.

We can say that there is a 'genetic' colour link between those offspring and their respective parents. As we know further theoretical mixing between the primary and secondary colours gives rise to a range of tertiary colours which also exhibit a genetic colour link with their respective 'parent' hue. Similarly, there is also a genetic colour link between those tertiary colours that share the same parent.

If we look more closely at the pure hues – orange, red orange and yellow orange – we notice that they visually look similar.

Similarly, the same can be said of the pure hues – violet, red violet, blue violet.

Also for, yellow green and blue green.

This similarity can be expressed in terms; those colours that appear 'warmer' and those that appear 'cooler'.

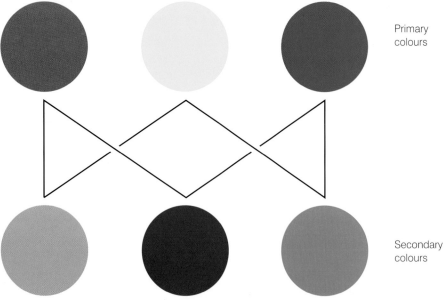

Primary colours

Secondary colours

colour dimensions

The dimensions value, intensity or chroma and undertone give rise to a method of describing colour according to how dark or light; bright or muted; or warm or cool it appears.

colour characteristics

We now therefore have six characteristics that we can use to visually describe a colour or to be precise, its colour quality or colour pattern.

For example we can say that this about the following colour samples:

This yellow green is more yellow, however, it does reflect some green. Its colour quality is light, warm.

This blue green is more blue, although it does reflect some green. Its colour quality is light cool.

In terms of characteristics when we look at a colour there is often one characteristic which stands out, one which we see first. This is called its **dominant characteristic**. Here are some samples (colour swatches) to illustrate this:

deep

These are colours that are of medium to deep value that are neither too warm nor too cool.

From left to right: deep royal purple, pine green, charcoal grey.

light

This describes colours that are of light to medium depth value that are neither warm nor too cool.

From left to right: powder blue, lemon yellow, light bright pink.

bright

This describes those clear, true colours that have a more balanced undertone.

From left to right: bright yellow, true blue, true red.

muted

Muted colours can be described as being soft blended that are neither too warm nor too cool.

From left to right: soft peach, soft cocoa, soft teal.

warm

These are colours that reflect a golden tone and are of medium value.

From left to right: medium golden brown, pumpkin, orange.

cool

These are cool colours that have a blue 'undertone' and are of medium value.

From left to right: sky blue, orchid, soft blue red

secondary and tertiary characteristics

As your eye becomes more accustomed to looking at different colours, you will begin to discover that many colours exhibit more than one characteristic. This can be expressed in terms of a *secondary* or even sometimes a *tertiary character*.

For example:

Cranberry
1st Cool 2nd Deep

Clear Blue Red
1st Deep 2nd Cool

Medium Yellow Green
1st Warm 2nd Light

Light Yellow Green
1st Light 2nd Warm

In the case of the examples above, those colours with a warm or cool dominant characteristic that are of medium value, if they are made darker or lighter, respectively the undertone becomes less obvious and the deepness or lightness, respectively becomes the first characteristic.

This interchange of colour characteristics, although sometimes subtle occurs throughout colour, wherever colours of different characteristics are mixed.

a balanced characteristic

If the dimensions of colour, undertone, value and intensity were represented along a scale, with the respective characteristics at either ends, a balanced 'characteristic' would be said to be of a medium nature.

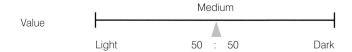

This is an important idea to grasp as it introduces the concept of *tonal bias*: a leaning a particular colour has towards a characteristic.

◼ contrast relationships and colour harmonies

During the nineteenth century the French chemist, Michel Chevreul, investigated the relationship between colours. He experimented by placing different colours alongside one another and noticed that certain hues had a 'draining' effect on other colours. Chevreul's work published in his famous book, *The Principles of Harmony and Contrast Colour,* inspired the impressionist painters of his day such as Monet, Renoir and Van Gogh.

The relationship between colours has wide application in the field of design. From painting to packaging, from interior to fashion, the relationships are as important as the actual choice of colours. Later in the book I will be applying the principles of colour relationships and colour harmonies to make-up design and fashion styling. However, for now let us examine the different types of relationships.

contrast relationships

When we speak of contrast we are comparing two sources that are perceived to have distinct differences. For instance, white–black, cool–warm, large–small, short–long are all poles apart. They are at opposite ends, which our senses have interpreted as 'comparisons'. The eye and mind achieve distinct perceptions through comparison and contrast.

Applied to our study of colour and its application there are four types to be aware of:

1 light or dark
2 complementary
3 simultaneous
4 cold–warm

light and dark contrasts

A light dark contrast occurs when colours of different values are placed together. The strongest examples of this are the colours white and black with greys and chromatic colours between them.

This effect can be used to add drama to fashion styling by combining garments or accessories of varying values. How aesthetically it works for your client will depend on a client's level of contrast in their colouring.

complementary contrasts

Complementary colours balance and excite each other. When it comes to choosing eye shadows to intensify and bring out the natural colour, look to colour contrasts.

simultaneous contrasts

This colour effect, although subtle, can slightly alter the appearance of your natural colouring. If two colours of equal brilliance which are not complementary, including grey, are placed together each colour will try to shift its partner towards its own complementary.

This effect *only* occurs in the eye of the observer causing an after-image to be seen. This alters our perception of the two colours, and depends on how well the colours are chosen; skin texture; print and fabric; and lighting.

cold-warm contrasts

The ability to observe this relationship is always relative. However, research shows that people do feel subjectively warmer in a red-orange environment than in a blue-green one, even though the actual temperature is the same in both.

This has to do with the vibrational energies of the different component wavelengths of each colour present within the respective pigments and how the brain decodes them.

The colours that are warmer are more 'energised' and excite. When blues are 'placed' next to reds they look cooler and the red looks warmer. However, if blue is mixed with varying amounts of red, the resulting blues will look warmer, although when mixed with green they become cooler.

A specific hue can appear warm if set among cool colours, but cool if set among warm colours. The strongest cold-warm contrast is red orange/blue green.

This technique can be used with great affect in make-up techniques to excite a person's natural colouring as well as in dressing to introduce a contrast.

colour harmonies

As you begin to develop your 'colour eye' you will begin to appreciate that all colours are related to each other in a smooth continuous way. How close can be understood by looking at the following colour harmonies or combinations.

monochromatic harmony

This relies on the combination of colour tones derived from a single hue. Such colours are distinctly warm or cool. Of the warmer harmony consider the following examples using combinations of different intensities of the same colour.

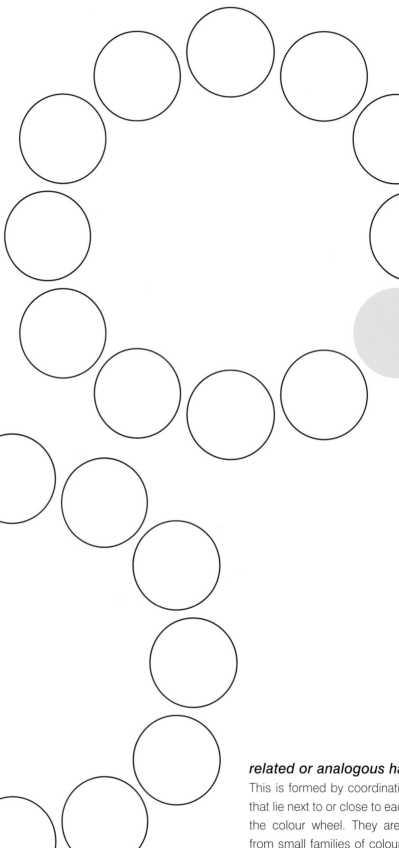

related or analogous harmony

This is formed by coordinating colours that lie next to or close to each other on the colour wheel. They are made up from small families of colour or sets of colours producing a subtle and elegant effect.

contrast harmony

This is often called *complementary* harmony and is formed by colours that are not related to one another and are found opposite each other on the colour wheel. When placed alongside one another the pairs have the effect of balancing and exciting each other, but annihilate each other to grey black when mixed. All complementary pairs contain a warm and a cool hue such as yellow and violet, blue and orange, red and green.

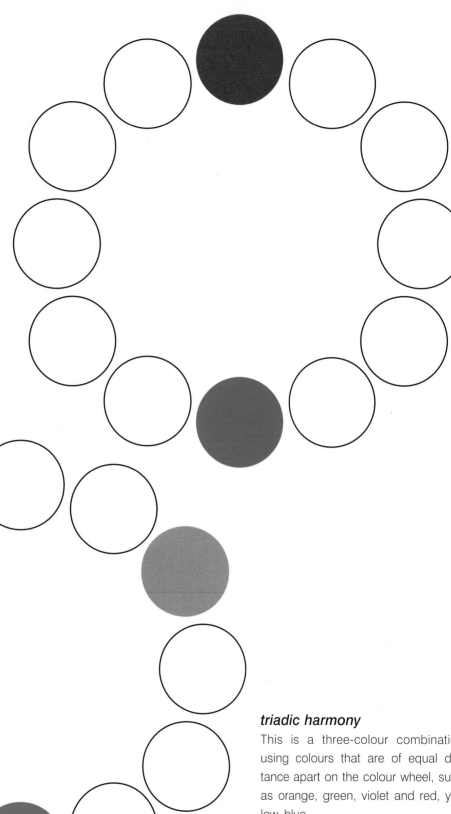

triadic harmony

This is a three-colour combination using colours that are of equal distance apart on the colour wheel, such as orange, green, violet and red, yellow, blue.

To ensure that this colour combination works the colours must be of the same value, intensity and in the correct proportions.

3.2 body colouring and pigments

colour variations

As we begin to study this fascinating subject, it will become apparent that there are tremendous variations in hair and skin colouring around the world. Studies of human pigmentation show that there is a strong regional component, linking this to the intermixing of groups of people within an area, and the intermixing between races and nationalities.

It has been suggested that the regional colour variations governed by genetic factors has over time become modified by environmental factors. Those people in tropical regions have the darkest pigmentation whilst people in cooler zones have less. This feature has probably evolved because of the body's need to protect itself against the effects of ultraviolet radiation, which is more intense at lowest latitudes. Thermoregulation, the body's ability to deal with heat, may also account for the fact that darker skins absorb more heat than light-skinned persons, but also can regulate heat loss more efficiently (black-body radiation).

It is therefore not surprising to find, when combining regional, hereditary, environmental and population numbers that there are more people in the world with dark skins and dark hair, than there are with light skins and light hair.

skin colour

The colour of skin depends on the amount of the pigment melanin present in the stratum germinativam of the epidermis and the papillary layers of the dermis. It is the melanin together with two other pigments, haemoglobin and carotene, which combine in varying amounts to produce such a variation in natural skin hues and tones. A brief description of each pigment is provided below.

- *Melanin* is present in the skin. Depending on the amount, skin colour can range from very deep black, dark brown, medium browns, light beige, ivories and porcelain white.
- *Haemoglobin* is the oxygen-carrying pigment contained in our blood cells. It is commonly expressed as red in colour but it can vary in value from pink or rose, orange or peach, violet or mauve. Skin will take on a different colour depending on whether the dermal blood vessels are dilated or constricted. If dilated, skin becomes red due to oxyhaemoglobin in the red blood cells. If the blood vessels are constricted, the blood flow is slower. The skin appears blue due to the presence of deoxygenated blood.

- *Carotene* is yellow pigment found in the epidermal cells.

Everyone has each of these three pigments, although in different amounts. It is this fact which gives us so many variations of skin tones. Each skin tone will therefore have a particular colour basis.

expressing skin tones

Skin colour can be described in terms of its:

- *Colour value* which describes the depth of colour and is a measure of relative lightness or darkness; it depends on the amount of melanin present.
- *Undertone* which is a relative term used to express the degree of warmth or coolness of a skin tone.

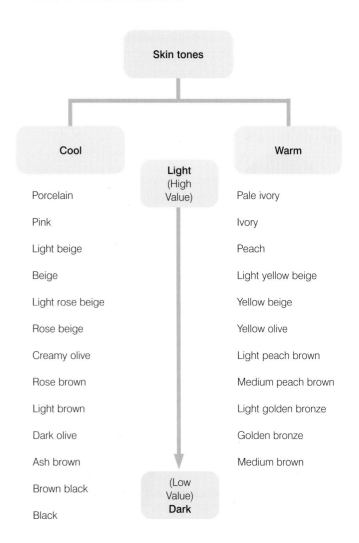

In spite of the many variations of skin tones it is still possible to position clients into three distinct bands of colour on the colour wheel. These bands fall into one of four colour families:

- yellow–orange
- red–orange
- red
- blue–red

hair pigments

In hair, melanin production occurs in the layer of cells (called melanocytes) surrounding the papilla at the base of the follicle. These cells are also found in the cortex region.

As in skin, these cells are the centre for the biochemical conversion of tyrosine into melanin. It is the oxidation of tyrosine aided by the enzyme tyrosinase, which brings about a change in its molecular structure resulting in the production of melanin.

Once melanin is produced it is coated with melanoprotein to form a granule. These pigment granules (called melanosomes) enter the cortex and become part of the hair structure. Changes in hair colour occur at the formation stage as the melanocytes enter the cortex and as the hair grows above the level of the skin. The melanin-filled granules are scattered throughout the cortex in no set pattern or amount.

variation in hair colour

Changes in hair colour can occur at any time of life brought on by:

- **Puberty**   often blonde hair in children becomes darker the older they get as more melanin is produced.
- **Age**   associated with this is often the 'greying' of hair brought on by the slow down of the production of melanin, until the melanocytes produce less and less resulting in the light appearance of the hair. This is apparently due to the loss of tyrosinase activity in the melanocyte.
- **Illness**   this is known to affect the pigment production mechanism, so can zinc deficiency.
- **Shock**   this too disrupts the process, along with the claim that hair can turn white overnight.

The variation of hair colour around the world is related to the pigment complexes within hair. They are classified into two groups of melanins: *eumelanin* (a black–brown pigment) and *phenomelanin* (a red–yellow pigment).

Phenomelanin is thought to result from the interference of the chemical tryptophan in the tyrosinase-tyrosine biochemical reaction.

Studies into the pigments of red hair have identified a pigment called trichosiderin which contains iron. Consequently, it is not surprising that red hair is found to contain greater amounts of iron than other hair shades.

The variation in hair colour is due to:

- the amount and size of the pigments. The pigments vary in size as follows

Black	>	Brown	>	Red	>	Yellow
Largest						Smallest

- the distribution of pigments within the hair structure
- the ability of the pigment complexes to absorb and transmit particular wavelengths of light

the composition of pigment complexes in hair

Black hair is made up of colour pigments red and green 70%; orange and blue 25%; plus yellow and violet 5%.

Light brown hair contains mainly orange and blue pigments, with smaller amounts in equal quantities of red, green, yellow and violet.

Light blonde hair contains large amounts of yellow and violet with small amounts of orange and blue pigment and minute amounts of red and green.

Light ash blonde contains larger amounts of yellow and violet with small amounts of orange and green.

Mousy hair is described as hair which no one colour dominates. The complimentary equal colour pigments present neutralise each other.

Grey hair is not actually grey but a mixture of white hairs and natural colour. With the onset of greying, the proportion of white hair emerging from the hair bulb increases which can be expressed as a percentage compared to original natural colour. Grey hair is caused by the absence of hair pigment in the cortical layers.

Although the pigments in hair are not visible to the naked eye, the full 'pigment story' unfolds during the bleaching of dark hair. During this process, hair can be observed to undergo a succession of colour changes resulting in the loss of colour pigments in the following order:

Dark brown ▶ Brown ▶ Red ▶ Orange ▶ Yellow ▶ Pale yellow

The blue pigment, located closest to the outer cortex just below the cuticle layer, is the first pigment to leave the hair shaft.

The red pigment is rather more resistant to lightening, being located deeper in the hair shaft. Consequently the hair shaft will need to be swollen sufficiently and sufficient time must be given to allow oxidation of the red pigment to take place.

Lastly, the yellow pigment is the most difficult of the primary pigments to remove as it is found deepest in the hair shaft and needs, for the same reasons as above, sufficient processing time to remove it.

■ eye colour

At birth, Caucasians often have blue eyes because there are few sparsely pigmented melanocytes present. However, in darker races the melanocytes of the iris are already more darkly pigmented at birth. Pigmentation increases in all races during the first six months to one year.

The colour of the iris is a result of the combination of a number of variable factors including the:

■ density of the cellular layer in the iris

■ density of the pigment cells

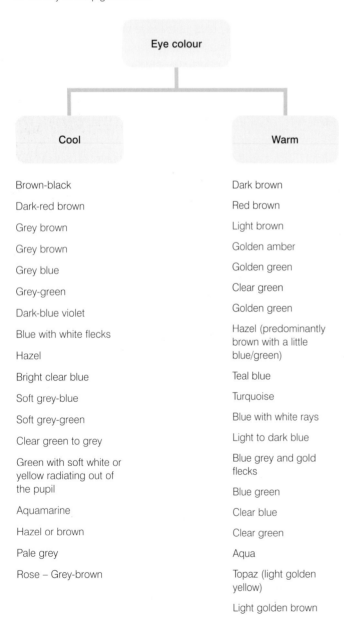

Cool	Warm
Brown-black	Dark brown
Dark-red brown	Red brown
Grey brown	Light brown
Grey brown	Golden amber
Grey blue	Golden green
Grey-green	Clear green
Dark-blue violet	Golden green
Blue with white flecks	Hazel (predominantly brown with a little blue/green)
Hazel	Teal blue
Bright clear blue	Turquoise
Soft grey-blue	Blue with white rays
Soft grey-green	Light to dark blue
Clear green to grey	Blue grey and gold flecks
Green with soft white or yellow radiating out of the pupil	Blue green
Aquamarine	Clear blue
Hazel or brown	Clear green
Pale grey	Aqua
Rose – Grey-brown	Topaz (light golden yellow)
	Light golden brown

■ size of the fibres that form the cell structure and the arrangement of these cells

The diverse range of eye colours is associated with the pigment melanin. Green to dark brown irises have more melanin present. Those eyes of yellow appearance have less. Blue irises appear blue because of the way light is reflected within the eye and then absorbed by the melanin pigment.

Like skin tone and hair colour there are many variations of eye colour. Eyes are rarely all one colour and usually display combinations of two or even three colours, such as a mixture of brown, blue and green, which we call hazel. In another person, you may see gold or green flecks in a medium brown eye or the very striking combination of deep royal blue with a violet ring around the pupil, shading into a blue iris or even a person with white flecks in a blue grey eye.

In terms of undertone, skin, hair and eye colour can be categorised according to whether they are warm or cool. Value describes the degree of lightness or depth of a client's eye colour.

■ why hair and skin appear a certain colour

Colour pigments are present in all living matter. These pigments have the ability to selectively absorb and reflect different wavelengths of light; the colour of hair and skin we observe is due to the interaction of light with the pigments.

In the absence of light and pigment, hair and skin would be colourless. The pigment melanin has the ability to absorb blue and violet wavelengths present in white light.

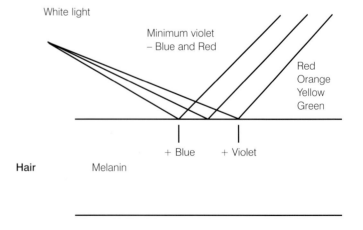

So the resulting hair and skin surface colours are due to the intermixing of the remaining 'colour wavelengths'.

Taking this a stage further, if the melanin has the ability to absorb most of the blue and violet wavelengths the other wavelengths – red, orange, yellow and green – are predominantly left. These are scattered and reflected back from the surface of hair or skin to our eyes where they are decoded and registered.

The other naturally occurring yellow and red forms of the hair pigment phenomelanin have the ability to absorb from white light, the orange, green, blue and violet wavelengths. The remaining wavelengths, red and yellow, are then scattered and reflected back from the hair surface.

White light

'Yellow'

White light

'Red'

Absorbs all the waves except yellow

Absorbs all waves except red

Melanin 'brown'

Hair pigment complex

White light

Red
Yellow

Hair structure

Phenomelanin pigment

orange•green•blue•violet

hair resonance

In natural blonde hair, the concentration of melanin is low as well as being widely dispersed. Hence our perception of blonde hair is mainly made up of 'white/yellow light', as most of the wavelengths of light that strike this colour surface will be transmitted and reflected (together with yellow) rather than absorbed.

Compare this to a person with very dark brown/black hair, where there is a high concentration of melanin pigments even in the cuticle layers, which selectively absorb most of the incident light. Hence we get a perception of blackness.

Red hair contains a higher concentration of the red pigment phenomelanin, which selectively absorbs most of the incident surface light except the red wavelength so that the predominant colour wavelength and tone perceived is 'red'.

Vidal Sassoon

▲ Variations of skin and hair colour

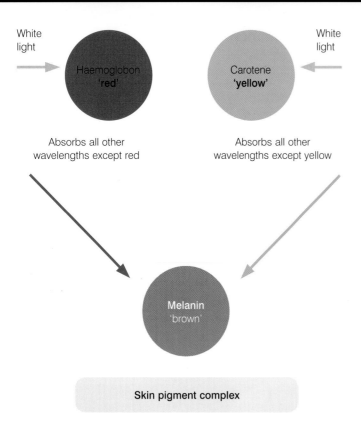

White light → Haemoglobon 'red'

Absorbs all other wavelengths except red

White light ← Carotene 'yellow'

Absorbs all other wavelengths except yellow

Melanin 'brown'

Skin pigment complex

skin surface colour

In skin, the pigment complex, depending upon skin tones, relies on the interaction between the absorption properties of haemoglobin, a red pigment and carotene, a yellow pigment, and the ability of each to selectively transmit red and yellow wavelengths, respectively.

▆ summary

Our visual perception of hair and skin colour will therefore be influenced by:

- the proportions of pigments within a 'complex'
- the resonance of the respective pigment complex to absorb and transmit particular wavelengths of light
- the interaction within the pigment complex between the various pigment molecules to capture, absorb, reflect or neutralise scattered wavelengths of light
- how the wavelengths that are finally reflected from the surface of hair or skin are registered and decoded by the eye/brain relationship

An understanding of these concepts will be essential in furthering your colour services and in the practical application of colour starting with analysing the distinctive colour characteristics that give every person such different colouring and give rise to different colour types.

James Darrell

Total design analysis combined with your consultation skills provides a powerful tool in identifying client requirements. It is an essential stage in the designing, composing and creative process. A thorough analysis needs to be carried out prior to offering style guidance or producing photographic imagery.

Understanding your clients and their needs may seem relatively easy and straightforward, however, this is not always the case. It can be unwise to think or assume you understand without qualifying or verifying your notions. There are no short cuts or gains to be made by ignoring this crucial information-gathering process. There is absolutely no substitute for assimilating the facts with which to make informed judgements, and subsequently offer style solutions. Real progress and success will require you to find out much about clients and their needs. Identifying their needs, their preferences and expectations will be essential. This will only be achieved through your observations, pertinent and tactful questioning and well-constructed assessments.

Assessments will require you to take many different factors into consideration as you begin to collect and collate valuable information. This process can best be described as a complex jigsaw puzzle – a puzzle that can only be completed once you have collected all the necessary pieces of information. How well you achieve this and fit the information together will have much to do with your experience and expertise as well as having an effective plan.

Total design analysis is an action plan. It takes the whole person into consideration. It is a thinking and decision process.

Visualise the overall process in terms of a journey with a start point and a destination. The starting point will depend on where you are at with each client. Your destinations will depend on each client's particular requirements or needs. It is important to specify this end goal early in the consultation, and to remain focused to this end throughout. The task ahead of you is to plan how you are going to get to your destination.

Clearly you will need to identify what are the client's particular problems, requirements or needs. Once you achieve this you will have a fix on your destination, that is to come up with specific style solutions, ideas or recommendations.

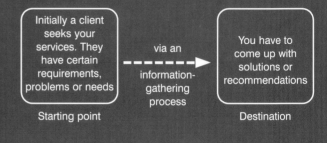

Initially, you must start to map out in your mind what information you require in order to get where you want to be.

It may help to break your 'journey' into a number of stages or mini-assessments and organise them into a sequence in which they can be carried out effectively and efficiently. Therefore allowing you to reach your destination smoothly and quickly and by the shortest route.

The following framework will help you to come up with solutions, advice, recommendations or suitable compositions.

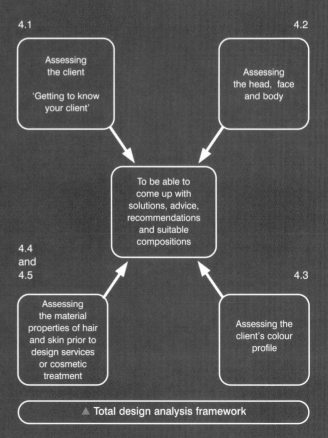

▲ Total design analysis framework

4.1 assessing your client

■ getting to know your client

From the onset of the consultation it will be important to build up a complete picture in your mind of the type of person you are dealing with. Gaining a greater insight into their inner psyche and inner world will be essential and invaluable as you seek to come up with style and image solutions that are in harmony with 'who they are and with what makes them the individual they appear to be'. This involves understanding them as a person in terms of:

- ■ how they think
- ■ how they rate their self and body image
- ■ their self-esteem and self-confidence
- ■ their motives for seeking your services
- ■ their personal preferences and values
- ■ their personality
- ■ their emotions and temperament

Unless you understand these psychological issues, even on a very basic level, you may fail to uncover what a client's real needs are and subsequently link 'needs' to human qualities. Consequently further progress may be slow, difficult and even unrewarding for you both.

Next extend the client's personal profile to finding out as much as possible about their background, lifestyle and important people in their lives. This will help to make recommendations that are appropriate, practical, manageable and financially acceptable to their way of life. This must include domestic, social and work needs as well as meeting the needs of any life changes, or forthcoming special occasions, engagements or work commitments. On the question of 'people and their lives' it will be useful to find out about their personal relationships and the possible effect these may have on style decisions.

To complete the picture, age needs to be considered from the style position of whether you can help to make the client look younger, if that is an important consideration, or older if their lifestyle warrants it.

personality

Personality as you must by now appreciate is a complex issue, and judging it is equally complex. Many companies now use what are known as psychometric tests to analyse personality and to predict how people will behave. They are widely used as a personnel management tool in the selection, assessment and development of staff. Whilst the formal procedure and mechanics of such a test would be unsuitable in a salon environment you will nevertheless need to carry out an assessment of a client's personality in a more informal and indirect way, calling on your perception of human character, knowledge of interpersonal skills and using image signals to guide you.

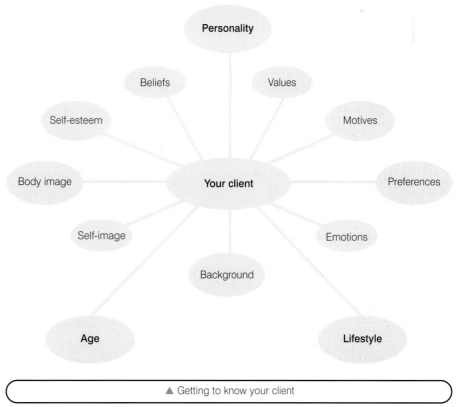

▲ Getting to know your client

use your own experience

Call on your experience of life, and of people. Try and remain objective, free from prejudices and stereotyping. Remember that every client is unique. The way they look, talk, act and behave are said to be expressions of their preferred emotions and temperament. In terms of emotionality, is the client the more extroverted or introverted type? Do they like to seek attention or are they the more shy retiring type? Do they share any similarities with any of the style personalities (refer to Part 1, Section 1.1).

style preferences

Do their style preferences give you any clues about their personality?

Does the client during conservation express or hint on their style 'likes' or 'dislikes'? These 'likes' or 'dislikes' highlight the different preferences we all have: preferences which will contribute to the client's decisions on how they would like to look and the manner in which they present themselves to others. Conversely, such preferences would also influence the personal judgement of others. Such attitude sums up our feelings of others orientated by our own values and associations. The intensity of feeling can even lead to a 'mood' or level of emotion when they may appear glad, sad, scared or mad.

emotions

Have you noticed how clients' emotions change? You need be aware of these and appreciate why a client may be feeling this way. What is triggering this complex mechanism? Is it you or is it more to do with their:

- self-image   what sort of person do they think they are?
- self-esteem   how good do they feel about themselves?
- body image   how good do they feel about their body and looks?

These are complex issues that directly affect a person's self-confidence, which you **must** aim to build and boost.

motives

And so to the question of motives. What are your client's motives for seeking your services? Clients' motives fall into the following categories:

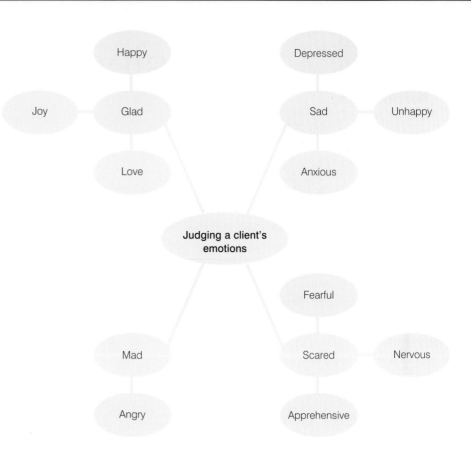

- objective – rational and prepared to acknowledge; or
- emotional – based on 'feelings' and less likely to acknowledge

Clients are motivated by both types. You must be able to 'read between the lines'.

◼ lifestyle considerations

We now turn our attention from life skills to lifestyles in order to gain further insight and information about our clients. Lifestyle revolves around their roles, responsibilities, activities and interests either at home, school, college, or at work. These are true-life situations which clients must learn to juggle and invariably adapt to. Needless to say every client's lifestyle will be different. Some may have relatively simple 'parts' to their life. Others will have more complex lifestyles which calls on clever style juggling and role playing to present an 'image' or convey an appropriate impression. Consequently, many clients may need to be something of a chameleon and be able to convincingly adapt to different environments and surroundings. It is the situation or occasion which provides the backdrop to their performance and appearance and the need to consider how they can change the way they look.

Consider some of the following examples where the client may need to:

- conform to certain rules, regulations and standards of dress and grooming for work
- create an impact and stand out at work
- melt into the background
- know how they can change their look for a career interview
- dress in a particular way to reinforce their work position
- be able to change easily a more classic business style of haircut into a dramatic evening look

style appropriateness

Style is about change, so is life. Life is dynamic, clients' circumstances may suddenly change – so too can their situations outside work. Perhaps they:

- have left school recently and are applying for their first job
- are about to embark on a new career after leaving college or university
- are a young mother at home with small children
- are planning to resume a career after a period of absence
- find themselves made redundant after many years of work with the same company
- are beginning a new relationship and wish to impress
- have broken off a relationship with a partner

Whatever the reasons, we all at some time face changes to our lifestyle. Maybe these are periods of change are unsettling. However, often, change can be beneficial leading to new discoveries and development. Without change we can become stale and static. Similarly, a client's personal style needs to be constantly re-appraised to keep pace with lifestyle changes.

Not only must a client be concerned with looking the part, say at work, out socially or at a special occasion but they must juggle with practical aspects of style. For instance:

- Will a new outfit be comfortable to wear, hard wearing, easy to clean and crease-resistant?
- Will a new haircut not only be fashionable but quick and easy to maintain at home?
- Will a proposed new hairstyle be suitable for their holiday?
- Will their wedding day make-up last until the early evening?

When it comes to helping clients look their best, you will need to consider 'budget restrictions' before making specific style recommendations.

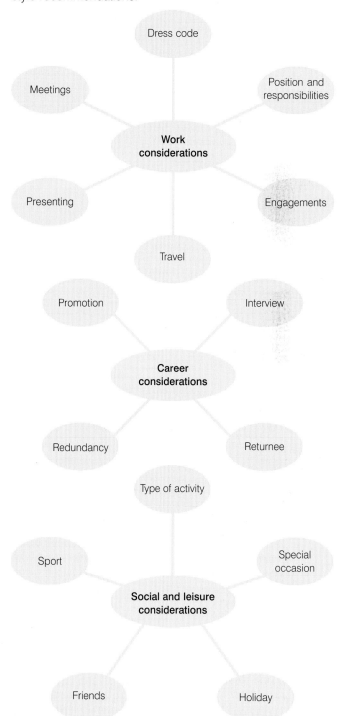

lifestyle influences on hair condition

A discussion on lifestyle in relation to hair would be incomplete if I did not comment on how a person's lifestyle can impact on their hair condition and hair image. Subsequent haircare advice will need to take many factors into consideration if the quality of this material is to be nurtured and improved. Hair is a very versatile and remarkably tough material. But is it really that tough and is it little wonder that its quality is severely threatened by all that it is subjected to by just living, self-abuse and abuse by others?

lifestyle influences on skin condition

In order to successfully advise and treat a client or customer's skin condition or problem, it is essential to consider their lifestyle activities which may well be affecting their skin's well-being and fitness. Such activities must take into account how their skin is cared for both internally and externally.

health matters to consider

Much of helping clients to look good is encouraging them to change their appearance in some way and care better for their hair and skin. A great deal can be achieved by working on the 'outside'. However, as consultants and advisers you must also appreciate the importance of inner body care and the relevance of health matters to how people look and their overall image.

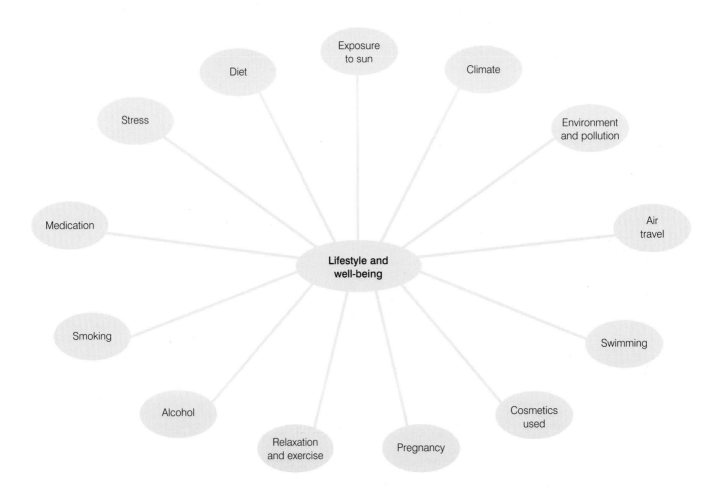

If clients want clearer, brighter, healthy looking skin and much improved hair quality, they must be educated to look after their body and well-being.

age considerations

Age is an important style consideration. You have all heard the saying: 'you are old as you feel'. That is very true, however, this may be of no consolation to a client who is searching for ways to look younger. Looks and the search for eternal youth have much to do with how clients look after their bodies, both internally and externally – through diet, rest and exercise. No industry is more concerned with 'skin and hair fitness' than the cosmetic industry. Millions are spent on anti-ageing research spurned on by the desire to find solutions to externally reduce and halt the ageing of the skin and the camouflaging of lines and wrinkles. Similarly, over the years, the race to find a cure for baldness or reduce hair loss has seen the introduction of hopeful remedies. For many, the desire to look younger can become an obsession and can be taken to the extreme, such as cosmetic surgery. In such cases, frequent trips to a cosmetic surgeon over the years often results in an unnatural approach to growing old gracefully.

For many clients this is not an option, and although anti-ageing solutions are still important, clients prefer less radical measures to make the most of their natural assets and improve their attractiveness.

Ageing is no reason for an inhibited approach to style nor does it mean caring less. There's a difference between a client wanting to make the most of themselves and wanting to look like 'mutton dressed up like lamb'!

Advise the client on how to finely tune aspects of their style by taking into consideration:

- what clothing colours would be more suitable
- the line, length and cut of their clothes
- the choice of fabric
- the length and shape of their haircut
- the use of hair colour, and the effects of colour changes on the skin
- the use of beauty lotions and potions
- their choice and application of make-up

It is ironic to think that there may be a time in the life of a client when they might need to look older than their years. This is often the case in business, particularly if a client has a young face and holds a more senior position within a company in charge of a team. Whilst nobody will deny that they are not brilliant at their job, some team members may resent working under a younger person.

For the young fashion-conscious client, they will not want to look dull, drab and unadventurous. Their style priority may be wearing the latest hair and make-up trends and less on aesthetic considerations.

These considerations must be appreciated before offering style solutions.

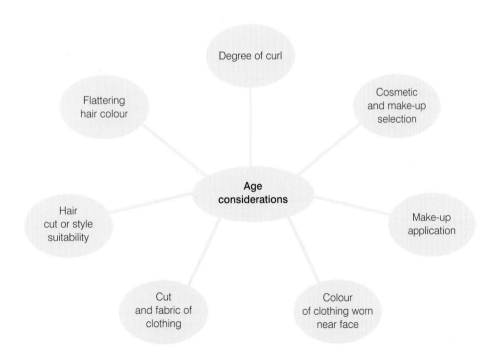

4.2 assessing the head, face and body

■ attention to detail

Earlier in the book I said that a hair professional shared much in common with an architect and structural engineer, whose work invariably starts by surveying the environment. Surveying starts by taking measurements, closely examining structures before a design can be conceived and transferred onto the drawing board. For a design to work an architect must have an eye for detail and be able to produce detailed scaled drawings, material specifications, castings and site instructions. Before building can commence the architect must get planning approval and satisfy building regulations. The aim is to ensure that when built a structure will be environmentally acceptable, aesthetically pleasing and technically sound.

Whilst hair designers do not generate scaled drawings, your design proposals or concepts still need to work. You also need to ensure that you appreciate any design limitations and that your designs and design detail are technically sound, aesthetically pleasing and what's more get approval from your client.

For instance, there is no point finishing a client's hair only to discover that the shape and proportions of a cut or style do not suit the person, their face shape, facial features or body proportions. Attention to aesthetic suitability must start by 'surveying' the client's head, face and body, taking note of such detail as:

- height
- head shape and size
- face shape and facial dimensions
- facial features
- neck length, width and shoulder proportions, and
- body contours and proportions

This amount of detail will be essential in order to help you compose and create winning looks.

■ surveying the canvas

height

This relates not only to how tall your client is, but also how tall they appear to be. The ideal female figure is considered to be eight heads tall.

For women, height can be broken down into:

- short – 5'3" or under
- medium – 5'4"–5'5"
- tall – 5'6" or over

The minimum height for fashion models is 5'8".

Always assess your client's height during the initial consultation stage and don't hesitate to ask them to stand up.

Head position

Height

Head shape and size

Shoulder proportions

Face shape

Neck length and width

Surveying the client's head, face and body

Facial dimensions

Facial symmetry

Body regions and proportions

Facial features

Body shape and symmetry

the head

head shape

The bones forming the cranium determine the shape of the head. The three important head regions to appreciate are the occipital, temporal and mastoid areas – they influence the shape and curvature of the head. You will need to carefully consider the symmetry of your client's head and cleverly visualise how you can build up or reduce the overall shape to be as close to creating the correct proportion. The aim is to control the natural shape of the hair by aesthetically moulding it around the head.

Observe the client in profile, decide where there is flatness or roundness and where the volume of hair needs to be adjusted to create the right balance.

The perfect head shape is evenly balanced. It is in proportion with the body and widens a little at the top. Typical head shape types formed by the outline of the skull are:

- pointed head shape, hollow nape (A)
- narrow head, flat back (B)
- flat top (C)
- large head (D)
- wide at the front, flat head at the back, receding base to the skull (E)
- small head (F)

A   B

C   D

E   F

head size

Apparent head size is visual, it is therefore especially important to ensure your hair design is in proportion. You must decide how full or compact the chosen style needs to be. Assess the client's head size in relation to their body proportions.

the face

Our faces are as much a work of art as they are a wonder of nature. Our faces are individually unique and so are our features, so much so that the ancient Chinese practised the art of character reading by studying the face. For instance the notion that a high forehead represents intelligence or a square jaw determination; a broad chin ambition; a round chin initiative. There are just a few of the character associates based on facial characteristics and features.

Although facial shape and structure are inherited, scientific research has found little evidence to support the relationship between personality traits and facial characteristics. Similarly there is no scientific link between eye, hair and skin colour to personality patterns.

However, what scientists have been able to provide is that the old idea that beauty is in the eye of the beholder is a romantic myth.

Recent research has quantified beauty. Beauty in women is characterised by:

- large eyes
- small nose
- full lips
- a small chin
- high cheek bones
- a delicate jaw
- smooth unblemished skin

And that the most attractive faces are not average ones.

However, it is very likely that such views will probably change again with time. Each decade and generation has its own views of what is perfect.

Irrespective of the pursuit of the perfect face, the evolution of new beauty does draw on role models who look like real people. It is accepted now that beauty and attractiveness are less about perfection but more about individual sex and style appeal.

The essential point to appreciate is that every client can make positive improvements to enhance their facial features and that less than perfect faces, large noses, big lips, can become an attractive feature with your help.

No matter whether you are an artist looking to, successfully, frame the face with hair, adorn hair with accessories, paint faces or accessorise with jewellery you must start by assessing the client's or model's face.

face shape

Facial features and expressions are determined by the shape and size of the facial bone structure supporting the muscles and subcutaneous fat tissue. The foundation of face shapes is this bone structure which, as a person loses or gains weight, can become more or less pronounced.

Conventional facial analysis classifies face shapes or contours into the following categories:

- square
- diamond
- triangular
- oblong
- oval
- pear
- round

These can be further described by using the idea of 'facial line' to describe the overall types. The terms often used are:

- sharp straight
- straight
- soft straight
- straight soft
- soft curved
- curved

Whilst useful as descriptions relating to the fact that faces are often a combination of different lines, they tend to describe faces in one plane only. As I will discuss later it is essential to view the face through 360°.

facial line

Whilst we may talk about 'the ideal face shape' this is not the norm. Clients' facial contours are made up of straight lines and curves. When we compare a range of face shapes, we notice that the lines may be horizontal, vertical and diagonal. One such direction may dominate but, as is more often the case, clients' faces are a combination of both movement and line. Recognising facial types comes with experience. Get as much practice as possible at observing the position, prominence and dimensions of facial bone structure. Start by gently pulling their hair back from the client's front hairline. Study the contours of the head and face. Assess:

- how angular, soft or curvy their face is
- the width across the hairline
- the depth of the forehead from the hairline to the eyebrows
- the width across their cheekbones
- the width across their jawline
- the overall length of the face

comparing facial dimensions
what shape is their face?

The following should help you to visualise these facial dimensions.

Face shape	Dimension
Square	A square face – the width is two-thirds or more of length. (Generally considered to be a strong facial shape for men.)
Oblong	An oblong face is longer than it is wide with the cheek, jaw and forehead more or less of equal width.
Triangular	A triangular face has a wide forehead and narrowness across the jawline.
Diamond	A diamond-shaped face has a narrow forehead, extreme width across the cheekbones and narrowness across the jaw region.
Pear	A pear-shaped face has a narrow forehead, wide jawline and chinbone.
Round	A round face is about two-thirds as wide as it is long with the distance across the cheeks being the widest dimension. Often has a round hairline and round jaw.
Oval	An oval face is about one and a half times larger than its width across the brow. The forehead is slightly wider than the chin. Considered to be the face shape that is in correct proportions.

assessing facial proportion

Facial proportion describes the overall dimensions; width and length of the whole face and relationship between different parts of the face and facial features. Visually assess:

- facial dimensions
- relationship between width and length
- facial symmetry

Every face is different and needs a cut or style that is correctly proportioned, has balance and line that flatters the facial dimensions. The potential cut or style must suit the client from all angles – front, back and profile.

This is often overlooked, not only by the client, who is most familiar with seeing a front-on mirror image and does not fully appreciate what others can see.

It is vital during all stages of hair design assessment to make full use of the mirror. Rotate the chair if possible, stand back, observe the profile and rear view in the mirror. Analyse the client's face for its strong and weak areas, and if necessary mentally adjust the length, width and height of the design accordingly.

Base your designs on the ideal facial proportions and symmetry:

- The face is divided into three areas of equal length: forehead to eyebrows; eyebrows to end of nose; end of nose to bottom of chin.
- The mouth will always be a quarter of the way up the total length of the face from the hairline to the chin.
- The length of ear is equal to the length of the nose and both are on the same level. This is also approximately equal to one-quarter of the length of the head.
- The distance from pupil to pupil will be equal to the distance from the bridge of the nose to its top.
- Ideally the top of the ear should align with the eyebrow and the bottom align with the bottom of the nose.

Similarly prior to make-up application the client's or model's face shape and proportionality must be assessed in order to consider how best to apply the principle of light and shade to sculpture the face (see Part VI, Section 6.1).

assessing facial features

Just as face shapes vary from client to client so do facial features. Facial features include the:

- shape of forehead
- eyes
- ears
- eyebrows
- ·mouth
- nose
- jawline and chin

They should be assessed from the front and in profile in order to prescribe hair styles or make-up designs that can enhance good points or draw attention away from weaker or less attractive features.

▼ Facial symmetry

1/3rd

1/3rd

1/3rd

the forehead

The forehead is subdivided into three parts, the upper part (near to the hairline), the central part, and the lower part down to the eyebrows.

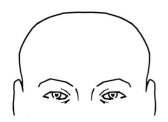

A A wide forehead is one with a width of more than 12 cm from temple to temple

B A high forehead is more than 6 cm

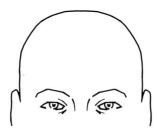

C A low forehead is less than 6 cm high

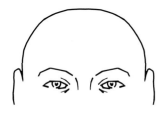

D A narrow forehead is less than 12 cm wide

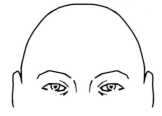

Other shapes of foreheads include very prominent, straight, square, concave, backward sloping and combinations of the types.

If the temple region is concave, adjust the volume of hair in this region.

eyes

The shape and line of the eye and eyebrow should be assessed from the front, and in profile, particularly when contemplating incorporating a fringe into a design. Take note of the movement of the eyebrows. Are they horizontal, arched or downward sloping? Hairline lengths may need to be designed to follow the highest point. For repetition of line aim to cut the shape of the hairline to that of the line of the eyes. When considering fringes take account of the temple area and the amount of space, for instance, if it is very narrow or sufficiently deep.

The eye, its shape, size, the distance between both eyes and lid size are of prime importance in make-up design, so too is the need to assess these features prior to eye shadow application and placement. This is discussed in more detail in Part VI Mastering make-up Section 6.1 Eye design.

ears

The size, shape and position of the client's ears need to be assessed, particularly if you are contemplating a short hair cut or dressed style which might mean taking the hair up off the face. Proportionally the ear should be equivalent to the length of the nose. The top should align with the eyebrow and the bottom on the same line as the nose.

Do their ears protrude? Ideally the ear should not stand away from the head by more than the width of its own thickness.

Are their ears out of balance? If so this can affect a cut particularly if they are used as a guide.

eyebrows

Further reference to eyebrows and their significance in make-up design is discussed in Part VI.

mouth

When assessing the mouth, take into consideration the

- size of mouth
- shape and line
- lip size
- lip shape
- quality of the client's teeth
- cosmetic preferences – do they wear lipstick or prefer a natural look?

nose

The client's nose must be assessed both face on and in profile. *In profile* the nose is wedge shaped and does not extend beyond the normal curvature of the face, which is considered to be straight. However, this may not be the norm. Observe whether the client may have a prominent/pointed nose or turned up nose. *Face on* observe whether their nose is crooked or wide and flat.

jawline and chin

The jaw and chin make up the lower part of the face and need to be assessed for shape, line and irregularity. Is their jawline and chin

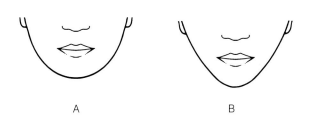

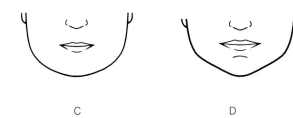

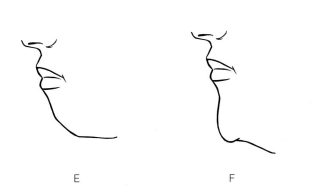

(A)   Well proportioned, oval chin
(B)   Long pointed chin
(C)   Round chin
(D)   Square chin
(E)   Receding chin
(F)   Double chin

- square?
- round?
- pointed?
- receding?
- protruding?
- double chin?

Assess the distance between the earlobe and the client's chin.

- Is the jawline angular?
- Is the distance short?
- Is the jawline long or sloping?

Cheekbones can be emphasised by considering style lines which follow the line of the client's cheekbones.

Cosmetically cheekbones can be emphasised and even shaped by suitable application of blusher and highlighter.

the body

body shape and symmetry

When we talk of an object as having a certain shape, we actually mean that the space it occupies is this space maintained by the lines that surround it. Traditional figure analysis classifies body shape into a number of types and relates to the area defined by the:

- shoulders
- ribcage/midriff
- waist
- hips/thighs, and
- calves

Body shape varies from person to person according to bone structure and surrounding adipose tissue. This gives rise to different types depending on whether their overall shape is maintained by lines that are straight, curved or a combination of both.

Female body types range from the very angular woman with athletically broad shoulders that are wider than her hips; to the woman who is straight from the shoulders to the hips; to the woman who has a triangular (pear) or hourglass figure to the woman who has a curvy figure like a figure eight and finally to the woman is more oval or rounded. These body types give us six basic shape models to work with. They are the:

- inverted triangle
- rectangle
- triangle
- hourglass
- figure eight
- oval

Another system of classifying body types uses the notion of body lines to describe the contours or outline of the body. This can be predominately angular or made up of straight lines or predominately rounded or made up of curves as well as a combination of both. The terms used to describe such bodies are:

- sharp straight
- straight
- soft straight
- softly curved
- curved

Body shape	Front on
Inverted triangle	The shoulders or bust are broader than the waist and hips giving a top-heavy look.
Rectangle	The shoulders are as wide as the hips.
Triangle	Often called pear-shaped, the shoulders and waist are narrower than the hips/thighs.
Hourglass	The shoulders are straight and are relatively as wide as the hip/thighs with a well-defined waistline which is distinctly narrower than the shoulders and hips.
Figure eight	This differs from above in as much as the shoulders are curved and are relatively as wide as the hips/thighs with a well-defined waistline which is distinctly narrower than the shoulders at hip area.
Oval	The figure takes on a fuller shape. The shoulders are narrower or as wide as the hips/thighs with no noticeable waistline. The waist may even be slightly wider than the shoulders and/or hips.

variations to body shape and line

Whilst categories are often useful as a means of classification, they can be too restrictive. As you would expect there are variations to these body shape types, such as the woman who has a mainly rectangular shape but with a very slight curve at the waist.

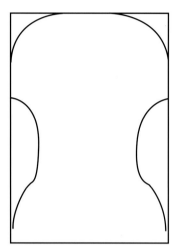

Softly straight

Or the woman who has a more rounded triangular or pear-shaped body

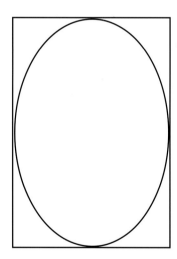

one body … two silhouettes shapes

It is not uncommon to find a person who has two different natural silhouettes. The one from the front, the other from the back.

Example 1

The woman who has a rectangular body shape from the front, but from behind she has an hourglass figure.

The aim: To create the illusion of a waist in the front by wearing an outfit that is drawn in at the sides.

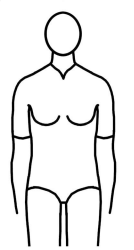

Example 2

The woman who has a perfect hourglass shape from the front but is rectangular shaped from behind.

The aim: To recommend garments that are sufficiently gathered in the front to mimic and give definition to her body's natural waist, but are tailored in such a way at the back to give the illusion of a waist.

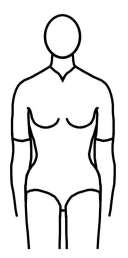

body regions and proportions

Whilst we talk about body shapes in much the same way using such terms as pear and round, the ideal body exists mainly on the drawing board. We all have aspects about our bodies which we love as well as features with which we are not so happy. The first step in giving someone body confidence is to encourage them to accept themselves and not to dwell on their figure faults. The second step is to show them how, by wearing the right style clothes, their good points can be enhanced whilst their not so good areas camouflaged. Although this is the work for the image and style consultant, as a hairdresser you can play an important part by recommending hair designs that have correct style lines and proportions to flatter their figure.

making a visual assessment

When you consult a client, make a visual assessment of their figure. Note how the visual balance of the body regions relates to the length and width to their contours.

- How angular or curvy are they?
- Are they top heavy, bottom heavy or evenly balanced?
- Observe, if possible, their shoulder width. Do they balance with their hips?
- What is their face size in comparison?
- Do they have a long or short neck length?
- Would you describe their neck as being slim or broad?
- Are their shoulders narrow or wide?
- If they are female, are they small or large chested?
- Do they have narrow or wide hips?

So as not to appear to eye the client up or down, do this subtly or explain the need for making these observations based on the principle that good proportion creates harmony and balance throughout the body.

the significance of upper body proportions in hair design
head position

This is best viewed by observing your client's body from the side. Most people carry their head forward. This is usually a congenital condition, often brought on by poor posture.

A person's natural posture should be straight, with the head directly over the shoulders, so that their spine is coming directly up their back, and up into their head. A forward tilted head is also associated with dropping shoulders, and possibly the formation of what is called a 'dowager's hump'.

Besides looking ageing, a poor posture does nothing to enhance body shape. If the tilt is very pronounced, you must minimise it by styling the hair to fill out the nape region.

neck length and width

The length, sturdiness and slimness of the neck is another consideration in the total overall look of the body. The position of the head and the type of shoulders will affect the neck's apparent length.

A forward set head has a shortening effect on the neck, as do square shoulders. With shaped shoulders the neck appears to be larger.

The neck length and width must be considered when planning a hair design during the consultation.

shoulder width
Visually assess the width across your client's shoulders from the back (obviously this can be difficult if they are wearing a number of layers).

Ideally shoulders should be slightly broader than the hips and fall into three categories:

square, sloped or tapered.
A person with extremely broad shoulders and slim hips can carry more weight and may appear taller. A person with narrow shoulders can look shorter and heavier.

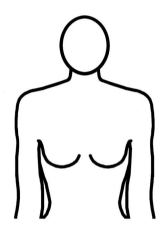
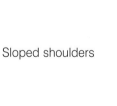
Square shoulders

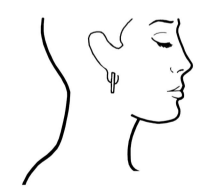
Short neck

Sloped shoulders
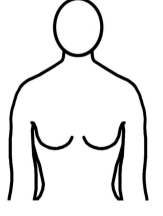

Long neck
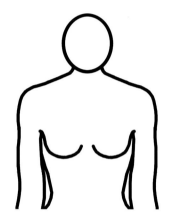

4.3 assessing a client's colour profile

◼ colour analysis

Why do we need to assess a client's colour profile? What do we need to consider and what are the benefits?

A colour profile describes a person's overall colouring or colour direction using names or a nomenclature to classify distinguishable colour characteristics. It is based on visually assessing a person's skin, eye and hair colour.

The process of assessing a client's colour profile is closely linked to the colour analysis movement. It is a movement that came to prominence in the sixties. To date there have been many systems used by companies and consultants to determine and describe an individual's unique colour profile subsequent to recommending a selection of the most flattering colours to wear and make-up to apply.

the different systems

It is not my intention to offer a DIY guide to colour analysis. This is best covered practically, using models, during an indepth training course. The aim of this section is to introduce the following systems:

- ◼ seasonal
- ◼ seasonal and flowing
- ◼ expanded seasonal
- ◼ tonal

These will be used as the basis for comparative study. Whilst there may be other names adopted by different companies and by independent consultants, these are the most widely used terms.

training foundations

Such a study should form the foundations to furthering the standard of colour education and training within the image industry: training that explores it as a science and as an art.

the benefits

The aim of this section is to provide a foundation to exploring colour in the book and introduce the application of colour analysis as a 'tool' to enhance:

- ◼ hair consultations
- ◼ hair colouring services
- ◼ make-up consultations
- ◼ make-up selection
- ◼ fashion styling

◼ seasonal analysis

The seventies saw the establishment of the colour analysis industry and the growth in colour consultants, adopting a seasonal means of classifying natural colouring based on undertones. A colour wheel was split vertically into two halves.

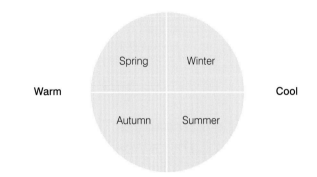

Each half was further split horizontally into two, giving a total of four quarters. Assigned to each quarter was a 'season', which reflected the degree of warmth or coolness. Two of these groups contained *warm*-based colours, symbolised by *spring* and *autumn*; and the other two reflected *cool*-based colours symbolised by *summer* and *winter*.

This early work on seasonal analysis started in America. It offered an individual a subjective assessment of their colour profile based on specific seasonal characteristics. The aim was to evaluate which range of colours from a seasonal array of colour palates or swatches, would best enhance their natural colouring. Each season contains colours of the spectrum, but in different *shades*, *tints* and *tones*.

Applying this reasoning, one of the seasons will include 'hues' that are closest to the person's colour profile. Just as the colours within each season are of the same family, it is true to say that these colours will be complimentary. Each 'season' therefore becomes a means of classifying natural colouring and recommending compatible colours.

seasonal characteristic variations

The following chart summarises the geographic variations of the seasonal groups found throughout the world as well as the tremendous variations in skin, hair and eye colouring that are found within each season.

Season	Ethnic group
Winter	This is by far the largest colour group in the world, including Africans, Asians, Southern Europeans, South Americans, Polynesians, descendants of the American Indian as well as the Irish and Welsh with their deep hair and light skin colouring.
Summer	Moving into Northern Europe, this group includes those racial mixes from Scandinavia, the Netherlands and the British Isles.
Autumn	This group has no specific origins and accounts for a mixture of racial backgrounds, in particular those persons of Asian, African, Middle Eastern origins, as well as the classic European red head.
Spring	This group contains persons mainly from Northern Europe. Many are descendants with Scandinavian, Dutch and British blood.

overall colour characteristics

In subsequent sections, I have adopted the basic seasonal name i.e. 'winter', 'summer', 'spring', 'autumn' to denote a generic means of classification starting with a study of overall colour characteristics for each group.

winter

skin tones

This group has predominantly *blue or blue pink undertones*. The largest group are those with *taupe beige skin* ranging from light to dark, rosy or just plain beige.

Most olive-skinned, blacks and orientals are 'winters', although a few are 'autumns'. Winters may have milky white skin and dark hair. The skin may have a visible pink tone. Winters do not usually have rosy cheeks.

eyes

Eyes are deep in colour: red brown, black brown, hazel (a combination of grey brown and blue or green); grey blue and dark blue. Blue or green-eyed winter people often have flecks in the iris and/or a grey rim around the edge of the iris.

natural hair

Most of the group have *dark* hair. Brunette 'winters' have hair colour ranging from *light brown* to *dark charcoal brown*, sometimes with a touch of red highlights. *Blue black* hair is typical of the oriental 'winter', as is salt and pepper or silver grey. This group is most likely to grey prematurely. It is rare to find an adult blonde, but if so, the hair is white blonde.

summer

skin tones

This group has predominantly *blue undertones*. 'Summers' usually have visible *pink* in their skin. Some are very fair or pale, with a translucent quality to the skin. Others have *very pink skin* with high colour, or *rose beige* skin, ranging from fair to relatively deep. The skin tone may be sallow, particularly on the arms, but there is usually a visible pink in the cheeks.

eyes

Eyes are most often blue, green, aqua or soft hazel (mainly blue or blue green with greyed brown surrounding the pupil). There is sometimes a cloudy look inside the iris. Many 'summers' have soft grey eyes or eyes with a grey rim around the iris and white flecks in an irregular pattern inside the iris. Eye colour can also be intensively blue or soft brown.

natural hair

'Summers' are often blonde as children. As they mature their hair tends to darken to a 'mousy' colour (greyish cast). Brunette 'summers' also have hair colours ranging from light to *dark brown* with *ash* overtones. 'Summers' occasionally have auburn highlights, especially after being in the sun.

autumn

skin tones

This group has predominantly *golden undertones*. 'Autumns' come in three varieties: *fair ivory or creamy peach* skin; *true redhead*, fair to dark often with freckles; or *golden-beige brunette*, with skin ranging from *medium to deep copper* (charcoal black hair).

Many are pale or sallow. A few orientals and blacks are 'autumns' but most are 'winters'.

eyes

The majority of 'autumns' have brown or green eyes. Brown eyes range from dark to topaz. Green eyes may have isolated flecks, gold, brown or black, in the iris. Some 'autumns' with hazel eyes contain golden brown, green or gold flecks in the iris. A few 'autumns' have vivid turquoise or aqua eyes, but not a true blue or grey blue colour.

natural hair

Autumns can be *golden blonde* as children, usually darkening as they mature. *Redhead* autumns have auburn or red brown hair. *Brunette* autumns have a gold or metallic red cast. Some autumns have *charcoal black* hair.

spring

skin tones

This group has predominantly *golden undertones*. They possess the most delicate quality of all tonal types. A 'spring's' skin may be *creamy ivory* (appears to have golden flecks); *peachy pink* or *peachy beige* (likely to have rosy cheeks). The skin is highly textured and seems to 'flush'. Springs can easily be confused with summers. Look at parts of the body to see whether tone is peachy or truly pink.

eyes

Eyes are most often blue, green or aqua. Some 'springs' have eyes as clear as glass. Others have golden clusters surrounding the pupil. Many have blue eyes with a sunburst of white 'rays' coming from the pupil. There are some brown-eyed springs, but they are always golden brown or topaz. A spring's hazel eyes contain golden brown, green and gold.

natural hair

Hair colour may be warm blonde, brown, golden blonde, strawberry, bright red or golden brown. Many children are blonde but darken with age. Some have very dark brown hair. A few have vivid *carrot red* hair.

Armed with an understanding of colour, we are now in the position to explore further systems used to assess and analyse a person's colouring.

seasonal limitations

Difficulties occur when people cannot be slotted into one of the four seasonal categories. Another problem is the wide variety of skin, hair and eye colourings within each season. For instance, a 'spring' may have ivory skin and auburn hair, another peachy skin and dark blonde hair. A 'winter' may be olive-skinned and dark-eyed, or have a pink undertone with blue eyes. There is a third limitation with this system in that a very high percentage of people are a complete mixture of warm and cool elements and therefore in practice can wear colours from either group, depending on their personal preference, their mood or what's in fashion. It is obvious that each season therefore exhibits different characteristic variations.

■ seasonal and flowing

There was, therefore, a need to expand the barriers to allow less cloning and a greater sense of personalisation. Consequently, the idea of 'flowing' from one season into another developed.

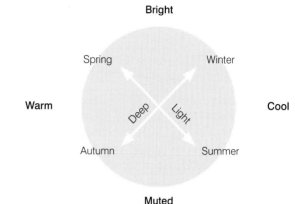

For example it is possible to be a light spring flowing into a light summer or a bright spring flowing into a bright winter.

flowing

The concept of flowing introduces the flow of colours from one season to another. This relationship between colours and subsequently their relationship to a person offers the versatility of expanding a seasonal palette by considering colours that are of the same 'family' based on the characteristics, undertone, value and intensity.

Once a person's season has been determined together with the dominant characteristic, extra colours can be added by starting from the centre band of that person's respective flow chart and moving outwards in the direction that best describes their colouring.

Non-flow colours are colours that are not related to the other season in the flow chart. Flow colours are colours that

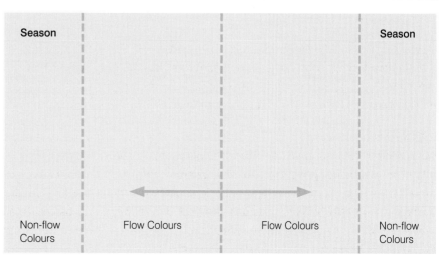

are found in the centre region that are related to another season in the chart.

the expanded seasonal concept

The development of the expanded system of colour analysis was borne out of the earlier work conducted by the artist Albert Munsell. To recap, he defined colours and their relationship in terms of hue, value and chroma. His theories were adapted in the early eighties and incorporated into a nomenclature which interpreted seasonal analysis in terms of:

- *undertone*: how cool or warm a person appears
- *value*: how light or dark a person appears
- *chroma*: whether they have a clear, soft or muted colouring

Armed with these further subdivisions, the analyst was now able to extend the original four seasons. Each season was broken down into three distinct types, giving in total twelve key impressions or new seasonal palettes, combining a seasonal direction with a dominant tonal characteristic.

For instance, if the analyst was now confronted by a woman who under the original analysis would be described as a 'winter', they would be able to qualify what type of winter. If she was a clear, bright type she would be referred to as a 'clear winter'. This person can borrow some of the clear colours from the spring palette and should carefully consider wearing the cooler shades from the original basic winter palette.

If she was a cool, rosy winter, she would be referred to as a 'cool winter'. She could wear some of the cooler shades from the summer palette, but should avoid the deepest winter colours. If she exhibited a strong, rich colouring, then she would be called a 'deep winter'.

The expanded seasons and key impressions are summarised below.

▼ expanded seasons and key impressions

Basic season	Expanded season	Key impressions
Winter	Deep	Strong and rich
	Clear	Clear and bright
	Cool	Cool and rosy
Summer	Light	Light and fair
	Muted	Soft and muted
	Cool	Cool and rosy
Autumn	Deep	Strong and rich
	Warm	Warm and golden
	Muted	Soft and muted
Spring	Light	Light and fair
	Warm	Warm and golden
	Bright	Clear and bright

tonal theory

The frontiers of colour coding or colour analysis still needed to be pushed out further. It needed to become more precise. There was a need for better terminology to extend the colour analysis theory. Just as the artist uses precise terms to describe colour, there was no reason why the colour analyst should not do the same. With this reasoning a new phase of colour analysis, the *tonal theory* was born, based upon the following tonal dimensions and characteristics.

Tonal dimensions:	Undertone	Value	Intensity
Tonal characteristics:	Warm	Dark	Bright
	Cool	Light	Muted

Tonal theory, based on a colour in its purest form, evolved by considering a person's colour tones in terms of the six characteristics. The aim of such a system is to recommend *colour profile*, i.e. colours from a particular region of the colour spectrum.

This is initiated during a colour analysis consultation by assessing which of a client's characteristics is the more dominant and assigning a tonal value, i.e. first, second or third, by examining their natural hair, eye and skin colour.

These three dimensions enable the colour wheel to be further subdivided, as follows, into six categories which form the basis of colour classification and hence numerous colour combinations.

▼ tonal characteristics

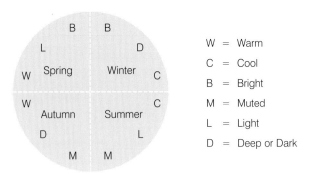

W = Warm
C = Cool
B = Bright
M = Muted
L = Light
D = Deep or Dark

dominant characteristics

Identifying a person's dominant colour characteristic is based on those first colour impressions, how you, the analyst, sees that person. However, often first impressions can be wrong. It is not until analysis begins, that hunches can be confirmed or rejected. Put it to the test on yourself. Are you:

■ *Dark* You can best be described as having a deep strong rich colouring, characterised by black, dark brown, chestnut or auburn hair, deep brown, hazel or green eyes.

■ *Light* In comparison, if you are light, 'delicate and fair' best describes you with either ash to golden hair colouring. You will have little contrast between your fair skin and eye colour, which can range from a light blue to blue grey.

■ *Bright* If brightness is your dominant characteristic, you will have contrast between your deeper hair colour and fair skin tones. However, some 'brights' can be fair haired with golden skin tones. Your eyes will be jewel like. You will have clarity.

■ *Muted* You will have very little clarity with hair, skin and eye colours. Hair colours can range from medium to dark blonde, ash or golden, medium brown, with ivory, beige or golden skin tones.

■ *Warm* Your overall quality will be 'golden', with a warm undertone in the skin, golden brown chestnut hair, possible with natural red highlights and green, hazel, warm brown eyes.

■ *Cool* If you are cool you will notice that your hair has an ash or greyish tone, your skin has a cool pinkish glow, which can often appear soft looking offset against your cool, often blue, eyes.

It is these six categories which can be used to describe a person's unique colour profile or direction. However, as you will appreciate these categories can be grouped together singularly, in pairs or in trios depending on their respective tonal qualities, which gives rise to potentially numerous combinations or groupings.

▼ colour variations

	Hair	Eye colour	Skin tone
Deep	Black Medium to dark brown Chestnut Auburn	Dark grey Deep brown Deep hazel Deep green	Beige Olive Bronze
Light	Very light blonde Medium to light Blonde Ash to golden blonde	Blue Green Blue green Aqua	Ivory Soft beige Pink or peach
Bright	Black Medium to dark brown Salt and pepper grey	Brown black Blue Grey green Blue green Aqua Violet	Porcelain Light ivory beige
Muted	Light to medium Ash blonde, or blonde	Soft hazel Brown Teal Greyed green	Ivory Light to medium beige Rose to golden beige
Warm	Light to medium Golden blonde Strawberry blonde Light to dark brown Chestnut Red to deep auburn Warm grey	Hazel (golden brown) Teal Aqua Brown Green	Warm beige Ivory with freckles Light golden blonde Bronze
Cool	Black Medium to deep Ash brown Salt and pepper Silver grey	Rose brown Grey blue Grey brown Cool hazel	Light to medium beige Pinky beige Pink/Rose

4.4 assessing the material properties of hair

people and hair

The crowning glory for most people is considered to be a head of healthy, well-styled and manageable hair. However, many people never seem to achieve this. Those that do, know the good feelings that this brings. Those people who never realise their hair potential live in daily frustration with their locks and looks. Whether it be too straight, too curly, too wavy, too thick or too thin, they always seem to want what they have not got and are always in search of ways to change their hair in some way. Most females during their youth dream of having beautiful silky flowing hair, others may seek to experiment with the latest fashion trends regardless of suitability. As they get older and a little wiser, there's nothing like a style change to focus their needs, to this end they may seek out a hairdresser who can enhance their looks. Similarly, males of all ages are becoming increasingly style conscious and adventurous. They too seek style and grooming solutions that will tame their hair and nurture their locks into peak fitness and performance.

structural and physical characteristics

The foundation of changing and improving a client's hair image must take into account each client's unique 'hair personality and temperament'. These will be influenced by its structural and physical characteristics. This needs to be technically assessed, which will require you to take into account the client's age, lifestyle influences on hair and skin, health matters, previous chemical work and product history as well as important diagnostic considerations. These include hair type, texture, porosity, hair weight, length, visual quality and structural condition.

hair type

Traditionally hair is grouped into the following populations and raves:

- Caucasoid (European)
- Negroid (African)
- Mongoloid (Asian)

However, today ancestor origins are not always so defined due to the intermixing of races. Consequently hair type varies greatly not only in appearance but also in respect of cutting, styling and chemical treatment.

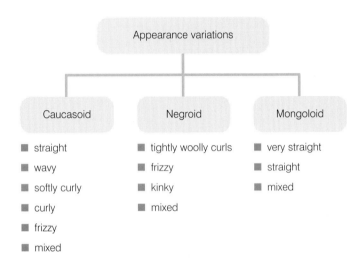

surface quality and texture

In Part II, Section 2.3, I expressed surface quality in terms of tactile and visual quality. Your ability to register tactile quality by just looking has much to do with how developed your tactile memory is. You can use this to judge the texture of hair.

judging the texture of hair

Method: Take a single hair strand between the thumb and forefinger and *feel* its texture.

Observation: How would you describe its diameter?

☐ Very thin ☐ Thin ☐ Medium ☐ Thick

Conclusion: The diameter of hair can be used to judge hair texture or, as it often referred to, the 'degree of fineness or coarseness'. Fine hair has the smallest diameter. Coarse hair has the greatest diameter.

The 'feel' of hair is affected by the position of the cuticle scales and will tell you whether the hair is soft or hard; or coarse or fine.

The surface quality can also be described in terms of its degree of smoothness, roughness or a combination of the two. This property can be felt and visually assessed. These properties are related to different hair types.

The porosity of hair reflects the state of the cuticle and position of the cuticle scales.

- hair with low (or poor porosity) – the cuticle scales are tightly closed
- hair with normal to good porosity – the cuticle scales are raised from the hair shaft
- hair that is said to be very porous indicates extreme cuticle damage

Porosity can be affected by texture in as much as the finer the hair, the more susceptible it is to damage. Hence the porosity of fine hair is more easily increased than that of coarse hair.

Porosity can be affected by:

- excessive hair drying
- using heated rollers and curling tongs
- harsh shampoos
- colouring products including tints and lighteners
- perming lotions
- chemical straightening
- prolonged exposure to the sun
- salt water
- chlorinated water used in swimming pools

The degree of porosity needs to be established before undertaking any chemical work on the hair and can be tested in the following way.

testing porosity

Method   Select in turn a few hair strands from the front hairline, in front of the ear and from the crown area. Run your thumb and forefinger from the hair end towards the scalp. What do you feel?

Observation and conclusions

- ☐ Smooth feel – In this state the cuticle is tightly closed, dense and hard. It will not absorb moisture or chemicals easily.
- ☐ Rough feel – In this state the cuticle is more open and will more readily absorb moisture or chemicals.

Use this test prior to perm.

hair density

Hair density is a term used to describe the amount of hair on a client's head. It is expressed as the number of hairs per square centimetre of scalp. It is estimated that this can vary from 175–300 hairs per square centimetre, although 223 is considered the average for a normal adult scalp. Consequently the more hairs per square centimetre the denser the hair is, although it may differ on different areas of the same head, particularly around the hairline where it is more sparsely distributed.

Surface quality can also be described in terms of how shiny, glossy, matt or dull hair appears.

porosity

Porosity of hair is a term usually used to describe the hair's resistance or ease to absorb moisture or chemicals.

- resistant hair is said to have low porosity
- normal hair is said to be of medium porosity
- porous hair refers to hair that can absorb an above normal amount of moisture or chemicals
- very porous hair indicates hair that is in extremely poor condition; hair that is severely damaged as a result of chemical deterioration and attack
- uneven porosity refers to areas along the length of hair that absorb moisture or chemicals at different rates

To assess a client's hair density, put your fingers into the hair. How would you describe it?

☐ Sparse   ☐ Fine   ☐ Moderate   ☐ Thick

hair length

Your style recommendations may be restricted by the present length of the client's hair. If it is too short suggest they grow it, with a definite aim. Be cautious of the client who is aimlessly growing their hair with no particular style direction in mind.

For those clients, growing hair does not mean they have to stop going to the hairdressers. It is still important to keep it regularly cut and in as strong as shape as possible. If they need to grow out layers suggest you start by equalising the length to a region where it is possible to form a stronger line.

Often 'in-between' shapes are difficult to manage and cause the client great frustration. Suggest they experiment with different drying, styling and dressing techniques in the interim, aided by one of the many excellent styling products that can give support, volume and enhance the wave or curl.

For clients with long hair it is important to appreciate the visual and structural changes that the client's hair may have undergone along the entire length. It is realistic to presume that long hair may not be in best condition by virtue of the fact that it has been more exposed to handling and environmental factors, not to mention electrical and possible chemical mis-treatment. Consequently, it is very likely that the condition of the cuticle may be worn away in places or there may even be variations of hair colour along its length. Similarly, hair that is described as 'older' may appear more faded towards the end lengths. Hair in this state is likely to be over porous. In which case before any chemical services are undertaken it may be necessary to use preconditioning treatments or pre-wrap products to equalise porosity and thus ensure a more even hair colour.

visual quality

Why is some hair shiny while some hair looks dull?

Shine is that visual quality that most people notice. It depends on the health of the outer layer of the hair shaft – the *cuticle*.

The cells of the cuticle are transparent, mostly made up of keratin. In healthy hair the cuticle cells lie flat to form a smooth, clear layer that reflects light and colour on the surface of the hair shaft causing the hair's shine.

In damaged hair these scales stand away from the rest of the hair shaft, causing an uneven surface. Light is not reflected evenly from such a surface, hence making the hair appear dull.

The amount of oil on the hair also determines to a degree the shine of the hair. The sebum secreted by the sebaceous glands coat each strand of hair with a smooth film of oil. This oil fills the gaps between the cuticle scales and creates an even light-reflecting surface.

The function of the sebum is to protect the hair, lubricate it and stop it from becoming brittle.

Products affecting shine include:

- harsh shampoos – not pH balanced
- hair sprays and setting lotions except those that are composed of water soluble, biodegradable fixing agents
- mousses – except those that are alcohol free. Some mousses can build up on the hair
- petroleum polymers – coat the hair with a film and are difficult to remove
- dandruff shampoos – can cause colour fade

The visual quality of hair is also affected by the textural quality of hair. For instance, light is reflected better from smooth hair as opposed to wavy or curly hair due to its surface unevenness.

structural condition

I'm sure you have noticed that some clients' hair holds a blow-dry or set better than others. This physical characteristic is related to the amount of moisture in the hair and the condition of the protein fibres of keratin. Perfectly normal hair is considered to be at a 100% level composed of about 97% keratin and 3% moisture plus carbohydrates. The physical condition of hair is related to what is known as the moisture protein balance. This can be assessed by testing the elasticity of hair.

■ how will hair react, behave and perform?

To get the best out of this fascinating material whether by cutting, colouring, perming, conditioning or dressing, it is essential to be technically knowledgeable. You will need to know how the structural and physical properties of hair influence its behaviour. Similarly, it will be essential to anticipate how hair will react, behave and perform when considering a particular design service. Let your experience and technical expertise guide you.

For instance you will need to anticipate:

- how the client's hair may react to certain hair-care products
- how their hair type will react and be improved by cutting
- which cutting technique will encourage the best results taking into consideration their hair texture

- what external factors such as heat, climate or cold will have on their hair
- how you can visually enhance a client's natural hair colour
- which colour products and colour techniques will achieve a desired look
- which colours will best suit the client's skin tones
- which permanent waving lotion will be better for the client's hair type, texture and porosity
- which perm roller size and winding method will suit the client's hair length and desired effect
- what drying, styling and dressing techniques will be more suitable, taking into consideration the client's hair type, texture, the cut and the type of finish required.
- which styling and finishing products will help you achieve the final look

These are just some of the points that need to be considered during a consultation before you make recommendations.

Of course, one cannot always be right. Unfortunately, you are not in the business to make errors, give your clients unsatisfactory advice, or proceed with a service that is technically or aesthetically incorrect.

Prevention is better than cure. Errors, mistakes or disappointing results can be minimised even eliminated by carrying out appropriate pre-service assessments, analysis and tests – the details of which are summarised in the following graphics.

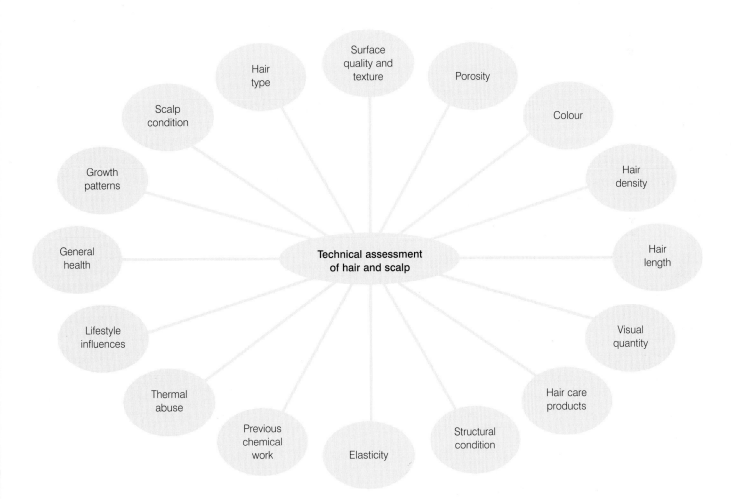

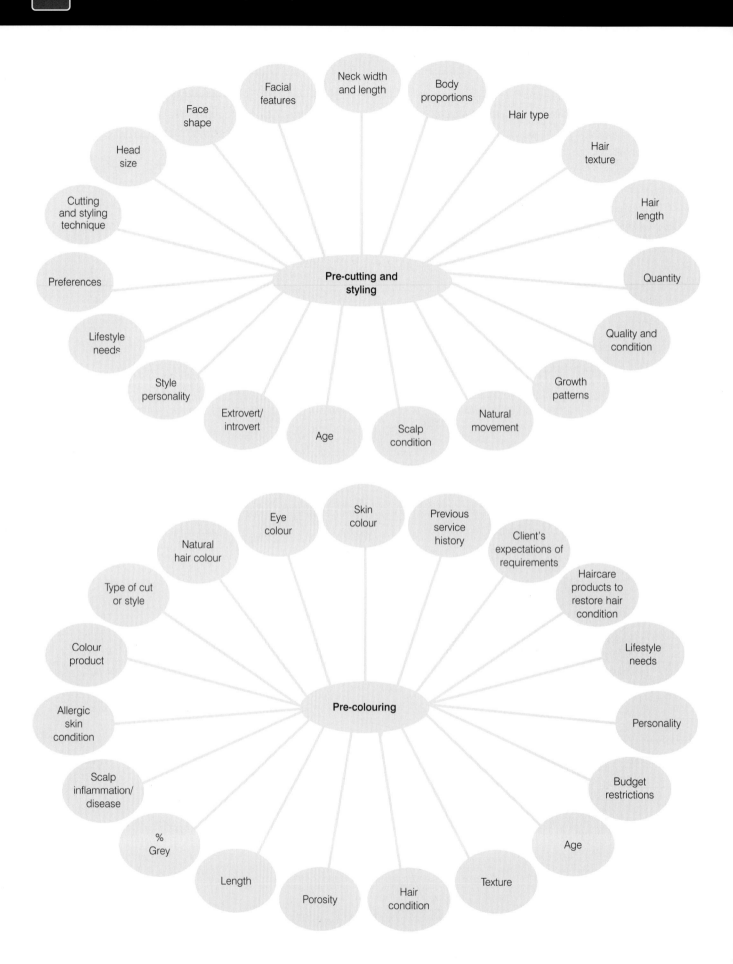

Pre-cutting and styling

- Neck width and length
- Facial features
- Face shape
- Head size
- Body proportions
- Hair type
- Hair texture
- Hair length
- Quantity
- Cutting and styling technique
- Preferences
- Lifestyle needs
- Style personality
- Extrovert/introvert
- Age
- Scalp condition
- Natural movement
- Growth patterns
- Quality and condition

Pre-colouring

- Eye colour
- Skin colour
- Natural hair colour
- Previous service history
- Client's expectations of requirements
- Type of cut or style
- Haircare products to restore hair condition
- Colour product
- Lifestyle needs
- Allergic skin condition
- Personality
- Scalp inflammation/disease
- Budget restrictions
- % Grey
- Age
- Length
- Porosity
- Hair condition
- Texture

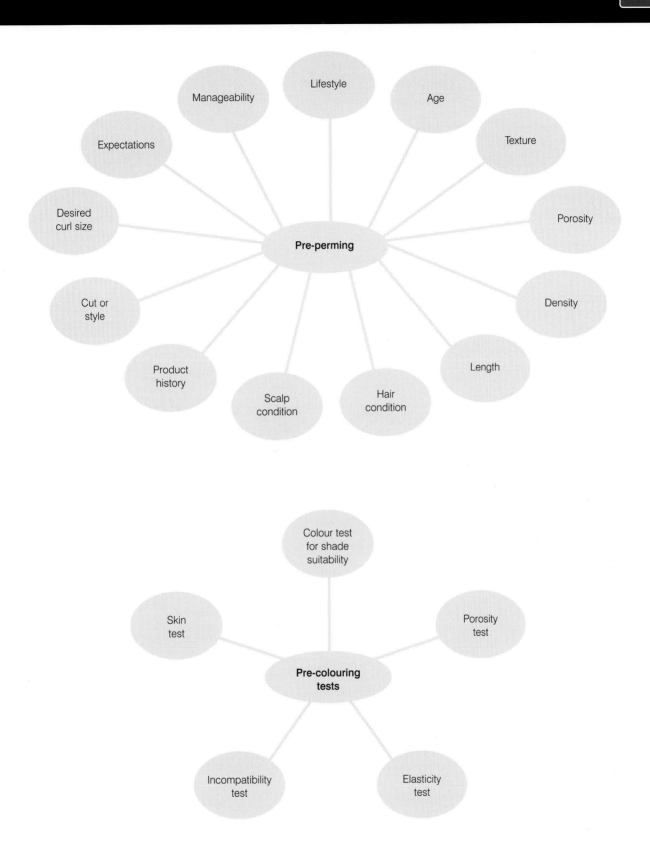

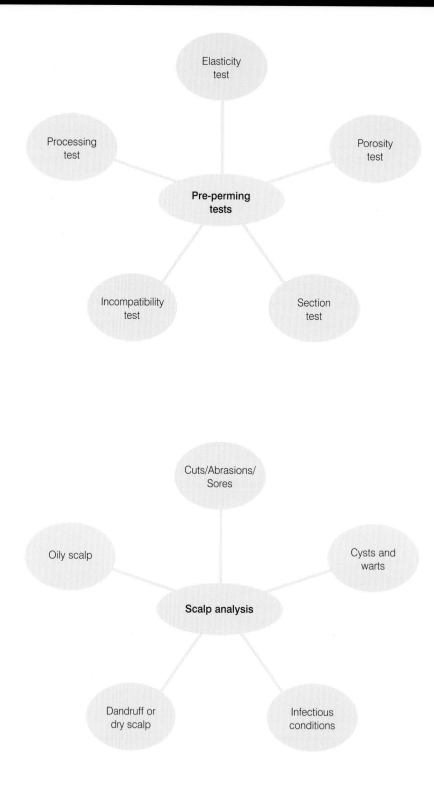

4.5 assessing the material properties of skin

people and their skin

Skin has been described as the 'ideal wrapping material', a material that covers the entire body surface. Skin accounts for about one-eighth of the body's total weight. Skin is the body's largest organ. It is also the one that is so often abused and neglected over the years to the detriment of its owner. In healthy condition skin feels firm, soft and elastic and moist. Its texture which describes how it looks and feels is said to be even, fine and blemish free. A good complexion is a phrase also used to indicate a fine texture and a clear, healthy skin colour.

When it comes to quality, think of the smoothness of a baby's bottom. However, this quality soon changes, particularly on the face as it is acted upon by the external forces of gravity, harmful environmental factors, poor or misguided skin care regimes and harsh cosmetics. All this in addition to the effects of poor diet, smoking, excessive alcohol consumption and general lifestyle abuse.

We cannot escape the downward pull effect of gravity and the natural ageing process of skin, especially on the face. However, where we can make positive changes and improvements to the outward appearance of skin or slow the ageing process down is how we look after and treat this precious material. The battle to combat this is no secret. Clients and customers of both sexes will be searching for effective skin care advice and treatments to improve, restore or nurture their skin into tip-top condition. Your success at doing this will initially depend on your ability to assess and diagnose skin problems and recognise skin typing clues. Consequently, giving the correct advice or treatment will require you to have a sound knowledge of skin physiology. This will mean observing, asking pertinent questions, listening carefully, touching and feeling their skin.

skin assessment and analysis

The importance of this must not be overlooked if you are to effectively prescribe suitable cosmetic products or carry out appropriate beauty treatments. The assessment and analysis should be carried out on thoroughly cleansed skin. Ensure that all traces of oiliness are removed by gently wiping with a toner, which otherwise may give you a false impression of the skin's natural moisture level. If your client has sensitive skin which is prone to becoming flushed, reddened or become irritated easily, allow it time to settle down before proceeding with your assessment.

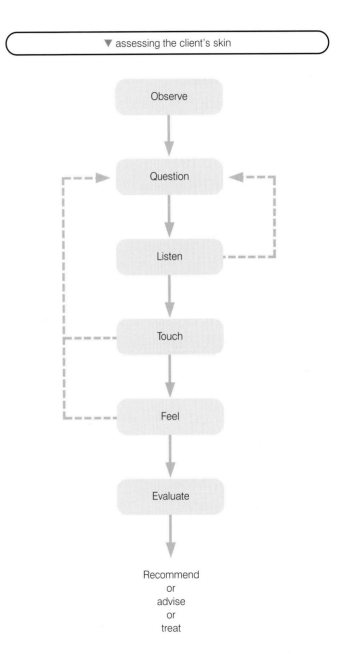

▼ assessing the client's skin

Observe → Question → Listen → Touch → Feel → Evaluate → Recommend or advise or treat

An effective assessment and analysis must take into account the client's age, lifestyle, health, cosmetic history, diagnostic considerations including pore size, skin type and texture as well as your ability to recognise facial skin conditions. Such contributory factors may make it difficult to type a client's skin.

assessing the face prior to make-up application

Before starting a make-up design, assess the client or model's face. Pay particular attention to their colouring, facial anatomy, features and skin.

diagnostic considerations
pore size and condition

Pore size, whether small, medium or large, is genetically governed. However, it is also controlled by the amount of sebum secreted by the associated glands. The larger the pores generally the greater the amount of sebum secreted. Hormones and massage can trigger oil production which in turn causes the

pores to increase in size. The condition and size of facial pores gives rise to different skin types which are summarised shortly.

skin texture and surface quality

The texture and surface quality of facial skin depends to a large extent on the role of secretions of sebum from the sebaceous glands. The sebum is essential for maintaining the skin's well-being and giving it its appearance.

In terms of appearance or surface quality, we can now describe skin as:

- *Plain smoothness* which describes a skin that is even, flawless, firm and overall smooth.
- *Patterned smoothness* which describes a skin that feels smooth but looks textured because of freckles or other pigmentation.
- *All over textured* which in contrast to the above describes a skin that has surface depth or unevenness due to wrinkles, blemishes, etc. It may also be described as flaky, crepy, coarse, pitted, leathery.
- *Combination textured skin* which is plain and smooth in certain places and textured in others.

muscle tone

The loss of muscle tone, crepy loose skin; increased facial lines around the mouth and eyes; folds of skin on the eyelids; loose skin around the neck and jawline; dropping and sagging of facial muscles are all telltale signs of ageing. In many clients, these may be very pronounced and for these clients this 'melting wax' look can be very depressing. Your aim as a consultant or adviser is to help improve the facial contours and offer advice on how to delay the inevitable ageing process, through appropriate facial treatments that may include massage or electrical stimulation. To achieve this you will need to have a good understanding of facial anatomy including the muscles of the face and the role they play in giving the face its form of expression.

skin type

Skin typing is the key to prescribing an effective skincare programme and specific product regime. Such a programme is closely linked to understanding the activity of the sebaceous glands. Skin types are classified according to whether the skin is

- normal
- oily
- dry
- normal combination
- sensitive
- older

skin pigmentation and imperfections

Skin pigmentation is associated with its main pigment melanin. This is discussed in greater detail in Part 3 Section 3.2. However, it is important to appreciate that when assessing the face you may come across pigmentation disorders.

In addition there may be skin imperfections, many of which can be treated by a specialist beauty therapist or in more serious cases by a dermatologist or cosmetic surgeon.

Common skin imperfections are summarised below.

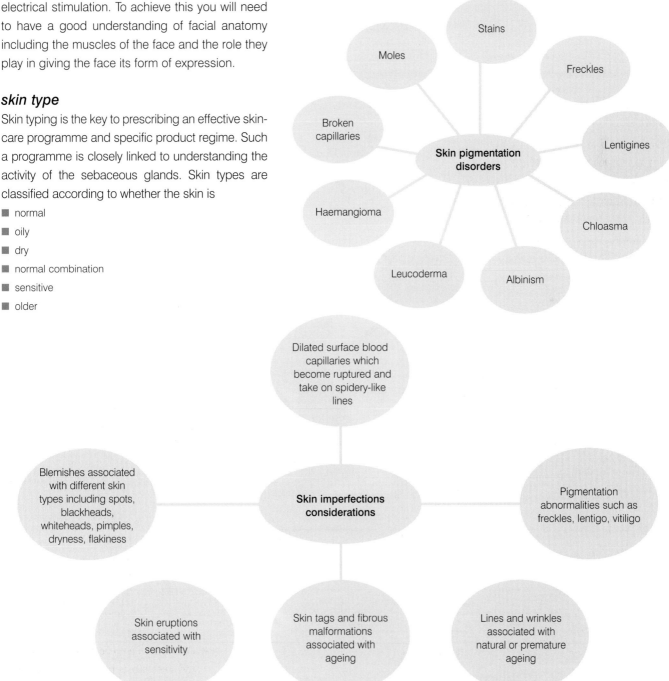

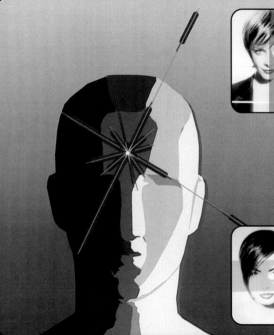

Cheynes

Cheynes

Ian Mistlin

Composing is the next stage in the design process. It requires you to draw upon your knowledge and understanding of design and style principles. Thus enabling you to advise clients and compose looks that are aesthetically suitable and technically sound.

From surveying the client's head, face and body you are now ready for the conception and composing stage.

To compose means to arrange or put in order. For example, a composer of music is a person who notates and arranges a musical score. Similarly, as a professional hair or make-up artist, a colour consultant or fashion stylist, you are a composer of a client's image.

I use the word 'image' in the context of changing the form or appearance of a client through their hair, make-up, the colour or style of clothes they wear. In effect you are helping the client to visually improve the way they look by composing an alternative visual image.

Your ability to compose looks, be it as this stage just conceptual images in your head, and make recommendations to your client, is a very complex process that requires a wide range of different thinking skills including:

- assessing
- analysing
- categorising
- comparing
- linking
- reflecting
- evaluating
- visualising

It requires you to be able to bring together key areas of knowledge and information, which you have previously gathered during the total design analysis, and arrange it or put it in a logical manner. This is described in the 'composition framework' diagram.

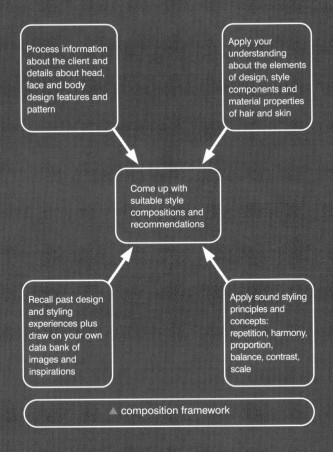

▲ composition framework

Think of the overall process in terms of having to add and make sense of essential items of information to form an *'image equation'*.

An equation is an expression that has two sides separated by an equals sign (=). The object is to match one side to the other so that the equation balances.

This process is now summarised in the following graphics which illustrate the 'components of information' that contribute and need to be considered when composing a client's hair image, make-up image, colour range and fashion image.

Your objective is to compose an 'image' that matches the client and their needs in every possible way.

How creative your compositions are will depend on your ability to develop right-brain activities and the power of whole thinking (see Part 2, Section 2.2)

Personality and
style preferences

+

Lifestyle

+

Age

+

Material
properties of hair

+

Head, face or body
particulars and features

+

The technical and
aesthetic merits of 'a cut'

+

Colouring and colour
harmony considerations

+

Drying, styling and dressing
considerations to achieve the desired finish

+

Correct choice of hair cosmetics for
conditioning and finishing

=

Client's hair image

▲ hair image equation

Personality and
style preferences

+

Lifestyle

+

Age

+

Skin texture

+

Skin imperfections

+

Skin condition

+

Colouring

+

Bone structure
and facial features

+

Compatible
colour selection

+

Texture
considerations

+

Cosmetic
compatibility

=

Client's make-up image

▲ make-up image equation

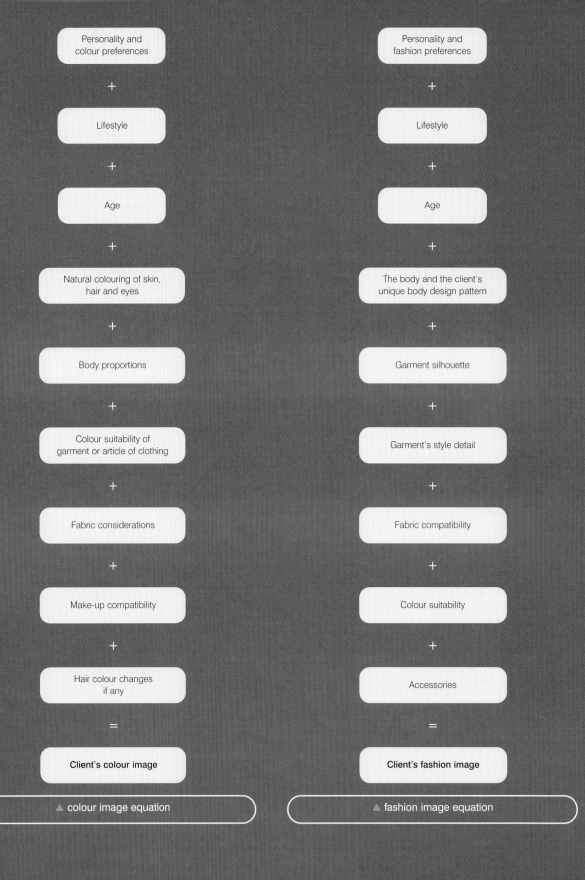

Personality and colour preferences	Personality and fashion preferences
+	+
Lifestyle	Lifestyle
+	+
Age	Age
+	+
Natural colouring of skin, hair and eyes	The body and the client's unique body design pattern
+	+
Body proportions	Garment silhouette
+	+
Colour suitability of garment or article of clothing	Garment's style detail
+	+
Fabric considerations	Fabric compatibility
+	+
Make-up compatibility	Colour suitability
+	+
Hair colour changes if any	Accessories
=	=
Client's colour image	**Client's fashion image**

▲ colour image equation ▲ fashion image equation

5.1 hair – design and style recommendations

■ what suits the client?

How hair looks, reacts and behaves will be influenced not only by its material properties but also by you.

It will be down to you to know how to treat it, bring out its best qualities so that what you do is technically sound, and most importantly, aesthetically suits the client.

people are different

On the question of suitability, wouldn't it be easy if everyone's face shape was the same? However, this is far from the case. The so-called perfect face for a woman is considered to be oval. It is the most symmetrical of all the shapes. Regardless of a client's face shape, you must be able to rebalance it as well as enhance their bone structure. Similarly, you must also design with their body shape and proportions in mind.

There is no point finishing a client's hair only to discover that the proportions are wrong. Before you start, as early as the consultation stage, you will need to have a visual image, a picture in your head of what the finished cut or style will look like on them. Call it a design blueprint.

what to take into account

To conceive this blueprint you will need to consider the design detail or *specification* of the cut or style, taking into account:

■ the shape of the cut or style

■ the style lines

■ movement and direction

■ the dimensions of the cut or style

■ style proportions

■ the symmetry of the cut or style

■ the scale of the cut or style

The aim is to compose and recommend a look that is aesthetically suitable. That is, it flatters the client's

■ height

■ head shape and size

■ face shape and dimensions

■ facial features and bone structure

■ neck length, width and shoulder proportions

■ body contours

In addition, there are technical considerations that must be taken into account including:

■ the material properties of hair

■ its temperament – how it behaves

■ how it will react

■ its limitations and potential

This obviously is of prime importance when considering methodology and technique such as how to control the dimensions and distribution of hair by adopting different cutting or finishing techniques.

The importance of finish must not be overlooked. Consequently, it is essential to visualise the type of finish and appreciate whether you will be able to reproduce the desired effect taking all factors into consideration.

Design issues and style challenges

1. Technical and aesthetic recommendations for different hair types and textures
2. Helping clients to overcome growing pains
3. Line treatment to balance and compensate different face shapes, profile irregularities and nose shapes
4. Line treatment to balance neck proportions
5. Enhancing facial features: the eyes, ears and mouth
6. Line treatment applied to different body shapes and proportions
7. Technical solutions for dealing with scalp, crown, hairline and neckline irregularities
8. Controlling the dimensions and distribution of hair by cutting
9. Controlling the dimensions and distribution of hair by finishing, styling and dressing
10. Style enhancing using colour and perm

Similarly, compositions involving the use of colour and perming, must not only take into account technical factors associated with chemical work but also aesthetic considerations. This means colour compositions or colour effects that enhance the client's unique colour profile.

design issues and style challenges

In this section I will be offering guidance and recommendations to help you deal with a wide range of design issues and style challenges.

1 hair types and textures

The basis of changing and improving your client's hair image should take into account each person's unique hair characteristics.

It is therefore essential to consider the properties, behaviour and temperament of different hair types and textures before carrying out any design service. The aim is to consider what will be most suitable technically, aesthetically and practically.

Human hair is grouped into the following types:

- Caucasian (European) – straight, wavy, soft, curly hair
- Negroid (African) – tight curled, frizzy, kinky hair
- Mongoloid (Asian) – very straight to straight, coarse hair

technical and aesthetic recommendations

straight hair

- has a rounded hair shaft
- feels smooth
- responds well to precision, blunt, geometric type cuts
- can be permed to change its form
- shines well when healthy, reflecting the state of the cuticle layers
- can sometimes appear limp when styled
- difficult to blow dry, particularly if blonde
- resistant to perming, particularly if blonde
- needs correct daily haircare

wavy hair

- has an oval hair shaft – hair grows at a slant
- responds well to a variety of styles and designs, depending on technique
- needs to be well moisturised to promote maximum wave, especially in a dry, hot environment
- if coarse, can often become frizzy in humid climates, because of its ability to absorb moisture

curly hair

- has a flat hair shaft and a curved follicle – hair actually grows backwards and then drops over to produce the curl
- usually much stronger than straight or wavy hair and less prone to breakage
- needs to be expertly cut to encourage the curl to form in the correct way
- needs good haircare, especially moisturising products
- sometimes prone to frizz in damp weather
- does not shine or reflect the light like smooth hair
- colouring needs to be more adventurous – semi-permanent rinses are great to add shine, without chemically altering the structure
- avoid straightening curly hair either chemically or thermally as it will become damaged and very brittle

Texture refers to the degree of coarseness or fineness of hair, which may vary on different parts of the head. Variations in hair texture are due to:

- the diameter of the hair, whether fine, medium or coarse – coarse hair has the greatest diameter, very fine hair has the smallest
- the position of the cuticle scales affecting the feel of the hair, whether they lie flat or are raised

You will need to consider how the client's hair texture will affect the desired result.

fine hair

- feels soft and smooth and usually looks shiny. The cuticle layers in healthy fine hair are tightly closed, making it often difficult to set and resistant to perming. Similarly, it is more resistant to colouring because of the more tightly packed concentration of melanin cells in the cortex. Conversely, it is less resistant to chemical lightening so milder agents have to be used.
- usually looks its best in sleek one-length cuts which emphasise the bluntness, giving the illusion of thicker hair.
- layering can be successful particularly if the external length of the cut is adjusted to accommodate shorter internal lengths. This can be useful in giving lift and movement to a look
- over-layering often makes it look weak and visually thin, particularly if the overall length is left too long
- needs to be well maintained and looks best when cut regularly every 4–6 weeks
- needs to be 'airy' which means daily shampooing to remove dirt, oils and the build-up of styling products, which otherwise will clog the hair, making it look limp
- choice of haircare products is essential – the aim is to use products that enhance body

- looks better with an overall colour rather than highlights or lowlights
- it is better to avoid perming
- fine hair is delicate. Care should therefore be taken to avoid damaging it when combing and brushing

medium hair

- not as soft as fine hair
- responds well to most cutting techniques, blunt cutting, graduated and layered looks
- responds more favourably to colour products than fine hair
- does not always look as smooth as fine hair
- needs regular haircare with suitable balanced products
- responds well to blow-drying and setting if in good condition

thick hair

- has thick hair shaft and is usually very strong
- has texture with the most body and bounce
- less prone to mechanical damage and other abuse
- thick curly hair is often resistant to change of shape and needs to be relaxed and softened pre-cutting and styling with correctly balanced moisturising shampoos and conditioners
- it is important to appreciate how the volume of hair will be affected by different cutting techniques. Generally, careful layering can reduce volume or heaviness as well as create shape
- in-between and extreme layered lengths on thick coarse frizzy/curly hair may be difficult to control. Aesthetically it may be better to keep it one length to help to suppress the volume, though maintaining the weight of hair
- thick hair with natural waves or curls can work well graduated around the hairline and bottom lengths
- thick coarse textured hair has less compacted concentration of hair pigment because of the hair shaft's bigger diameter. Consequently a slightly lighter result will be obtained compared to the lightening effect on fine/medium hair. However, it will offer greater resistance to chemical lightening

2 growing out hair

Growing their hair does not mean the client should stop going to the hairdressers. Suggest they keep it regularly cut to keep in shape.

Often in-between shapes are difficult and frustrating. It is important to carefully adapt the shape/style and keep it looking good.

It is a time to be an understanding hairdresser. Give the client a goal. It is important for the client to have an end style firmly in mind – that is something to aim for.

> ### ✓ tip
>
> - Growing out layers can often be a problem. Bob hair until layers have grown out, keeping the external shape as strong as possible.

Advise them on appropriate styles. Educate them to follow the correct hair fitness programme for their hair type. Suggest they:

- use styling products such as mousses, gels, fixing sprays to give extra shape, volume, width and texture
- experiment with different drying techniques, e.g. scrunch drying, blow drying, to achieve a 'new look'
- experiment with different styling equipment, such as heated beddies to give curl, wave or texture
- consider whether it may be easier to grow out a style with the help of a soft perm
- experiment with hair accessories, e.g. slides, combs, scarves

Lastly, encourage them to have perseverance.

3 face shapes, profiles and nose shapes

Our face shapes are unique. They are made up of a combination of face lines and proportions. The key to total style suitability is understanding the relationship between the line and proportion of a proposed design in relation to the client's head, face and body contours.

The inconsistency in face shapes can be rectified by considering the exterior line and interior style detail of your haircuts. By working cleverly with the principles of *style* and *concepts* it is amazing how each client's face shape can be balanced and their bone structure enhanced.

Every client's face has potential regardless of imperfections. It is your job to know how to accentuate the stronger areas whilst compensating for the weaker regions.

This is now discussed with regards to line and style treatment for enhancing different:

- face shapes
- profile irregularities
- nose shapes

▼ facial shapes and facial geometry	
Face shapes	**Facial geometry**
Oval	About one and a half times longer than its width across its brow Forehead is slightly wider than the chin Considered the 'perfect face shape' – width is in proportion to length Usually small with delicate features
Round	About two-thirds as wide as it is long with the distance across the cheeks being the widest part Round hairline and round chin line
Oblong	Longer than it is wide with the cheek, jaw and forehead more or less equal
Pear	Narrow forehead, wide jawline and chinline
Diamond	Narrow forehead, extreme width across the cheekbones and narrowness across the chin
Triangular	Wide forehead and narrowness across the chin line
Square	Width – two-thirds or more of the length Straight hair lines and square jawline

▼ ways to balance different face shapes	
Face shapes	**Aim**
Oval	To maintain what is considered to be the perfect proportions for a female. If the forehead is slightly wider than across the chinline keep the line narrow
Round	To create the illusion of length by adding extra height and straight square lines below the jawline using diagonal lines
Oblong	To shorten, creating the illusion of more width than length
Pear forehead	To create the illusion of width across the forehead To decrease width across the jawline
Diamond	To reduce the width across the cheekbone line To add width across the forehead and jawline creating the illusion of ovalness to the face
Triangular	To decrease the width across the forehead To increase width across the cheek and jawbone
Square	To rebalance width and length in favour of adding width to the sides between the eyebrows and the lips by creating a fuller shape at the cheek bones and temples

line treatment and style recommendations

oval

hairstyles to go for

- usually any length, particularly short or chin lengths to complement shape
- wispy fringes
- sleek brushed back styles

hairstyles to avoid

- heavy straight fringes and centre partings that make the forehead seem wider

round

hairstyles to go for

- styles with height and narrowness
- chin-length wispy cuts that frame the face
- chunky layered styles that fall onto the face
- layered fringes
- asymmetric long wispy styles across the face to offset roundness

hairstyles to avoid

- round shapes
- tight perms
- one-length round haircuts, e.g. pageboys, halos, Isodora
- solid straight across fringes that create too much width at the cheeks
- very short hair that accentuates the roundness of the face
- flat hair on top of head

oblong

hairstyles to go for

- jaw length styles, e.g. short layered bobs
- curly or wispy fringes to reduce long face
- styles with volume at ear level
- asymmetric shapes
- hair parted off centre
- wispy styles onto the face
- fullness through perming or layering fine hair or medium texture hair at the sides to create width and broaden cheek bones

hairstyles to avoid

- upswept hairstyles, with short backs and sides, that add length to the face
- large surrounds of hair as this tends to make the head very big and the face small
- styles with 'narrowness' that accentuate the long lines of the face

pear-shaped (inverted heart)

hairstyles to go for

- styles with height and volume across the forehead
- asymmetric fringe to partially cover the forehead
- styles with softness coming onto the cheeks, but still narrow at the jawbone
- fringes that are cut back

hairstyles to avoid

- styles that create extra width across the cheekbone line
- styles that give the illusion of narrowness across the temples

diamond-shaped

hairstyles to go for

- styles that create fullness across the forehead and jawline, whilst maintaining narrowness, keeping hair close to the face across the cheeks, e.g. bob with the ends flicking out at jaw length
- short styles with fullness at temples and brushed back across the ears

hairstyles to avoid

- straight styles, e.g. bobs to ear length
- flat hair at the temples
- centre partings
- long hair styles that do not accentuate forehead width
- styles with fullness across the cheek bones

triangular or heartshaped

hairstyles to go for

- straight styles that have extra volume, curl, wave at the jawline region
- fringes that reduce breadth of the forehead
- mid-length styles are best

hairstyles to avoid

- full styles across the temples
- high hair, exposing weak chin and mouth region
- hair pulled off the forehead
- heavy and very straight fringes that add width to the forehead

square

hairstyles to go for

- soft perms to soften jawline
- soft wispy cuts framing the face
- texturised cuts with the layers brushed forwards to soften an angular face, e.g. a layered bob style that gives fullness off the forehead and coming onto the sides and jaw to create narrowness and softness

hairstyles to avoid

- square cuts, e.g. bobs finishing at jaw length
- short cuts, cut over the ears and left long through the back
- geometric shapes
- deep cut straight fringes
- centre partings

profile irregularities

The aim is to position hair to optically diminish the size of the feature as well as cover up. This can be achieved by using style lines to direct the eye away from the feature as well as by surrounding the feature with more space to optically change its size. For instance, by surrounding the face with full hair the size of the feature can be optically reduced.

line treatment and style recommendations

concave (prominent forehead and chin)

aim
To reduce bulginess of the forehead
To soften and reduce the axis through the jaw and nape of neck

what will help
Soft flat fringes
Styles with wisps, strands, soft curls or waves around the nape region coming onto the face

what to avoid
Style lines that emphasise the line of the chin

In profile the forehead and chin will be seen to protrude

convex (receding forehead, prominent nose and receding chin)

aim
To create a balance between fullness on the forehead, combined with a closely sculptured hair in the nape and sides to compensate the receding jawline

what will help
Curly or straight fringes, dressed slightly forwards to conceal the receding forehead or irregular hairline
Create a better balance by designing the hair at the sides and nape to sit as close to the head shape as possible

In profile there is little indentation from the chin to the base of the neck

low forehead and protruding chin

aim
To create the illusion of height to a low forehead and length to the face
To direct attention away from the chin by creating a style line that is either above or below the chin

In profile the chin will be seen to protrude

what will help
Go for styles that give height and volume to the forehead as well as softness in the nape coming onto the face to soften the sharpness at the sides of the protruding chin

nose shapes

prominent

aim
To minimise the prominence of the nose by reducing the distance from the nose to the ear

what will help
Hair should be styled onto the forehead with softness onto the face, swept to one side thus forming a diagonal line across the forehead over one eye to the other eye which diverts attention

what to avoid
Styles pulled back off the face exposing a large forehead or styles elevated at the crown

turned up

aim
To create an illusion by lengthening the distance from the nose to the ear

what will help
Styles that are designed off the face at the sides

what to avoid
Styles that come onto the face

crooked

aim
To create asymmetry whereby the focal point is off centre thus drawing attention away from the nose

what will help
Asymmetric styles
Side partings
Diagonal fringes

what to avoid
Symmetrical styles and centre partings with full fringes

wide and flat

aim
A wide or broad nose tends to widen the face particularly across the cheek bones. Aim to reduce this width

what will help

Styles that are styled off the face, preferably with volume across the temple region

what to avoid

Styles that increase the width of the face across the cheek-bones and jawline

4 neck proportions

The length, sturdiness and slimness of the client's neck is an important consideration when it comes to deciding on suitable hairstyles, fashion neckline and jewellery. In this section our discussion will focus on hairstyles. You will also need to take into consideration the client's head position in profile and in particular how they carry their head. The position of the head, type of shoulders, will all affect the apparent length of the neck. There is, of course, the view that a long neck is an asset. In which case you will want to highlight the area. To visually enhance neck dimensions, your aim should be to balance the length and width of your hair designs therefore compensating for variations in upper body shape and proportion.

line treatment and style recomm endations

short neck, double chin

This neck shape often accompanies the woman with a fuller figure.

aim

To create the illusion of length by using vertical lines to direct the eye away from the area

hairstyles to go for

- short above the shoulder cuts
- styles with height on top, particularly at the crown
- keep the nape length short
- maintain smoothness at the sides
- graduated napes, with the appropriate balance and proportions from the back and side to create narrowness and open up the neck region

hairstyles to avoid

- styles with horizontal style lines that give fullness to the nape area, e.g. square bobs

long, thin necks

aim

To minimise the appearance of a long neck by incorporating horizontal style lines into a style

hairstyles to go for

- horizontal styles lines that give the illusion of width

- longer hair in the nape region with volume to give added width, softness and fullness

hairstyles to avoid

- long, lank hair styles, which can make a long thin neck look even longer

To highlight a long neck, aim to keep the area exposed. This can be done by taking hair away from the neck either by creative cutting or clever dressing.

In addition, a long neck can be emphasised by using long dazzling earrings or neck jewellery.

neck slanting forwards

This profile problem often accompanies a person with what is called a dowager's curvature of the back.

aim

To fill out the space caused by the forward slanting of the head and neck in relation to the back

hairstyles to go for

- styles that add dimension to this region and fill the void in the neck region

5 facial features

the eyes

Don't overlook the focal point of the face. You will need to help the client to draw attention to this important asset which, together with the mouth, is considered to be the most expressive part of the face. It is essential to also note the shape of the eyebrows when planning a hairstyle.

wide set eyes (usually found with square, round or diamond shaped faces)

The object is to reduce the distance between the eyes. This can be achieved by closing down the area between the side of the head and the corner of the eye by filling in with hair, and also by creating extra fullness on the top of the head. Avoid centre partings.

close-set eyes (usually found in persons with oval, long, narrow faces)

The aim is to open up the face and give the illusion of more width between the eyes. This can be achieved by creating more space at the side of the face by working the hair upwards off the face and outwards. This draws the eyes wider apart. Avoid centre partings.

wrinkled eyes

For the older female client who has wrinkled eyes suggest that she wears her hair up softly off her face. It's a great way to give her a 'face lift' without surgery.

the ears

It is very important to compensate for the movement of ears when combing sections over the ear. It is common when cutting bobs to find a 'gap' in the section over the ear. When the ear returns to its normal position, it will spring up, reducing the length of the hair section.

Protruding ears are best partially covered, or certainly left with sufficient volume of hair behind them if possible.

If the client wears a hearing aid, design the cut or style to hide it, by ensuring there is sufficient hair left over the ears. This also applies to clients who wears glasses. Make allowances for the arm of the glasses interfering with hair, in the region of the temples and above the ear.

the mouth

Since we spend so much of our lives in communication, it is understandable why the mouth is such an important facial feature, and contributes greatly to our first impressions of others.

According to research men find well-defined full lips very attractive in women, whereas women find men's mouths appealing, not because of the shape and type of lip, but because of the expression.

If you want to make your client's mouth a focal point, consider styles brushed onto the face. Aesthetically the shape of the mouth and lips can be improved by correct make-up application (see section 6.1, mastering make-up).

If the client's mouth has an unattractive shape and line, avoid haircuts or styles that finish at lip level, which will only draw attention to it.

6   body shapes and proportions

Getting the correct scale of your cuts and styles is essential. This will mean taking into consideration overall proportions in terms of balancing width and length from top to toe as well as the ratio of head to body size.

type of body shape

tall and slim

Hair can be styled in numerous variations because the proportions allow for styles with volume and length, which balances the frame shape. For example medium long hair is best with volume and lift so that the head and body are in proportion: hair can be tied back or use neat chignons. Avoid too short hair or too long lank styles.

tall and well built

Women with big broad frames should try soft, voluminous hair, preferably shoulder length. Balance width to frame the face, with sufficient volume to cut down proportions. Also try full chignons with lots of body. Avoid short hairstyles.

short and thick-set

Short plump women should avoid overcrowding their faces. Too much hair, especially too full, produces a curtaining effect giving the illusion of an even shorter body. Try softer styles which balance height with width, or chignons which create extra height and narrowness. Avoid square shoulder length cuts or too short severe looks.

narrow top and wide hips

Ideal styles are those that give texture or fullness between the chin and the shoulder region. Avoid short hair.

full chest and narrow hips

Ideal styles are those hair styles that give fullness between head and shoulders. Avoid too short hair which can draw attention to the bust line.

petite

Short, feminine cuts are ideal. Avoid too much hair which can overcrowd a small face, and certainly swamp a small body.

7   head detail

shape of scalp

This is particularly important when considering 'very short cuts' where there is the possibility of irregular 'bumps' being visible. Look for any old head wounds that may have unsightly scars.

growth patterns (e.g. hairlines)

Irregular growth patterns should be carefully considered during the consultation stage, particularly when the hair is dry. Determine how best they can be incorporated or how they will affect the desired cut. The overall design may need to be tailored to disguise a problematic hairline such as cowlicks, a widow's peak, excessively curly neckline, very uneven neckline or a neckline that swings to one side. The weight of hair can be used to suppress the directional growth of a resistant neckline. Similarly, it is important to consider the natural fall of the hair prior to setting.

As with hair types, it is often better to go with the irregular growth pattern rather than fight it. Go with the natural movement. It is often possible with cowlicks or widow's peaks to incorporate them into the style, thus creating a feature of the irregularity.

Care must be taken when considering a short haircut to finish off the hairline in an attractive way. Clever undercutting and controlled graduation is essential, so too is scissor over comb work to create a soft, fine finish. Avoid cutting solid base lines into your haircuts which give a hard and aggressive look.

Similarly, when it comes to working with hair around the ear do *not* cut harsh lines into short layered or 'cropped' looks. Layer and point out hair to removed excess weight.

the crown

The crown is the region at the top of the head which balances with an imaginary axis drawn from the chin through to the top of the head. It is the base region from where the hair radiates.

Irregular crowns or double crowns can cause problems if dealt with incorrectly. It is important to establish the directional growth of the hair and then cut or set in the direction of the growth. Avoid cutting crowns too short unless the style warrants it. Otherwise there will be a problem with unsightly hair sticking up. The length of the hair at the crown should be predetermined to compensate for any irregular head shapes.

When roller-setting, the crown rollers should be positioned so as to create the desired head shape, carefully noting where volume is needed or not required. View the head in profile and note the curvature of the head and neck shape. If a defined neck shape is wanted you must decide on how much of the nape to set, if at all.

partings

A parting is a division within the hair. It usually falls along an imaginary line drawn through the centre of the eye back to the crown either on the left or the right side of the head. Partings can also be situated centrally along an imaginary line from the centre of the nose back to the crown. However, it is common for the parting to fall naturally off centre.

To locate a natural parting, simply comb the wet hair back off the face towards the crown and gently push the section forwards from the crown. The hair should divide down its natural 'line'. If the style incorporates a parting it is better to work from the natural parting.

Side partings emphasise the eyes, whilst a centre parting emphasises the nose and mouth.

Partings need to be positioned to suit the client's shape of head, facial shape and features; hair type and the natural fall of the hair must also be taken into account. These considerations must then be worked into the desired overall hairstyle.

There is no rule to say that every style should have a parting. In fact for many styles it would be most inappropriate. For instance, partings in shorter layered hair look hard and break up the natural flow or movement of hair. However, a definite parting in a classic one-length cut is a construction necessity, although when styling hair can often be finished to make the parting look less obvious. This can be achieved by taking the hair back off the face and allowing it to fall naturally. A zig-zag parting can be introduced to beak up a dramatic straight line parting and give the style an element of chaos. This works particularly well on classic bobs, shoulder length or graduated hair cuts. A zig-zag parting also complements chunky multi-toned blocks of hair colour in preference to highlights or for those clients with a roots problem.

8 the dimension and distribution of hair by cutting

The creative stylist knows that they will be able to keep pace with changing attitudes and trends. Fundamental to their success is the desire to experiment. Experimentation means possibly having to break the rules before one can break new ground. Their confidence is supported by having a solid foundation and understanding of the basic cutting principles.

Most creative cutters I have worked with over the years share a technical supremacy and the belief that it is the precision of the cut which helps to control the dimensions, distribution or how well the hair falls around the contours of the client's head, face, neck and shoulders. This is achieved by knowing which cutting technique is going to be the most suitable to produce the desired effect and result.

The final look will depend on:

- the exterior or shape or line
- the interior shape or detail
- the amount of graduation
- the length of layers
- the position of concaves
- the amount of movement and texture
- the angle of cutting

the exterior shape or line

The simplest shapes are basic one-length cuts, where all the hair hangs evenly to one level. This blunt cutting or club horizontal cutting technique demands that all the hair is cut evenly to produce a solid heavy perimeter line. Ideally hair at this length falls best below the curve of the shoulders. It should be explained to clients that the hair is not encouraged to separate at this optimum length. Hair that is allowed to fall on the shoulders can appear to be a region of 'no man's land', i.e. it is neither long enough nor short enough to be a bob shape.

A range of one-length cuts can be designed by varying the line *angle* of cutting; and the length of hair from the shoulders to the neck, and then from the neck to the jaw region, or onto the face.

These one-length classic cuts work well on smooth straight hair that it is in brilliant condition. They are characterised by being cut usually from a parting, are flat on top of the head with more volume and weight around the base line.

One-lengths cuts on curly or permed hair can result in a look that is particularly full at the base.

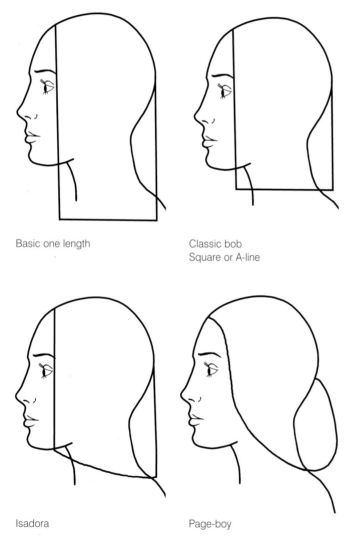

Basic one length

Classic bob
Square or A-line

Isadora

Page-boy

interior shape or detail

Just as the sculptor gently chips away at a piece of stone to build up shape, so too can the haircutter. The sculptor working methodically leaves excess of material in certain places to

emphasise form. Similarly the hairdresser, by cleverly using different cutting techniques can create and control the internal 'build-up' of hair in different regions around the head.

In effect hairdressers are creating shape by transferring weight and volume to a particular region around the head to enhance the facial proportions and create balance.

The *use of weight* in cutting is particularly valuable and forms the basis of the principle of a graduation cutting technique.

graduation

This is the slow process of distributing weight, creating movement, volume and contrasts in texture. The technique can be used around the perimeter of the head to create a variety of shapes. Graduation starts from the hairline, which is the shortest area. As you move up and around the head, the weight moves, with increasing lengths and volume. The position of the weight can be varied by the angle of graduation. The smaller the angle, the minimum the graduation and the weight line will be lower down the head. Conversely, by increasing the angle the weight line will be raised. Graduated haircuts like the classic graduated bob, wedge and fire-fly are characterised by variations in hair lengths, in comparison to the outline shape. The inner hair length is in all instances longer than the outline hair length but does not need the design line.

Another type of graduation called *reverse graduation* can be used when cutting one-length cuts such as classic bobs, page-boys and box bobs. This technique concentrates maximum weight on a blunt base line and can be used to control hair lines with difficult growth patterns. Visually from the top of the head to the base line the hair looks continuous. It is produced by an overlapping effect. To be effective there must be a longest point and a shortest point in the cut. Ideally there should be no more than 1 cm of reverse graduation present.

layering

Layering can be used to reduce bulk or weight, introduce movement and enhance hair type. A combined knowledge of optimum length for different hair types and textures is essential and should be thoroughly appreciated during the consultation stage. For instance, you will need to know how you can best layer naturally curly hair to encourage curl or wave function. A basic layered cut is a short cut, where the hair is cut into even lengths over the entire head by holding hair at 90° sections to the contours of the head, creating a soft smaller head shape. By varying the internal lengths and angles of cutting a variety of different layered head shapes and looks can be achieved. Starting 'internally' with the head shape, working out from the shortest point, forms a basis of creating a softer outline for the cut. For a harder exterior line, the exterior shape can be cut first.

In contrast to graduation, weight is transferred from the internal shape downwards. Layering can be used to distribute weight between short and longer points giving rise to differing levels in the hair. Volume and movement can be produced within the 'body' of the design. This is formed by releasing the natural movement or curl in hair during cutting.

concaves

This internal cutting technique can be placed around the head to encourage the internal movement and direction of hair. It works on the principle that the shorter hair pushes the longer hair. The shorter hair is strong, the long hair is weak. The shorter hair is able to maintain its shape pushing the longer more flexible hair in the required direction, thus altering the internal shape.

freehand techniques

These are very 'relaxed' freehand techniques to enhance a particular style by adding and increasing textures, movement and shape internally.

- *slide cutting*   creates loose texture and movement; can be used to blend extreme lengths
- *weave cutting*   creates volume and texture, by incorporating shorter inner hair lengths that support the outer longer lengths
- *chopping*   as the name suggests, achieves a chopped irregular texture
- *chipping*   softens and creates texture in a club cut line
- *pointing*   reduces weight and gives a softer effect to the ends of hair
- *thinning*   reduces bulk of hair and gives a softer effect
- *razoring*   creates movement and texture as well as reduces bulk/weight or length. Traditionally the hair is cut wet. A softer outline can also be obtained by this method
- *twist*   as the name implies a small square twisted section of hair is cut either at a desired length to create a diffuse finish or alternatively the scissor blades are squeezed and slide along the twisted hair length. This technique creates volume, texture and reduces weight

angles

The importance of angles in hair design should be appreciated in order to produce the desired shapes. *Horizontal* angles build heavy weight lines. *Diagonal* angles create volume and bevelled weight line. *Vertical* angles are the lightest form of layering.

9 finishing, styling and dressing hair

See part 6, section 6.2.

10 colouring and perming

colour

The key question that you need to consider before you so much as pick up a colour product or tint brush is:

- Will changing your client's hair colour in some way be right for them and if so what colour and technique would be aesthetically suitable and technically correct?

The benefits of using colour are now discussed along with aesthetic tips and recommendations.

the aesthetic benefits of using colour

Colour can be used to:

- strengthen or emphasise a client's natural colour shine
- accentuate a client's hair cut – darker colours relative to their natural hair colour can emphasise the line of a cut
- create the illusion of extra volume by using brighter shades
- accentuate texture by using different tones of highlights
- make some clients look younger with lighter hair
- give an added dimension of movement by using contrasting tones of light and dark
- visually help balance the shape of the face. For example:
  – hair that is emphasised at the sides will slim a wide face
  – strong fringes can help to shorten a long face

Cheynes

  – curly hair in a soft shade styled off the face will help to minimise a prominent nose
  – chin-length styles in a vibrant red or gold tone will make a short neck look longer
- increase visual impact and even arouse provocation
- optically make weak-looking hair seem thicker and healthier

Cheynes

aesthetic tips

- a strong contrast of colour that is too dark in comparison to a client's skin tone can look hard and ageing
- too light a colour on naturally light and fine hair can make it look optically thinner
- lightening hair can release unflattering colour pigments
- a blonde look can make some clients look bland

Cheynes

precautions when using colour

- ensure you achieve colour harmony between the client's natural colouring (including their hair, skin, and eye colour) and the colour of the product/formula to be used. This way you will create a pleasing and natural effect
- understand how the laws of colour work before you consider introducing complementary colours to accent a client's hair colour
- understand how structure, technique and product knowledge affect colouring results

using colour to create drama and excitement

This can be achieved by introducing accents of contrast colours in small amounts either as highlights, lowlights or slices. This works on the principle of contrast colour relationships to create cold–warm or warm–cold contrasts or light–dark or dark–light contrasts.

The former is created by using complementary or opposite colours on the colour wheel.

How far you go with creating the latter will depend on the level of contrast your client exhibits, together with ensuring you do not unduly upset colour harmony.

corrective colouring

We know that when two pairs of complementary colours are mixed together in equal amounts they will neutralise each other. This can be used to great effect if you need to neutralise unwanted warmth in hair as a result of lightening.

For example red and green neutralise each other. Therefore to neutralise unwanted green tones use a warm or red shade. Orange and blue neutralise each other. Consequently to remove or tone down unwanted brassiness such as orange in hair use a blue-based hair colour. Yellow and violet neutralise each other. To rid hair of unwanted yellow tones select a violet-toned hair product.

colour recommendations based on a client's colour profile

The right choice of colour depends on taking natural hair colour, skin tone and eye colour into consideration. It's about creating harmony and balance. The following charts outline colouring recommendations for each of the four 'seasonal' groups.

Characteristic: Winter

Do's	Let the colouring be as natural as possible. Use *medium* to *dark brown* semi or permanents or burgundy plum, damson highlights or lowlights
Dont's	Avoid light highlights – they can be ageing. Avoid red tones. Avoid bleaching as the hair is likely to turn red
Greying	This group is most likely to grey prematurely. It is best to wear shorter styles if client is going natural. Long grey hair is ageing. To cover grey use ash brown tones or light to light-blonde highlights. Avoid 'warm' tones otherwise red will appear. As people age the skin fades too!

Additional notes

- avoid dyeing the hair blonde, red or black, unless you want to create a hard tarty look
- highlights on a 'winter' can be ageing, as the hair takes on a yellowish tone
- exposure to sunlight, as well as being damaging, will cause sun bleaching, making the hair appear as if it has red highlights
- dyed red hair on a deep cool person with olive skin may make the face appear dirty
- grey hair 'winters' who smoke heavily or who have been in a smoky atmosphere are likely to have a yellowish tinge in their hair which will need to be removed

Characteristic: Summer

Do's	Let dark brunette summers be as natural as possible. The once blonde 'summer' whose brown hair is light can be blonde again by using highlights to add life. It is best to use *ash tones*, *ash blondes* e.g. ash brown/dark ash brown shades
Dont's	Avoid 'warm' tones. Avoid henna as it is harsh and ageing – clashes with the skin. If skin has pink tones avoid colours with red tones
Greying	The 'summer' greys gracefully to a blue grey or white tone. It can look very attractive to leave the hair natural. To cover grey use ash blonde, Light ash blonde or ash brown tones as semis

Additional notes

- the effects of nicotine on grey hair need to be removed to enhance the beautiful natural silver tones
- if they have a very pink skin colour avoid extreme exposure to sunlight to prevent hair appearing 'red'

Characteristic: Autumn

Do's	Autumns look great with *red tones*. Try golden glints on redheads, or lowlights using a red colour or a shade lighter than their own colour. Child blondes wishing to stay blonde should use *golden blonde tones*. Other autumns should use auburn red and warm brown tones
Dont's	Avoid ash tones – this will make them pale Steer away from colours with gold tones, although in some cases the orange tone can complement the skin, avoid ash tones
Greying	Autumns should cover grey, as the colour tends to come in yellow-grey. The two-tone look may appear drab, especially on a dark muted redhead. However, once their hair is completely grey it can be most attractive. To natralise grey look to lowlights using warm medium brown or warm red/mahogany

Characteristic: Spring

Do's	To stay blonde use flaxen or *golden blonde* colours. Spring redheads should maintain their 'redness'
Dont's	Avoid ash tones
Greying	Springs do not grey gracefully, so it is wise to keep their hair dyed during the transition years Use light to medium brown, auburn, golden brown or light golden shades Once completely grey or white, its warm colour is flattering

perming

Just as new colouring techniques have been developed to emphasise hair cuts, so new perming techniques have evolved and been developed to give degrees of curl, volume, texture, style support and bounce.

Perming to enhance a cut or style is as much a science and art as colouring. The science associated with this characteristic is complex and must be thoroughly understood before attempting this chemical procedure, staring with thorough examination of the hair and scalp. These details can be found in a standard textbook.

For the purpose of developing perming as a style enhancing tool, I have outlined essential considerations that must be taken into account together with perming guidelines and recommendations to use or pass onto clients.

texture related recommendations

- for fine resistant hair, where the porosity is poor, choose a stronger alkaline perming lotion and/or allow a longer processing time
- for coarse resistant hair select an alkaline perming lotion
- for normal hair with a good even porosity use an acid lotion
- for hair that is porous as a result of previous colour or perming treatment or due to the cumulative effect of dying and styling use an acid balanced perm. As this type of hair readily absorbs lotion it requires the shortest processing time
- for hair that is described as 'over processed' and consequently over porous, it is advisable not to perm the hair until the offending portion of hair has been cut or restructured using protein treatments
- for hair that has uneven porosity along its length, use a pre-wrap lotion
- for hair that is coated with the residue of haircare and styling product it is advisable to use a 'deep cleaning' shampoo to remove all deposits

aesthetic recommendations

- make sure your client fully appreciates how curly the perm will be. The loose curl look that many clients pick out of a magazine cannot be achieved by perming. Invariably it has to be achieved by tonging or setting hair
- ask the client whether they like the look of perm best after it has been growing out for some time
- discuss how long the perm will last
- inform the client at this stage on how you plan to finish their hair, i.e. natural or set

health considerations

- pregnancy, breast feeding and other hormonal changes in the body can all affect the success of a perm

condition recommendations

- it is advisable not to perm overprocessed hair
- do not perm if the client's scalp is inflamed

haircare recommendations

- ensure that the pre-perm shampoo thoroughly removes any product residues that may have built up on the hair shaft. Remove by using a suitable deep cleansing shampoo
- if the hair is weak apply a pre-perm protein treatment to restructure the hair
- use a pre-wrap lotion to equalise porosity if necessary

cutting recommendations

- if the client is having a restyle ensure that the hair is pre-cut into a rough shape to successfully accommodate the perm. Perming hair that is too long may limit the success of the perm
- after the perm refine the cut and overall shape. Sculpture the hair to create flattering new proportions. If necessary cut into the perm by texturising
- always trim the hair after a perm to remove possible damaged ends

styling recommendations

- it is inadvisable to subject a new perm to intense heat and vigorous blow-drying that is likely to stretch it. It is better to use a diffuser

homecare recommendations

- use the correct haircare product to maintain the longevity and look of the perm
- spray the perm in the morning with a light mist of water to rejuvenate the curl
- avoid brushing the perm when dry which will turn the hair frizzy
- use a jumbo comb to gently detangle the hair when wet, and use a light detangler spray
- allow the perm to dry more naturally and if necessary use a dryer with a diffuser
- protect a perm from the effects of the sun, chlorine and sea water
- avoid having a perm just before going on holiday to a hot climate

rescue remedies

Over-permed hair is most undesirable. Aesthetically it looks awful and structurally it is disastrous. The only solution in this situation are professional salon treatments to remoisturise and strengthen the hair. Olive oil is best used on salads!

5.2 make-up selection

■ think colour

Nothing is more important than colour harmony with make-up selection and design. Knowing how to choose colours and successfully co-ordinate them requires an understanding of the laws of colour, and a knowledge of the rudiments of colour relationships in order to achieve the right colour balance. In this section I will be drawing on this knowledge and understanding. In addition, I will be referring to the application of colour analysis and the terms used to describe a client's unique colour portfolio. On a very basic level clients will have a natural affinity with the colours of one of the four seasons – winter, summer, autumn and spring. That is clients will look their best when their make-up reflects the colour qualities of their season. However, as discussed earlier more advanced analysis systems describe human colouring using the same terms of dimensions as scientists and artists. These dimensions are value, intensity and undertone. It is also possible to further describe colour in terms of tonal characteristics as shown in the following diagram.

▼ Examples of yin and yang in respect to colour

	Yin	Yang
Undertone	Cool	Warm
Value	Dark	Light
Intensity	Muted	Bright
Colours	Greens Cool blues Violets	Reds Warm yellows Orange

ability in a more artistic way. Consequently colour selection can be based on the prescriptive seasonal approach or the more fluid tonal approach. The result will be a selection of *compatible* colours that are related to the client's colouring. Such a colour relationship and combination are referred to as *analogous* colours. These are colours that live next to or close to each other on the colour wheel.

However, the tonal approach does not consider that colour in nature is a subtle balance of warm and cool, light and dark, bright and muted. In effect, colour is a balance of opposites. Interestingly, it was the ancient Chinese who appreciated the concept of balance and the principle of complementarity. This concept is based on the fundamental philosophy of Taoism. The principle was used to interpret the process of nature. It considers that life consists of two forces opposing but not antagonistic to each other. The forces are known as *yin* and *yang*.

Both forces move in circles and are in constant change in relation to themselves and to each other due to the ebb and flow of life forces of our universe. Everything is formed by both the yin and yang tendencies, nothing is solely yin and yang, i.e. they must be *balanced*.

```
                        ┌──────────────┐
                        │    Colour    │
                        └──────┬───────┘
          ┌────────────────────┼────────────────────┐
    ┌──────────┐         ┌──────────┐          ┌──────────┐
    │  Value   │         │ Intensity│          │ Undertone│
    └──────────┘         └──────────┘          └──────────┘

   Deep vs Light        Bright vs Muted        Warm vs Cool
```

The prescriptive seasonal approach is useful to 'signpost' a client's particular colour position and direction. However, it does not go far enough.

The tonal approach offers much more precise terminology to identify and describe a client's colour profile. It also provides a means to consider make-up selection and colour suit-

getting the colour balance right

Importantly it is interesting to note that there are many people whose colouring is a combination of warm and cool. This is certainly borne out by colour consultants who practise a less prescriptive approach to colour analysis.

The significance of opposites in make-up design is extremely important, especially if you want to 'get creative with colour'. The object is to use colour to balance natural colouring with enough of its opposites so that the make-up integrates naturally.

For instance, warm hues, those derived from yellow or yellow-red, can be used to intensify a cool eye tone. Cool hues, those derived from blue, violet and green, can be used to complement a client with warm brown eyes.

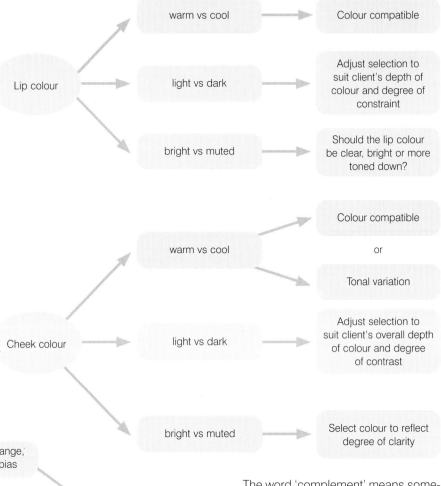

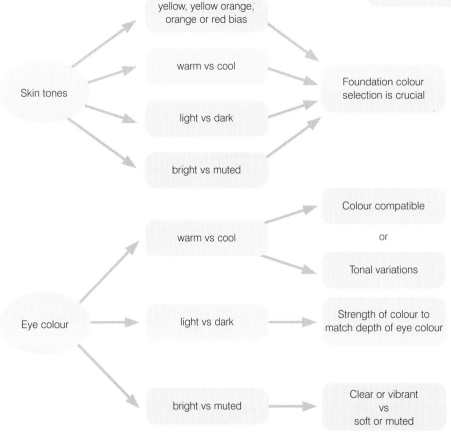

The word 'complement' means something that creates a balance. In terms of colour relationships 'complementary' colours intensify each other when placed next to or near one another.

Choosing cosmetic shades that best suit your clients, is the first step to composing a make-up look. They key is to get the colour balance right.

colourprinting

The philosophy of the company Prescriptives is based on exact colour matching. It offers a unique service of colourprinting, which exactly matches foundation, concealer and powder to the client's skin undertone. This falls into one of four colour families: yellow-orange, red-orange, red and blue-red. Once identified the products are correctly formulated and colour balanced to provide flawless coverage.

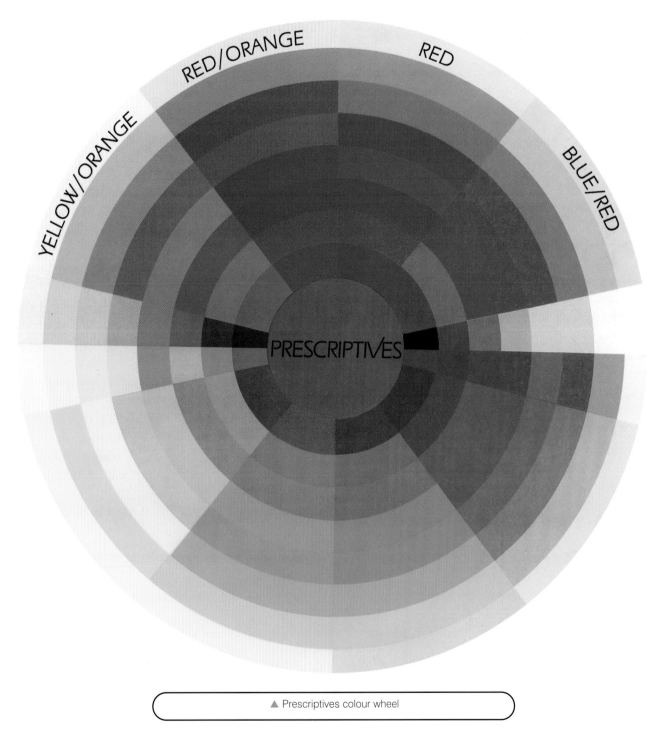

YELLOW/ORANGE

RED/ORANGE

RED

BLUE/RED

PRESCRIPTIVES

▲ Prescriptives colour wheel

Prescriptives adopts the basis of the artist's colour wheel to aid in the co-ordination of make-up colours and shows customers the ideal relationship of colour. By utilising its colour wheel it can advise a customer on all the shades for lips, cheeks and eyes that best compliment her colour family. Recommendations are based on three options or choices: a natural look, using colours in the same family as the foundation shade, an intensified look; and a contrasting look.

foundation colour

When you walk around the beauty and make-up counters in department stores are you bewildered by the variety of foundation colours on display?

Have you noticed that some colours have a pinkish cast compared to others that look slightly yellow or peachy?

Let's simplify the colour selection process by adopting a basic seasonal classification. Each season reflects a degree of warmth or coolness.

For a 'winter' or 'summer' you will need to use a cool or blue-based tone – too pinky tones are unflattering. 'Autumns' or 'springs' will look best in warm or yellow-based tones. However, this is an over-simplification.

You then need to consider how light or dark the foundation must be.

Perfect colour matching is the key to a flawless foundation finish. Nothing looks worse than an obvious demarcation line between face and neck tones. The right shade should blend perfectly to the skin tone, colour value and also enhance it.

The following 'skin tone scale' charts should help you come to terms with common foundation names.

shade variations

Choice of foundations depending on the intensity of skin tones.

'Winter'

Dark   Light

Rose Brown, Deep Rose Beige, Rose Beige, Neutral Beige, Cool Beige, Ivory, Porcelain

'Summer'

Dark   Light

Rose Brown, Deep Rose Beige, Neutral Beige, Pink Beige, Cool Beige, Pale Pink Beige

'Autumn'

Dark   Light

Golden Brown, Peach Bronze, Golden Beige, Peach Beige, Natural Beige, Ivory Bisque

'Spring'

Dark   Light

Golden Bronze, Golden Beige, Peach Beige, Peach, Ivory, Porcelain

testing the right colour

Applying foundation is not about changing the colour of the face. Choose a foundation that has the same intensity as the client's skin tone. The role of foundation is to enhance, even out natural skin colour.

If you wish to impart more depth of colour to a client's skin choose a foundation that is slightly darker than their natural skin tone. During the summer months it may be necessary for them to wear a slightly darker foundation to match a tan.

Too light a foundation can make someone look ill and pasty, whilst too dark can be hard and ageing. A little foundation goes a long way. Using too much will also make the skin look pasty.

Always test foundation on their face by placing a small dot along the jawline. Allow the foundation to remain on the skin for some minutes so that it can adjust and react to the skin's natural pH (acidic 4.5–5.5), then spread the dots and lightly blend.

Select the foundation that blends best and is nearest to their natural skin tone. It may be necessary to mix and match two shades of liquid foundation to create a perfect finish.

The best place to apply foundation is in natural daylight, in front of a window, with the light coming directly onto the face. Alternatively, if artificial light is used, make sure their face is evenly illuminated and that no part is in shadow. If possible use daylight bulbs.

eye-shadow colour, colour ways and schemes

Before you start to work, you need to consider the following selection criteria:

- the type of eye shadow and its texture
- eye colour in relation to colour harmony
- the warmth or coolness of the eye shadow
- the depth of the eye shadow
- the shape and size of the eye area
- the appropriateness of the colour to suit the time of day, mood and occasion
- what the client is wearing

Just imagine you are an artist with a colour palette in front of you. From your array of colours you will soon learn how to mix and match colours. As you become more confident your creativity will improve, especially when you realise how you can work with different colour values and colour harmonies to contour and enhance the eyes' natural beauty. I call these colour compatibles.

Eye colour	Skin undertone	Colour compatibles
Blue/Grey	Warm	Warm pinks; oranges such as coral; warm browns such as golden brown, bronze, mustard, rusts, terracotta; warm greens such as moss
Blue/Grey	Cool	Cool pinks; cool blues such as ice, powder and sky; cool brown shades such as beige, mushroom, cocoa, rose and dark brown; aqua and teal blues, lilacs and lavenders
Green/Hazel	Warm	Warm shades of gold; warm shades of brown such as bronze, golden brown, chocolate; warm rose brown, browny reds, rose brown, burgundy, clay plum violets; warm forest greens such as hue, sage, moss
Green/Hazel	Cool	Cool soft pinks, taupe, plum; soft grey; cool brown such as coffee
Brown	Warm	Warm peachy shades; golds and warm browns such as bronze, nutmeg, chocolate, coffee, rusts; deep warm greens such as forest, olive; deep brown reds such as burgundy; deep green blues such as teals, emeralds and navy blue
Brown	Cool	Cool grey beiges such as taupe, cool shades of brown such as cocoa; deep smokey shades of grey; Cool deep greens such as pine; shades of deeper mauves, purples, plums and blue violets

▼ Colour compatibles

depth of colour

When it comes to choosing the most suitable *depth of colour*, base your selection on the following:

- lighter colours are used to 'lighten' and bring out areas of the eye, the medium to darker values are used to recess, reshape and add definition to the eye

clarity of colour

When considering the *clarity* of a colour, base your selection on the following:

- lighter brighter colours can be used to 'spotlight' the eye. These colours are useful when used in small amounts to lift and brighten areas of the eye, under the arch of the brow bone or in the centre of the lid

colour schemes and seasonal groups
colour selection and placement

I have summarised and categorised colour selection and colour placement for each of the basic seasonal groups. Use these charts to help compose a basic eye colour scheme.

This key will help you to appreciate where best to place the respective colour when composing or creating a basic eye design.

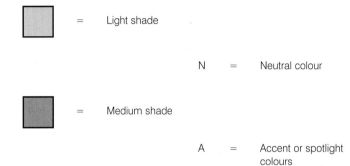

= Light shade

N = Neutral colour

= Medium shade

A = Accent or spotlight colours

= Dark shade

winter

Taupe	Cool Blue (A)	Navy (N)
Pale Grey	Cool Pink (A)	Charcoal (N)
Icy Pink	Silver (A)	Cocoa (N)
Icy Yellow	Mauve (A)	Grey/Blue (N)
White	Lavender (A)	Grey/Purple
	Aqua	Grey/Green
		Purple
		Deep Teal
		Pine Green
		Deep Periwinkle

summer

Pale Grey	Cool Pink (A)	Soft Grey
Pale Pink	Cool Blue (A)	Blue/Grey
Pale Yellow	Silver (A)	Cocoa
Soft White	Light Lavender (A)	Rose Brown
Taupe	Aqua (A)	Plum
	Light Blue Green	Grape
	Mauve (A)	Periwinkle Blue
		Lavender
		Soft Teals

autumn

Oyster	Apricot	Chocolate Brown
Pale Peach	Aqua (A)	Coffee Brown
Warm Pink	Light Warm	Golden Brown
Warm Beige	Green (A)	Bronze
	Golds (A)	Olive Green
	Softer Golds	Moss Green
	Peach (A)	Donkey Grey
	Nutmeg	Grey Blue
		Teal
		Warm Greens
		Emerald
		Coppers
		Mulberry

spring

Ivory	Peach	Clear Navy
Light Peach	Aqua (A)	Med. Golden Brown
Light Golden Yellow	Light Violets (A)	Med. Warm Grey
Warm Pink	Light Orange	Bronze
Lemon	Ivory Peach	Honey Brown
Light Aqua	Light Yellow Green	Moss Green
	Mauve	Teal Blue
	Golds (A)	Cocoa
		Violet
		Periwinkle Blue

choosing colours to intensify the eyes

So far I have discussed composing and creating an eye design using compatible colours but what if you want to intensify a client's natural eye colour? This is achieved by using complementary colours. *Complementary* or contrast colour harmony is formed by placing colours that are not related alongside one another. Two pairs of complementary colours are to be found opposite one another on the colour wheel and have the effect of exciting each other.

eye colour co-ordination

The trick is to choose a shade that contrasts eye colour to bring out the eyes. *Do not* use colours adjacent to the client's eye colour. **Never match the eye shadows to the client's eye colour**.

Adjacent colours will make the eye colour appear dull. However, adjacent colours of similar tonal qualities will give the eye a feeling of depth.

Complementary colours placed next to the eye will intensify the client's natural colour so it is important to select the right combination of colours.

> ✔ **tips**
>
> ■ note the warmth or coolness of the eye colour
>
> ■ locate it on the colour wheel
>
> ■ look directly across and choose a complementary shade to balance it
>
> ■ choose shades that are deep enough to balance its colour value, and not over-power them. If you use too dark a colour you will simply 'ground the eye'
>
> ■ choose shades to blend with the skin tones. Is their skin undertone warm, cool or more balanced? As a general guide if their skin has a pink undertone select pinker shades or less brown. If the client has a skin with a warm undertone, go for yellow-based colours

As you become more experienced at understanding the aesthetics of colour, you will notice that brown eyes can be both warm or cool, the same goes for blue and green eyes.

The key to colour selection is deciding what is the colour bias of the respective shadow, before application, and asking yourself, 'Is the shade going to make the eyes sparkle or make them dull?'

Cool eye shadow shades include taupe, charcoal blue, blue purple, plums, grey greens, grey blues, pine green and lilacs.

Warm eye shadow shades include variations on browns including red browns such as brick; yellow browns such as bronze, golden peaches, apricots and yellow greens.

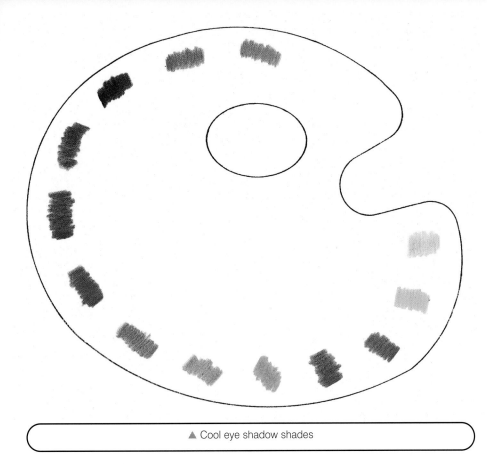

▲ Cool eye shadow shades

▲ Warm eye shadow shades

eye-defining
eyeliner colours

Classic shades include neutral tones such as variations of brown, taupe, charcoal and black. Choose the appropriate colour liner to make the eyes stand out.

✅ tips

- blue eyes will be best contrasted by using brown liner or deep navy liner

- brown eyes will be enhanced by using a navy liner or a compatible dark brown shade

- dark brown and black are best for people of deeper colouring

mascara colours

For classic looks and beauty shots neutral shades are best. Vary your selection according to the colour of their lashes.

✅ tips

- on fair lashes apply brown, reddish brown mascara

- darker lashes look great using brown-black or black mascara

- clear mascara can be used to give naturally dark lashes shine and definition

lip colour

Lipstick is an essential part of a make-up look, as it helps to pull the whole effect together, balancing eye, cheek and facial tones. The colour and texture of lipsticks can dramatically alter the shape of the mouth, strengthen facial expressions and generally add vitality to facial definitions.

☑ tips

- aim to balance the lip colour with the rest of the make-up. If you wish to go stronger on the eyes, such as a sultry smoky look, use a less intense lip colour. However, for stronger deeper or brighter lip colours, play down the eye make-up

- for total colour harmony go for co-ordinating lip colour to balance with the eye make-up and blusher. Work with the same family of colours to achieve harmony, i.e. colours of the same undertone

- do not attempt to match the lip colour to the outfit

- take into consideration teeth discolouration

- use lip pencils to shade the entire lip before applying lip colour. This helps to 'fix' the colour

- lip lining can look very unnatural

cheek colour

Nowadays blusher is used to subtly add colour to the cheeks to create an all-over natural gloss. The importance of blusher application should not be overlooked. The aim is to bring balance to the total make-up.

Nothing looks worse than cheeks overloaded with blusher colour or cheeks that look too pink. The aim should be to create a natural, soft and healthy glow using shades that integrate naturally with a person's skin tones. Work to the principle that the lighter the skin is, the lighter the blush shade should be. Similarly, the darker the skin, the deeper the blush.

blusher colours

- **Fair skin**   light beige shades for warmer skin tones, soft pink tones for lighter cooler skin tones
- **Medium skin**   brownish warm pinks
- **Dark skin**   for warmer skin tones use bronze, cocoa and brown reds
- **Redheads**   corals, peach, apricot shades
- **Olive or yellow skin**   balance yellow cast in skin with blue based brown shades such as copper, soft berry and plum

As with other aspects of make-up design, the ability to create different looks requires a consideration of the following:

- What *finish* will be the best for the client? Lipstick *texture* is vital to the end result. Do you want a matt, creamy or frosted finish?
- What *colour* will be most flattering to suit their skin tones?
- What is the professional way to *apply* lipstick to obtain the best results?
- How can you *shape* their lips?

colour families and skin tones

Most flattering lip colours will be found by considering mixes of the following colour families: reds – pinks – browns.

George Ong for Yardley, London

Skin colour	▼ Lip colour selection		
	Reds	Pinks	Browns
Fair skin	Light soft berry shades for cooler or bluish skintones	Light, and cool transparent and glossy pinks look best on people with bluish undertone. Beige pink for warm tones	Pink toned beiges for light and cool skin undertones. Honey, mocha browns, beige browns for light and warmer skin tones
Medium to dark skin	Brown reds for warm undertones, blue reds for cooler undertone. The darker the skin the darker the tone	Those with warmer undertones use deep warm pinks. For cooler undertones use soft mauve or pinks with blue or brown undertones	Soft mocha, coffee and caramel
Redheads	Brown reds, apricots, and sheer raisin shades	Peachy, apricot, salmon, coral pinks	Use peachy brown hue and raisin shades
Olive/Yellow tone	Raisin shades, brownish reds, like black berry and wine tones	Deep rose, berry, soft plums	Deeper shades of brown with red or with plum
Black skin	Deep and cool blue toned and mahogany reds	Soft sheer, nude pinks. Deep rose, berry, plum tones	Bright glossy beiges to deep chocolate shades. Deep berry with purple or bluish tones

✓ tips

- avoid applying colour too heavily

- blusher can be softened by dusting the cheeks with some translucent powder before blending into the cheek area

- match finish of blusher to finish of foundation, i.e. for a dewy foundation look use cream blusher, for a matt foundation look use powder blusher

■ think texture

Think products and finishes. Today's modern cosmetics technology has greatly increased the ability to achieve different looks by varying texture on the face. Consequently this has given rise to fast-changing make-up trends and design options.

Use texture to create different design expressions and moods. For instance a matt finish suggests sophistication; shimmery eyes can be seductive; glossy lips add glamour; dewy skin suggests youthfulness.

The secret is knowing how to work with different textures, where and how to apply them in order to achieve a look that does not look all glitter, greasy or powdery. The key is maintaining a balance by co-ordinating shine and matt.

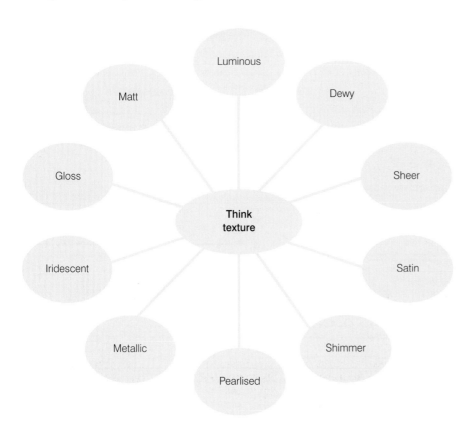

foundation

Foundation must not only to be chosen with care to suit skin type and tones, it also needs to be chosen to suit the finish you wish to achieve. Finish will also depend on the method of application. For example different foundations will provide different coverage.

- tinted moisturisers and mousse foundations give a very light coverage and are excellent for younger skins
- liquid foundations are available in different finishes and give good coverage when applied with a sponge
- compact foundations combine foundation and powder all in one. Applied with a dry sponge a soft natural matt finish is obtained; with a damp sponge coverage is heavier
- stick foundations can be applied with a sponge to give a sheer to medium coverage

✓ tips

- to obtain a glistening, dewy finish try mixing the foundation with a shimmering fluid before applying

- for a natural glistening look apply to the areas of the face that catch the light, such as cheekbones

eye shadow

There are two main types of eye colours or shadows – either wax or powder based.

waxes

These include creams sold in stick form, pots, wands, as well as pencils. Creams are more difficult to blend. Pencils are easy to handle and give pinpoint colour. Powder creams are suitable for the more mature skins. Waxier textures give more staying power as well as being water resistant. Creams and pencil types are best applied on an oil-free base.

powders

Powder eye shadows are sold either as singles or in compacts in the form of coloured blocks. They are easy to apply using the correct sized and shaped eye make-up brush. They are applied over a powder base.

✓ tips

- matt colours help to detract from a particular problem area

- light shiny or pearlised colours will emphasise a problem area

- dark matt colours can be used to help diminish a problem area

- light matt colours can be used to open up the eye and make eyes look larger

- matt colours are more suitable for photographic work

- matt neutral colours should be worn during the day, especially for work

- on older clients, it is advisable to use less eye shadow, and most certainly choose matt, less bright colours

- matt colours are better for clients who wear glasses

- to revive tired eyes, use a white pencil – apply a fine line at the base of the lashes

- to 'spotlight' the eye, blend a small amount of iridescent powder on the centre of the lid

- pearlised eyeliners can give the eye a flattering finish if a light shade of silver or soft blue is used. This should be applied to the inner corners of the upper and lower lashes and blended outwards

- matt shadows can be transformed by addition of Vaseline or sweeping a wash of pearlised ivory highlighter over the eyelid

lipstick

There has been much research and improvement in lipstick technology over the years. For example staying power has improved without losing the creamy consistency for the oils and waxes. This has been achieved by the addition of micro powder particles. Other advances include lipsticks made up of micro colour capsules, or new wax-free foundations that moisturise, colour and stay on the lips for some time.

what kind of finish?

Do you want a matt, glossy, creamy, frosted or a sheer finish?

- *Matt*   these are rich in colour pigments and are ideal for a strong, dry and opaque finish; gives long lasting and maximum coverage

- *Glossy*   gives a very sheer and shiny finish. When applied to narrow lips it helps give the impression of fullness

- *Creamy*   gives a moist finish, with added moisturising properties and sunscreens

- *Frosted*   gives a pearlised effect that sparkles in the light. Looks good in the summer and on tanned faces. Pearlised lipsticks can be brittle so take care when applying

- *Sheer*   gives a very light finish with little shine. Great for those summer days

■ combining texture and colour

Evaluate the client's best facial features and use these as focal points to draw attention to the face. This can be achieved by using colour and texture to create a balance between the upper and lower regions of the face, such as the eyes and lips.

For instance if a client or customer has a big nose define their eyes with a deeper matt eye shadow and use a more neutral lip colour. This will draw more attention to the top half of their face.

To draw attention to a great smile, healthy looking teeth and good shaped lips, do not emphasise their eyes but concentrate on the lips. To achieve this, use a wash of light neutral eye shadow and mascara balanced with more strongly coloured lips using a deeper matt or gloss lip colour.

A weak jawline, small chin or large jaw can be balanced by making the most of the client's eyes and brows. To achieve this, layer matt eye shadow over iridescent shadow to give a silky, vibrant blend. Balance with a light application of gloss on the lips.

6 contributing to creating a client's total look

From recommendations to reality and the art of creating. Creating a look on a client or model takes skills that include make-up and hair artistry, fashion styling and accessorising. This part of the book looks at how to master make-up and perfect hair finishing.

6.1 mastering make-up

Mastering make-up has been written for those hair session stylists who need to turn their hand to doing make-up on shoots. I hope it will also encourage many salon-based hairdressers to break new ground. It will I am sure be of great value to trainee make-up artists and students of beauty.

Mastering make-up offers techniques and tips to practise and to perfect.

■ make-up as a science and an art

Make-up requires a mastery of colour, texture, the principles of light and shade, design detail, techniques and skills, and prudent knowledge supported by an abundance of artistry.

There are many similarities between a make-up artist and a painter. Both need to be very familiar with the media and materials they are working with. A painter working with oils must first prepare the canvas. For a make-up artist the face is the canvas, the surface of which must be suitably prepared to receive make-up. The correct preparation of the skin is essential in helping to achieve a perfect finish. This means choosing carefully cosmetics to suit and care for different skin types.

Before painting of the face can begin, the make-up artist must ensure they have the right tools to enable make-up to be precisely and delicately applied to the surface of the skin.

■ what make-up can do

Choice of make-up is of prime importance, starting with colour. Knowing how to select and co-ordinate colour requires an understanding of colour theory and an appreciation for colour relationships. The object is to select and combine a range of colours that best harmonise or balance with a client or model's natural colouring. Used cleverly, make-up shades can balance colouring and camouflage skin discolouration and imperfections. Colour can give shape, definition and mood to the face.

The make-up artist needs to know about textures and capabilities of products to achieve different finishes on the face.

However, make-up can do more than add colour and texture. It can be used to emphasise good facial features and play down less attractive features. Everybody has some positive feature that can be made a focal point. Consequently, no matter what face shape a client has, carefully chosen colours, properly applied and blended, can bring out natural beauty and attractiveness.

For the wearer, make-up needs to be an expression of their personality and be sympathetic towards their lifestyle. Just as there are victims of fashion clothing trends, there are those who fall prey to seasonal make-up fashions. My advice is to educate your clients to be a timeless beauty. This calls for timeless make-up that can be varied to suit a specific situation, occasion, time of day, season or mood.

The key to mastering make-up is through learning about beauty and perfecting the basic skills and techniques that can be passed onto clients to help them develop their own beauty style and natural good look. Whilst many women shy away from make-up they do so because they have not been shown the benefits or because they do not realise that it is possible to wear make-up and look natural and healthy looking. Clients need to be given confidence to experiment with make-up. Similarly, a trainee or newly established make-up artist needs confidence in their ability to successfully undertake model assignments. My recommendation is learn the foundations and practise madly.

This section offers such foundations and a natural approach to make-up design that can be played up or down to suit client or model needs. It is written for those salon hairdressers and hair session stylists who wish to or need to add make-up to their repertoire of skills. In addition it will provide the essential foundations to those who want to pursue a career as a make-up artist.

■ tools of the trade

Having the right make-up tools is essential. These are available from specialist make-up shops and must include the following:

sponge

A wedge-shaped latex sponge to blend liquid, gel or cream foundation.

concealer brush

A narrow, firm brush with a tapered flat head.

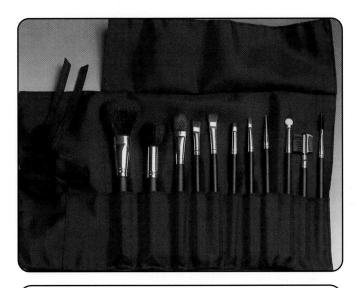

▲ Screenface brush kit

puff

A velour puff for application of powder.

eye shadow brushes

For applying base shade and highlighter choose a flat $^3/_4$-inch wide sable brush with rounded ends.

For shading choose a $^1/_3$-inch wide brush with flat, fairly rounded but not too long bristles for blending the colour into the eye socket.

For defining the eye, select a very thin 1/8-inch brush with small bristles that come to a point.

eyebrow brush

A small stiff slanted brush to enable the brows to be evenly shaded with shadow.

eyeliner brush

A finely pointed brush for controlled application of cake liner.

eyelash comb

A miniature comb used to separate eyelashes or comb through the lashes after mascara application to remove excess.

power brush

A large, soft brush used to dust away excess powder.

contour brush

This brush has dense hair about 3/4-inch long with a blunt end. It needs to be firm, used for shading under the cheekbones and around the hairline.

blusher brush

This is a medium, full-founded brush. It is used to add colour to the cheekbones, temples and jawline area.

lip brush

A small, firm brush with flat tapered bristles used to outline and fill in lips.

eyelash curler

A scissor-like item with rubber pads that can be used to clamp and bend lashes.

Q-tips

Q-tips or cotton buds are extremely useful to lift off excess colour or may be used as a blending tool.

■ preparing the canvas

For the perfect finish, it is important to carefully prepare the 'canvas' before starting to make up the eyes, lips or cheeks.

a step-by-step guide

1 *Basic skincare*   Make sure the skin is clean by following a skincare routine to suit the skin type. Use a hair band or clips to secure the hair out of the way. For colour correction see cover-ups.

For *dry* or *normal* skin, use a light moisturiser base then blot before applying the foundation.

For *oily* skin types, foundation will stay on longer if you first remove excess oil with an astringent lotion. If moisturiser is required use only a small amount. Too much can cause make-up to slide off the skin's surface.

2 *Foundation application*   Use a foundation to suit the client's skin type. Shake the foundation bottle well before applying. Place a small amount in the palm of your hand before transferring to the face. If skin is clear, use a tinted moisturiser or confine its use to only those areas that need balancing.

3 *Blending*   Either use your third finger or a damp cosmetic sponge, pat and blend carefully using light, outward and downward sweeping strokes. (A latex sponge should be squeezed between tissue to remove excess water.) For a sheerer finish try using a natural sea sponge. The trick is to coat the skin, without rubbing. Make sure the founda-

tion is worked into all awkward parts of the face, including ears if they show. Don't forget to apply foundation to eyelids and lightly around the lips. This will assist in the colour application later. Make sure you apply foundation into the eyebrows so as to avoid any demarcation edges.

Gently blend the foundation into the hairline (not too far) and down just under the jawline until it fades away on the upper neck. There should be no noticeable line between where the foundation ends.

4 *Cover-up concealer*   Use concealer, a shade lighter than the skin tone, to cover up any blemishes, marks, or dark circles under the eyes. Eye shadow bases are also useful when applied to the upper eye area to cover up veins or very dark lids, as well as provide a foundation for the eye shadow.

Dot the concealer over the respective area using the applicator or try using a fine concealer brush. This is especially useful when applying concealer around the

eyes and nose. To cover up spots, etc. press or pat the concealer into the skin with the fingertip. This gives a smoother effect. It may be necessary to build up a number of layers of concealer to cover a troublesome spot. Allow each layer to dry before applying more. Feather out the concealer and blend into the foundation. If necessary re-apply foundation.

5 *Setting the foundation to give a matt finish*   Allow the foundation to dry before using powder. Using a soft velour powder puff apply a light dusting of loose translucent powder. Don't rub the powder onto the skin. Press it gently using soft dabbing motions. It isn't always necessary to powder the entire face. Although, it is important to powder

down the shiny areas, such as forehead, nose and chin, as well as lightly over the eyelids.

If the client's skin is prone to wrinkles or lines avoid excessive powder as it 'settles' in fine lines. Leave the eyelids to last, making sure they are lightly powdered to facilitate eye shadow application.

Finally, remove excess translucent powder using a flat, empty powder brush by gently dusting outwards and downwards. On older skin types minimal powder should be used to avoid emphasising wrinkles.

✔ tips

- Choose a concealer according to the skin type. Dry skin needs one with moisturising properties, whilst oily skins need a powder-based concealer to absorb excess oil and stay in place.

- On oily skins, concealer can slide off! For better adhesion apply it after powder.

- The perfect place for doing make-up is to position the client in front of a window with lots of natural daylight.

- For a rejuvenating look, try a foundation with light reflective properties, which aim to soften wrinkles.

- For a light foundation look and a healthy glow, use a tinted moisturiser or try mixing the foundation colour with a little moisturiser in the palm of your hand.

- For a more luminous, glowing and youthful look, mix shimmer highlight liquid with foundation in the palm of your hand.

- For young blemish-free complexions use a light dusting of transparent powder over those parts of the face that are prone to shine. Similarly, for those clients who do not like foundation or do not need to use it all over their face, restrict it to those parts of the face that need evening out. Alternatively, suggest they use a cream blusher to give their skin a soft glow.

- Use a lilac, lavender or mauve tinted moisturiser as a corrective cream for sallow skins.

- Ethnic skin tones do not always need the use of a foundation although shine can be a problem on black skin tones and needs to be dealt with by powdering. If a foundation is used, do not go darker.

- Use a green corrective cream to neutralise redness.

- Beware of achieving a 'greyed' look because of the colour mixing effect that occurs on the skin surface when the complementary colours are mixed and neutralise one another.

- Always use less foundation than you think you need. It is easier to add more than remove it.

- If the foundation is too shiny, blot the face with tissue.

- For bare shoulder and chest beauty shots, do not forget to powder the upper body.

- To rejuvenate a foundation, moisten with a fine mist of Evian water spray.

■ cover-ups and concealing

Concealers are sold as liquids, creams and sticks. Choose the colour that is nearest to the client's natural skin colouring, in the same way that you would choose a foundation. However, you may need a number of colours to mix and match. Liquids are better for areas where the skin creases or wrinkles. Creams or sticks are more suitable for covering spots.

high colour and broken veins

Use a green tinted moisturiser under the foundation to cover up ruddy cheeks. Blend with a sponge. Allow it to dry before applying foundation.

freckles

To counteract freckles use a tinted gel foundation that is slightly darker than the overall skin tone.

sunburn

Cool a sunburn with cold water compresses before applying a moisturiser.

dark circles under eyes

To lighten these dark circles, use a concealer that is one shade lighter than skin tone. Dot the concealer just beneath the area, blend up and out onto the circle using a concealer make-up brush. Keep the application as light as possible to avoid making the problem more noticeable. Don't take the concealer right up to bottom lashes. If the dark area is still obvious, apply a light cream foundation to the area. Follow up with your chosen concealer.

acne

To disguise an acne skin use a matt foundation.

crow's feet

It is important to keep under-eye areas soft and moist at all times. This is achieved by applying an appropriate anti-wrinkle product containing rich moisturising oils over the foundation in the crow's feet region.

under-eye bags

Keep them as light as possible. Avoid using concealers as they draw attention to puffy skin.

spots and blemishes

Use a concealer on top of foundation, using a clean eyeliner brush, blend. Cover with foundation before powder.

expression lines

These are often found around the mouth, forehead and on top of the nose. Use a fine make-up brush to paint a liquid concealer, one shade lighter than the skin tone, right into the 'cavity' of the line to bring it forward. Blend with a sponge. Avoid using powder as it will collect in the lines.

birth marks

Cover up small birth marks with a heavy opaque pan-stick. Blend with a sponge. For larger and darker marks, port-wine marks, you will need to use a specialist product.

enlarged pores

First use an alcohol based gel to remove unwanted oil, then an oil free foundation, followed by translucent powder.

☑ tips

- Never apply concealer on the eyelid as it will cause eyeshadows to crease.

- Concealers can be applied with a fine brush or with the finger.

◼ face powders and powdering

Face powder comes in loose and cake form. It is available in a variety of shades and in different weights. Light and medium weights are more suitable for dry and normal skins, heavy weight powder for oily skins. It is used to hold concealer and foundation in place.

Face powders can help improve the overall appearance of the skin by concealing skin blemishes, toning down excessive colouring to the skin or even correcting a wrong choice of foundation.

☑ tips

- Translucent, loose powders are said to give a colourless matt effect, however, take care that it does not make the skin look pale and pasty.

- Compressed powder will give a dense cover to all skin types, however, if applied too often during the day, it will look 'cakey'.

- All-in-one compact powder and cream foundations will allow you to prepare the 'canvas' in one step. They are essentially firm fluids which can be used on dry skin to give a shine-free, sheer powdered finish. Applied with a damp sponge a more smooth and satin finish may be achieved.

- Creamy powders go on dry and give excellent coverage and staying power. Apply with a damp latex sponge for a sheer matt finish.

- Modern loose face powders are micro fine, light reflecting and non-cakey. Available in various tints, they can be used to subtly change base tone and soften the skin's surface appearance. For example, blue powder gives a cool ethereal look, green powder can be used to tone down a high colour, dark powders can be used to bronze the skin.

bronzing powders

Bronzing powders are multipurpose products which can be mixed or used on their own for all skin tones. Applied to the apples of the cheekbones and blended upwards towards the temples, they are excellent for giving super-sheer coverage and a healthy sun-kissed glow. They can be used in place of a blusher.

It is important to choose a face powder that blends with natural skin tones or match the powder to the same shade or slightly lighter than the foundation. However, a darker powder can be used if a deeper colour is required.

powdering

Loose powder is best applied using a large, soft powder brush, taking care not to overload the brush – remove excess using light downward strokes. This helps to prevent powder getting caught in the fine facial hair on the sides of the face and jawline. For a heavier application, a soft velour puff can be used.

Pressed or caked powder is easier to transport and use on location and is best applied with a brush.

☑ tips

- Pale yellow powders can be used to warm up too pink a foundation as well as equalising pink skin tones.

- Before adding powder, remove any oily shine on the surface of the skin by blotting with tissue.

- Do not apply a loaded powder brush directly onto the face; first tap off excess powder.

◼ eye design

Eye design plays a very important part in helping clients develop their facial image. With your help and the right eye make-up you can alter their shape, size, bring colour to the face, create greater impact and vitality. In addition, you can design the eye to draw attention away from other parts of the body that need to be minimised.

assessing eye shape

Even though your client may not be used to wearing eye make-up, a natural look that simply enhances their beauty can still be achieved. However, before beginning to apply colour, it is important to appreciate their eye shape, lid size and brow to eye proportions.

- Are their eyes close set or spaced wide apart?
- Are they low browed or high browed?
- Are their eyes deep set or prominent?
- Are their eyes small?
- Do they have a drooping eyelid?
- Do they have a narrow eyelid?

achieving balance

Once these assessments have been made, by working with the right colours and clever application, you will be able to create amazing tricks or optical illusions shaping and lifting the eyes, creating balance and proportion.

- A light colour will highlight the eyes. It will bring them forward and make them look larger.
- A dark colour will make the eye recede.
- A medium colour softens and blends.
- A medium to dark colour contours and defines the eye.

Any colour can be chosen to represent these tones as long as:

- the texture of the product is flattering to the eyes, age and skin type
- the colours are within the client's colour range
- the choice of colour is appropriate for whichever situation or occasion the client may encounter

basic eye design for the proportioned eye

Anyone can have beautiful eyes. All it takes is a little practice, an eye for the most flattering colours, and knowing where to place them.

The sketch below will help you become familiar with the areas of the eye to work on.

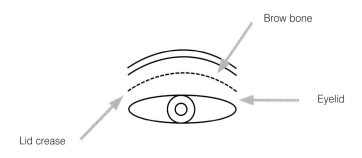

The eyelid extends from the eyelash base to the region where the eye socket indents. The lid crease is the indentation or socket line. The brow bone is the bony ridge above the lid crease that extends from the inner to outer corner of the eye.

eye make-up application
a step-by-step guide

Applying eye colours is rather similar to painting. The key to obtaining a good result is in the 'layering' and 'blending' of colours. 'Layering' describes the technique, how by starting with lighter shades you can build up depth and colour. Clever 'blending' is essential to ensure that no hard lines of colour are formed. Grading the colour is also important, starting from light at the inner corner of the lid to heavy at the middle and outer part.

1 Before adding colour ensure the eyelids have been correctly prepared with foundation and powder.

Select those colours you wish to work with. For instance three shades light, medium and dark from the same colour family. Placement will depend on the eye shape.

2 Start by sweeping medium base colour over the eyelid. This should be similar to the client's skin tone. For best results use an eye brush, work colour from the middle of the lid outwards in both directions. Use circular motions working with the flat surface of the brush (not point) to avoid getting lines. Add colour, a little amount at a time. Use what is left on the brush to blend upwards towards the middle of the eye.

3 Apply the darker colour, shading the socket line from the inner corner to the outer edge of the eye. Do not extend the colour onto the temples or brow bone area. Blend well so that the colour almost disappears.

4 To further define the eye, the darker tone can be shaded on the outer, one-third of the eye, in a triangular wedge shape. Blend well, sweeping the colour towards the centre of the eye, and softly fade it outwards. No solid lines should be seen. Reflect slightly under the eye along the bottom lashes using a Q-tip.

5 Highlight or lighten the browbone area, just under the eyebrow using the lighter colour to give the illusion of space.

6 Use eyelash curlers to 'open up' the eye area and bend lashes.

7 Apply eyeliner to give more emphasis to the lashes and give contrast between the eye and the eye shadow (refer to eyeliners). Apply liner along upper lashes.

8 Brush eyebrows into shape and if necessary apply a suitable eye shadow to shape and fill in. Alternatively, a pencil can be used to give more definition.

9 Add depth to eyes by applying several coats of mascara to upper lashes. Lightly point out bottom lashes (see mascara application).

10 Brush away loose powder from under eye area.

✅ tips

- Always tap your brush before applying eye colours to remove excess powder.

- To avoid excess eye shadow dropping onto and marking the foundation, either place a tissue under the eye to catch the spills or apply some loose translucent powder which can be brushed off afterwards. Alternatively excess powder can be blown off.

- Do not extend the blending of eye shadow past the end of the brow.

- Be gentle when putting eye make-up on. The skin around the eyes is very delicate and easily dragged. Use good quality brushes.

- For the older person, minimum eye make-up, carefully applied, is the key to younger looks.

- For day time, use a soft wash of colour, for evening try stronger shades.

■ eyebrow design

Eyebrow design also plays an important part in the facial image. Eyebrows can alter the face shape, change facial expressions and give added definition. Fashion trends come and go, bringing with it changes in eyebrow shape and grooming. However, regardless of fashion, eyebrows should be shaped to follow the natural line. Match depth of brow to the client's natural colour as well as eye make-up. Darker brows look good if the person is naturally dark or wearing minimum eye make-up.

shaping eyebrows

Using a brow brush or a clean toothbrush, sweep brows upwards and outwards following their natural movement and shape.

Before you start to shape the brow use the classic pencil check. To find where the eyebrow should begin, hold the pencil vertically against the side of the nostril, with the top end of the pencil crossing the brow. Remove any hairs growing to the

right or the left of the pencil, depending on which side of the nostril you are working from.

To determine the highest point of the brow, allow the pencil, still touching the side of the nostril, to cross the pupil. The point where the pencil touches the brow is the arch.

The brow should end at the point where the pencil, when it is pivoted out further, lines up with the outer corner of the eye.

eyebrow grooming

The correct eyebrow shape can enhance and improve the symmetry of the face, drawing more attention to the eyes. The secret is to get the arch of the brow right.

- Always follow the natural shape of the eyebrow.
- Using good quality tweezers pluck one hair at a time, following the direction of growth.
- Always shape from under the brow, never from the top.
- Start at the middle of the brow and work towards the ear, then work in the opposite direction from the middle towards the nose. Make sure the arch is highest at the centre of the eye.
- The width of the brow should be almost the same width across.
- Straggly brow hairs can be removed or snipped shorter.

eyebrow defining

If the brows are sparse in places, fill in with either a soft brown or grey eyebrow pencil, or for a softer effect use an eye shadow powder. Choose the colour as close as possible to the natural brow colour.

1 To define the brow, brush the hair in the opposite direction to natural hair growth. This removes foundation and powder particles. Rebrush into shape.

2 Fill in using short feathery strokes in the direction of hair growth. Start at the inner corner of the brow and gradually taper outwards. Alternatively use a complementary neutral eye shadow to define the brow.

3 Brush or rub brows to soften colour.

✅ tip

- Brows can be styled and kept in place by combing through a small amount of Vaseline to fix their shape. This also gives the brow a shine finish.

brow contouring to suit different face shapes

- To offset a *square* face and to give it a more oval shape, place the arch of the brow towards the end of the eyebrow, above the corner of the eye and extend the browline outward towards the middle of the ear.

- To contour a *triangular* face and increase the width across the forehead and the eyebrow slightly at the ends only, start the line above the inside corner of the eyes and continue to the ends of the cheekbones.

- To shorten a *long* face, shape the brow so that it is straightish with little arch, towards the tip of the ear. Do not extend the line further than the ends of the eyes.

- To lengthen a *round* face, make the arch higher and more pronounced. Start the line directly above the inside corner of the eye and extend to the tip of the ear.

- The browline on an *oval* face should curve down towards the bottom of the ear.

■ eyelash design

With the aid of modern cosmetics, such as mascara, the long thick eyelash has become the specially sought after part of facial design. Not only do eyelashes provide a frame to the eye, but on a more practical level they help protect the eye and prevent bacteria from getting in and causing infection. Make-up should be used to enhance the lashes, not to radically change their colour.

In a year it is estimated that we lose 1,600 lashes; every time one falls out it is replaced.

eyeliner

The use of eyeliner is optional and can be worn on its own or with eyeshadow. Its popularity depends very much on the current make-up trends and the desire to have a 'heavier looking' eye that emphasises the lashes and defines the eye. Depending on the area of application and colour chosen it can appear to open, lengthen or emphasise the eye.

Eyeliner is sold as a liquid, as a cake or in a pencil. The cake form needs to be moistened with water before applying. Liquid and cake types are applied close to the lash roots, using a fine brush to 'draw/paint' in a fine line. Pencils should not drag on the skin.

For a softly defined eye, shadow can be smudged along the bottom lashes with a foam applicator or cotton bud.

eyeliner application to contour the eye

1 Define the outer rim of the eye closest to the top lashes starting from the inner edge and working outwards.

2 Soften the pencil or cake line with a sponge tip applicator or cotton bud.

3 Emphasise outer corner by shading with medium to deep eyeshadow.

✓ tips

- If the client is looking tired avoid putting eyeliner underneath the eye.

- Do not apply liner to the inside rim of the eye.

- Apply eyeliner after eye shadow and before mascara.

- Eyeliner definition can be varied by smudging the pencil line or softening by dusting with a light application of eye shadow.

mascara

Mascara comes in two forms.

Wand mascaras are the most convenient to use and carry around. The liquid mascara is contained in narrow-necked barrel-shaped containers, housing either a brush-tipped applicator or a brushless applicator screwed in the neck. The brush-tipped applicator can be straight, curved or tapered. If the client or model has sparse lashes use a fine applicator, or a large applicator for longer denser lashes, to achieve better coverage.

Cake mascaras come in a small container and are used rather like a water colour paint. They are applied using a dampened fine make-up brush. The mascara is worked into a suitable consistency before applying. As they are water-based they run very easily.

types of mascara

Waterproof mascaras are good for people that play sport or swim. As they cannot be removed with water they are also tearproof. To remove a waterproof mascara you need to use a suitable eye make-up remover.

Fibre mascaras are good if you want to make lashes look thicker. As they contain fibre filaments they should be avoided by people who wear contact lenses as the filaments could irritate the eye.

Hypo-allergenic mascaras are specially formulated for wearers with sensitive eyes.

mascara application

1 To 'open the eye' use an eyelash curler to bend the lashes upwards and downwards. This will make them look longer.

Load the wand in the applicator by twisting it around gently. Remove excess mascara before applying by rolling the brush on a tissue, this helps to overcome clumping. Avoid over pumping the wand in the barrel as it causes the contents to dry more quickly, as more air is admitted into the barrel each time.

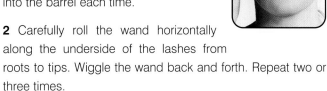

2 Carefully roll the wand horizontally along the underside of the lashes from roots to tips. Wiggle the wand back and forth. Repeat two or three times.

Allow each application to dry before reapplying a further coat.

Use the point of the wand held vertically to gently brush the lower lashes one at a time if required.

3 Use an eyelash comb to evenly separate out each lash after a final application. Watch out for mascara smudges on the skin, which should be removed with a cotton bud, dipped in eye make-up remover, before it dries.

✔ tips

- Lightly powder under the eye with loose translucent powder. Leave it on the surface of the skin until after you have finished and then brush off.

- Get older clients to switch from black mascara to a lighter shade. It is less hard and ageing.

- To widen the eyes only coat the top of lashes.

◼ colour contouring the eye

The following techniques can be used to visually reshape and change eye proportions.

close-set eyes

To widen their appearance, apply a lighter colour to the inner corners from the tear duct upwards towards the brow bone, graduating out to a darker shade in the outer cor-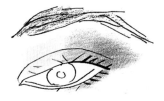

ners. Feather out the primary or secondary medium colour outwards slightly behind the outer edge of eye both above and below. Line the outer corners of the eyes with a dark eye pencil or eyeliner. Apply mascara more heavily on the outer top and bottom eyelashes.

wide-apart eyes

Use a dark shade on the inner corner of the eyes in the first third of the socket line and blend to a lighter shade in the outer corner. Apply 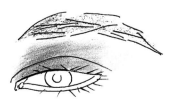 eyeliner tapering from the inner corners to the centre of the eye.

low-browed

Keep the area between the lash base and the bottom of the eyebrow lighter than the eyelids. Line the inner rim of the base lid with eyeliner to  draw attention away from the narrow upper lid. Do not curl eye lashes.

high-browed

Use deeper shades of eye-shadows near to the socket line, blending into a thin lighter highlighter area just below the eyebrow. Curl lashes upwards.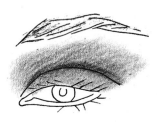

prominent eyes

Prominent eyes can be set back by using a dark shade in the socket area and along the crease. If the client has heavy lids, keep the lid colour to mid tone. The protruding browbone 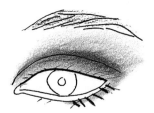 can be left bare, lightly covered with the lid shadow or a matt light to medium colour. This colour can be reflected under the lower lashes. Apply eyeliner close to lash base on the top lid to minimise it. Use more mascara on the bottom lashes. Avoid curling the top lashes.

deep-set eyes

Deep-set eyes can be brought forward by keeping the make-up to light to medium tones in and above the socket area. Blend the colour in an oval around the 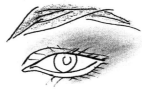 upper and lower lids and reflect slightly under the eye. Deep-set eyes often have small lids which can be made to look bigger by keeping the colour light. Apply a smoky colour above the lid crease, blend up and out. Curl lashes and lightly apply mascara. If liner is used keep it fine otherwise it can make the eye look more deep-set. You can also make the eyes appear larger by applying blue eyeliner to the rim of the lower lid.

small eyes

To make small eyes appear larger give the eyes maximum shape by ensuring that the lower eyelashes are not too bushy. Blend a pale lid colour from the  inner corners up to the crease. Define the outer corners with darker shade, sweeping the colour up into the crease line. Blend lid colour or a matt highlighter from the pupil diagonally outwards to the edge of the eyebrow. Apply a spot of white highlighter in the outer corner to give a more open-eye look. Avoid using dark eyeliner which will 'close up' the eye. The outer lashes can be emphasised with mascara.

round eyes

To make round eyes more oval and wider apply a light pale shadow over the entire lid, starting above the inner iris, blending diagonally up and onto the browbone. Apply a  mid-tone shadow along and close to the lash base, blending diagonally upwards and outwards. In the corner of the outer eye apply a darker shadow to elongate the eye. Blend upwards. Reflect the darker shadow under the outer two-thirds of the bottom lashes. Coat the lashes on the outer half of the eye with mascara.

drooping eyelids

To lift a drooping outer eyelid shape the eyebrows so that they are lightly arched and do not dip down too much at the outer corners. Apply a soft light colour in the inner corner of the eye,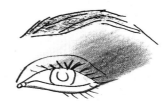

blend upwards onto the brow. Apply a matt mid tone and darker tone shadow over the eye lid. Blend all the colours upwards and outwards into the brow to lift the eye. The darker colour is used on the outer corner region of the eye. Line the lower lashes with dark eye shadow or kohl ensuring that the line is directed upwards at the corner. Apply mascara to the centre lashes, so that it brings more attention to the centre of the eye.

narrow eyelids

To widen a narrow eyelid apply a light shadow in the centre of the lid, blending upwards towards the brow. Colour the remaining lid area, the inner  and outer corners with a bright medium tone eye shadow. Blend a slightly darker shadow upwards on the outer third of the lower lid, sweeping it into the brow. Do not put any darker colour under the bottom lashes. A light line of eyeliner can be applied on the lash base in the centre of the eye.

■ cheek design

blusher

The aim of blusher is to add subtle glow and gentle shape to the face as well as to soften the contrast between a highlighter and shader (see face sculpturing).

Blusher texture varies. Blushers come as gels, creams, liquids and powders. However, the powder form is the easiest to apply and blend. Powder blusher is applied after powdering. All the other types are applied before powdering. Cream blushers are better for older skin types and do not leave a cakey finish. Gel blushes are good on young skin giving a natural-looking dewy finish.

blusher application

The aim is to use blusher so that it looks natural. This is achieved by building up colour very gently using a small amount at a time.

1 Always remove excess product by tapping the brush or blowing off excess powder before applying to the face. Always blend the colours well to avoid demarcation lines.

2 Apply blush to the apple of cheeks. The apple is the rounded, lifted part of the face which is easily located by asking your client to smile.

3 Blend colour up and back towards the hairline as well as in a circular upward motion.

✓ tips

- If blusher looks too intense, dust over with some face powder.

- For a more translucent effect, mix tinted moisturiser with creme blush and then apply to the apple of the cheeks with your fingertips.

- Do not apply blusher closer to the nose than the outer rim of the eye's iris or below bone of nostrils.

- Cream blusher is best applied by transferring it first to the palm of your hand and then onto the cheeks with your fingertips.

- Gel blusher should be applied over moisturiser and not foundation. Apply to the cheeks with your fingertips.

■ face sculpturing

Have you ever noticed a sculptor at work? Their eye for detail combined with their practical skills, enables them to create a face by meticulously chipping away or modelling the material until the right shape evolves.

You too can resort to clever face shaping to emphasise the good points or minimise the not so good points.

Before you begin to shape the face, it is first important to recognise facial shape and proportions (see facial shapes). To do this make sure the client/model is not wearing any make-up. Pull back the hair and observe the face shape.

The perfect face shape is considered to be *oval*, which is used as an imaginary template. Drawn an imaginary oval of the face. Any area of the face that falls outside the oval should be darkened. Areas inside the oval should be highlighted.

The secret is knowing how and where to use light and shade to minimise the more prominent features and empha-sise the better facial features. The trick is to use *dark to minimise and light to emphasise*.

To achieve lightness on the face use a highlighter. To shade the face, shaders and blushers are used.

Highlighters should be matt. Ivories and creams are nor-mally considered the most suitable colours. It is best to use a matt shader powder, a couple of shades darker than natural skin tones. It is also possible to use a foundation a couple of shades darker than the normal skin tone. This is then applied before the main foundation. Shaders are used to produce 'shadows' in those regions of the face where there is a need to minimise facial features and make them less prominent. The sequence of application is highlighter → shader → blusher.

Unless you are confident about achieving a flattering result, that is a face without heavy demarcation lines, you should practise and perfect this technique very carefully before using on clients.

For a more simplified approach use only blusher.

contouring different face shapes
a step-by-step guide

oval face
The aim is to enhance bone structure and maintain oval shape.

1 Apply highlighter on the cheekbones.

2 Apply blusher immediately underneath the highlighter.

3 Apply a small amount of shader underneath blusher. Blend colours well.

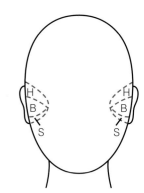

H = Highlighter
B = Blusher
S = Shader

Eyebrows These should frame the eyes and follow the natural arch.

Lips Accentuate the natural bow-line of the upper lip. Outline the lower lip so that it appears slightly fuller than the upper.

round face
The aim is to make the face appear slimmer, less round and more angular by shading at the sides of the face.

1 Using a contour brush highlight diagonally the top of the cheekbone. Apply high-lighter to the tip of the chin.

2 Shade under the cheek-bone in a triangular shape,

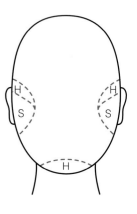

tapering from the hairline above the ear towards the centre of the cheek as well as at the sides of the temples.

3 Lightly apply blusher over the cheeks below the highlighter.

Eyebrows Follow the natural contour of the eyebrow. Make the arch more prominent. Start the line directly above the inside corner of the eye and extend to the end of the cheek-bones.

Lips Outline lips and fill in colour, avoiding excessive fullness.

heart-shaped face

The aim is to give reduced width across the forehead and increase the width across the jawline by applying blusher to the apples of the cheeks. Shading is used at the sides of the forehead.

1 Highlight diagonally the top of the cheekbones.

2 Shade over the temples.

3 Apply blusher just below the highlighter. Blend well.

Eyebrows The eyebrows should not be spaced too widely apart. Shape the brow to give a high arch.

Lips Follow the natural lip line.

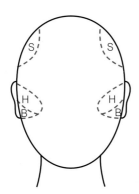

square face

The aim is to soften the angles and lengthen the face by applying blusher high on the cheekbones to define their shape.

1 Apply shader to the outer corners of the jaw around the outermost corners of the hairline and temples.

2 Apply blusher over the cheekbones in an upward diagonal direction.

Eyebrows A rounded arch will create softness and detract from the squareness of the jawline.

Lips Apply lip colour to create fullness and width. Use lip line to form slight triangular outline to lower lip, without going over the skin.

long face

The aim is to make the face fuller at the sides by applying blusher to the apples of the cheeks.

1 Emphasise temples and cheekbones by using highlighter to give the illusion of width.

2 Shade the bottom of chin and top of the forehead to make the face seem shorter.

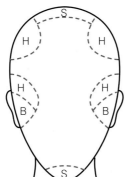
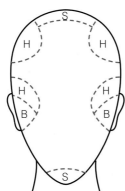

3 Horizontally apply blusher on the cheekbone below the highlighter.

Eyebrows Shape the brows so that they are straight with little arch. Do not extend the line further than the ends of the eye.

Lips Apply lip colour to give the illusion of fullness and width to the lips.

diamond face

The aim is to make the forehead appear wider at the temples and the cheek width narrower.

1 Apply highlighter at the temples.

2 Minimise the sides of the face with shades.

Eyebrows Slightly straighter brows will add width to the face across the temples. Play up the eyes.

Lips Create fuller lips.

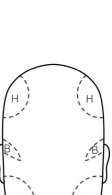

triangular face

The aim is to make the forehead seem wider and the sides of the jaw narrower.

1 Apply highlighter to the outer corners of the hairline and temples.

2 Shade the outer corners of the jaw.

3 Apply blusher to cheekbones.

Eyebrows Shape the brows so they are straight with little arch. Play up the eyes.

Lips Follow the natural lip line.

■ lip design
a step-by-step guide

1 *Moisturising* Ensure the lips are soft and supple by smoothing over with a suitable lip conditioning cream or balm.

2 *Priming* I will assume you have already prepared the canvas by applying liquid foundation and powder. If you have not, you will need to prime the lips in order to provide a matt surface for the colour to adhere. This is especially important if you want a longer lasting stronger look. If the foundation is too oily you may have a problem getting the colour to adhere to the lip surface.

3a *Outlining with a lip pencil* Use a narrow lip pencil with a sharp point to make a well-defined outline of the mouth. This will prevent the lipstick 'bleeding' into those faint lines around the mouth (more common in older skin).

For photographic make-up particularly on younger skin omit the lining. Instead use a correct colour lip pencil to fill in the lip area prior to applying lipstick. Fill in using light feathery strokes. For a softer lip line blend the pencil first before applying lip colour.

3b *Outlining with a lip brush* Start in the centre of the top lip and draw a line out to one corner. Keep the motion smooth and continuous.

Still on the top lip draw a line out to the other corner. Outline the bottom lip by starting in either corner.

4 *Filling in* Fill in the outline using a flat-edged lip brush, by applying the chosen lip colour right up to the lip line. Get the client or model to open their mouth so that you can apply colour into the corners of their lips.

5 *Blotting and powdering* Blot with a tissue and reapply lip colour or leave unblotted and lightly dust with loose powder. If you wish to retain a glossy finish leave off the powder.

✔ tips

colour

- Thin lips look fuller with paler shades and a well-blended lip line.

- To make a mouth look larger use light bright lip colours.

- To make a mouth appear smaller, use dark or more muted lip colours.

✔ tips

texture

- frosted lipstick looks better on young lips. They can be ageing on the older woman as it highlights lip lines.

- Sheer lipsticks or stains are useful to introduce colour to clients who are apprehensive of using a too strong colour.

to create fuller lips

If the client/model has thin lips, you can create a false lip line directly above the natural lip line using a lip pencil that is the same shade as the person's lip colour or a shade darker than the lip colour. However, this requires great skill and may simply draw more atten-

tion. Instead use matt and pearlised lip colours to give apparent fullness to central areas. Alternatively use a neutral lip colour and make the eyes stronger.

to narrow full lips

Use a lip pencil the same shade as the client's lip colour or a shade darker than the lip colour to outline just inside the natural

lip line. Fill in with a soft, matt lip colour. Blend well to avoid hard lines.

to solve drooping lips

Outline a drooping lower lip slightly upwards in the corners and use a colour slightly darker on the lower lip. Apply gloss to the centre of the upper lip.

This technique will help to draw attention to the upper lip.

to balance uneven lips

Work at balancing an even shape to the lips by building out with lip pencil and filling in with matt and pearlised lip colour.

to shorten lips

Do not take the pencil or lip colour into the corners of the lips.

✓ tips

- Nothing looks worse than applying lip colour on dry, cracked or lips in which the skin is peeling. Lip care is essential. Recommend to the client that they use petroleum jelly on the lips. Leave it on for about five minutes and then gently massage the lips with a hot face cloth the remove the flaky skin.

- Do not forget to use foundation on the lips as a primer.

- Use lip liner pencils in neutral shades to complement lip colour.

- For a matt look use lip liner pencil to fill in colour. Apply on well-moisturised lips. Next lipstick can be applied over the lip surface. When the lipstick wears off, the liner will remain.

- To increase the staying power of lip colour, dust with loose translucent powder after the first coat. Blot if necessary with a tissue and repeat lipstick application.

- For sexy, pouty lips use a highly moisturised lip colour or apply lip gloss over a matt surface.

- For a nearly nude, glossy look use a lip pencil to give all over colour and then add a top coat of gloss.

- For a natural lip colour use a tinted lip gloss.

6.2 finishing hair

This section offers an overview on the drying, styling and dressing of hair. Much of the traditional techniques are to be found in more standard textbooks. The emphasis is on fashion styling, product selection and usage. It concludes with a portfolio of finished looks.

■ hair fashion trends

the 1960s–70s

For many women the cut and blow-dry of the sixties was like manna from heaven. It released them from dreaded rollers, the back combing, the lacquer and having to go perhaps weekly to the hairdressers to have their hair set into shape.

The marketing strategy was developed around a technically superior cut which meant trouble-free hair for about four to six weeks, before they needed to return. During this time, women were able to wash and wear their hair in chic, easy-to-care-for styles that fell into place with a minimum amount of fuss, perhaps only needing to use a blow dryer to gently ease the cut into final shape.

The cut was considered a work of art, precisely engineered by a new breed of master craftsmen, who delivered the service with surgical precision and artistic feeling, sculpturing and working hair into the most flattering and desirable form. For the first-time client it was often a period of apprehension. It meant putting their trust in a new breed of hairdresser, an architect of hair design who sometimes operated with a dictatorial air of confidence. Nevertheless, eventually the cut and blow-dry became an accepted way of life, and a monthly ritual for million of women who preferred to seek out the newly emerging specialist salons located in the West End of London. This change was not without its causalities; that is the traditional local salons slow to adjust to new market trends. These specialist salons rose in status through the 1960s and early 1970s. They became purveyors of high calibre design and 'social clubs' – the places to be seen. Clients flocked through the doors, queued, and waited hours to be transformed in conveyor-belt fashion to get the 'cut of the moment'.

The cut and blow-dry remained in its purity through the late 1960s and early 1970s. More salons, new branches, new ventures opened up both at home and abroad to meet customer demand. To satisfy this demand, more personnel were recruited, trained and promoted. Many new salon ventures were opened up by hairdressers in search of fame and fortune. For the client, it was good news. For the first time they were able to shop round for services and prices to suit their needs and purchasing power. For the salon owner, competition was getting stiffer.

the 1980s

Choice for the customer was here to stay, and the early 1980s saw casualties, namely those salons that failed to foresee and respond quickly to changing market trends in a period of economic uncertainty and, what's more, changes in women's lifestyle needs and fashion trends.

For many women, the cut of the mid-1980s, although still highly desired, was not sufficient. Many no longer wanted a quick blow-dry, they wanted extra body, softness and curl. Some clients had, but this time, grown their hair and needed guidance on how to style and dress long hair. A new word was high on many a client's list of expectations – that was **finish**, not just any finish, but a *quality* finish. It heralded a new skill requirement for many hairdressers: the skill of *versatility* and the arts of blow-styling, setting and dressing; techniques which for many were rusty or had to be acquired. A period of 'versatile' hair grew. Provided the client had a good basic cut, a number of different looks could be achieved at home with practise, patience and with one of the many finishing products such as mousse, gel and fixing sprays coming onto the market.

where we are today

In many respects versatile hair is where we are at today. Hair that reflects individuality, a means of expression, attitude and a prop that can be changed frequently and easily to respond to the appropriateness of a particular situation or occasion.

This section responds to the needs of the new age hairdresser who wants to be able to create and capture magazine-style looks on clients in the salon or on a model in a photographic studio.

To achieve a quality finish, I take the view that hair needs to be taken through a number of stages. These may vary from client to client depending on their needs and what you are aiming to achieve. The starting point is an appropriately and well-cut head of hair. Similarly, this is also an ideal starting point for model-related work, assuming that the model is a house model. A house model is usually a professional model whose hair you look after, usually for free, in return for modelling services on photographic shoots planned by you. Such models are often used on a regular basis and become associated with your marketing and publicity material. That is, their look represents the image you are trying to project. It is also a common practice to talent spot clientele who may be of suitable photographic potential.

For those hairdressers working towards becoming a session stylist, the quality of finish on a model whom you may never have seen will be everything. It will require superior finishing skills to turn, often a badly cut, too long, very straight head of hair, into amazing creations.

Whatever situation you are in, the underlying principles of aesthetic hair design work discussed in Part V, Section 5.3 must be observed and applied to the finishing of hair. This must be supported by a technical competence and understanding in all the traditional and modern approaches to shaping hair, dressing out, and long hair work.

This section will provide a very useful companion for those make-up artists that need to, or are asked to, do hair on sessions.

■ shaping and styling

Many of the traditional methods of shaping hair start with wet hair. Shaping uses setting and blow-drying techniques to temporarily change the structure of the hair. In its wet state hair can be stretched around a roller or a brush and dried in its stretched position. The hair remains in this new stretched position until it is wet again. It is purely a physical change involving a change in shape of the keratin – this is a reversible process. This form of temporary set is known as a cohesive set and is the basis of all wet-setting methods including finger-waving, pin curling, roller setting and blow drying. That is

methods used to straighten, bend, wave or curl hair into new styles.

In addition there is a variety of other methods that rely on heat generated from different electrical appliances to shape and set hair in a dry state. These methods include the use of curling irons, heated rollers, a hot brush, flexible heated rubber rods known as beddies, crimping irons and flat irons. These appliances have an important role to play in the successful shaping and fashion styling of hair in a salon. However, they also form the essential equipment in a session hair-stylist's tool kit. They provide an effective way to give hair the 'right foundation' before proceeding to dress out the desired creation.

wet styling

pin curling

Pin curling involves the sculpturing of wet hair into circular coils or loops. The coil or loop is the basis of the wave or curl movement. It is secured in placed using two fine pins placed at right angles to each other, diagonally across the coil.

Before discussing the different types, let's look at the 'anatomy' of a pin curl.

▲ Techniques for shaping hair

There are three parts to a pin curl: its base, stem and body.

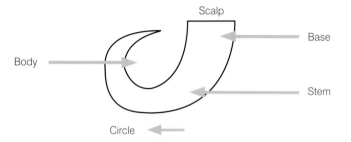

Base: this is the foundation of the curl attached to the scalp. The size and shape will be determined by the desired effect.

Stem: this is the portion of the pin curl between the base and the beginning of where it starts to curl.

It is the direction of the stem that defines the final direction of the curl and its mobility, i.e. degree of movement. The body of the curl, which in effect is the diameter, influences the degree of movement and how the hair moves from the stem.

types of pin curls

There are different types of pin curls which fall into two main categories:

- flat pin curls
- stand up or barrel pin curls

Flat pin curls as the name implies lie flat to the head and give no root lift. There are four varieties:

1 *Open pin curls*   Open body curls, producing a soft and constant degree of curl movement throughout the length of hair.

2 *Closed or clock-spring pin curls*   Resembling a watch clock-spring, the closed pin curl is coiled tighter towards the hair point. Consequently it produces a tighter wave pattern and spongier curl towards the end.

3 *Reverse pin curls*   Consist of open flat pin curls arranged in rows with the stems' position in alternating clockwise and anti-clockwise directions. After drying and dressing out, the rows should combine to form an effect similar to that of a finger-wave movement.

4 *Long-stem pin curls*   Possess a long stem with a smaller looped portion at the end. They produce a loose soft wave movement very suitable for hairlines or fringes.

Stand up or barrel curls are formed by winding the curl vertically onto its base, as if a roller was being used. This type produces root lift.

principles of pin curling

The technique of pin curling and its application to a more traditional hair shaping and setting culture is outside the scope of this book. However, it is important to grasp the principles and study:

- base variations
- stem variations
- clockwise and anti-clockwise curl formation
- pin curl patterns to achieve a specific effect
- anchorage methods to secure curls firmly
- how pin curls can be incorporated with other wet-setting methods

finger waving

Finger waving was a popular means of setting hair in the 1930s and 1940s. It was a technique that complimented the flatter hairstyles of these periods.

It calls for a high degree of hand dexterity and comb co-ordination to product S-shaped movements or waves in the hair.

The middle fingers of the left hand are used to control wave movement and sustain pressure. The comb is held in the right hand and is used to change direction of the wave. The general effect is to produce a succession of wave patterns with what are called crests and troughs, as a particular style feature or as an entire set. The waves are then held in place with clips or fine pins, taking care not to mark the hair. The waving process can be aided by using a sculpturing lotion, a gel or forming creme to hold the wave together during formation.

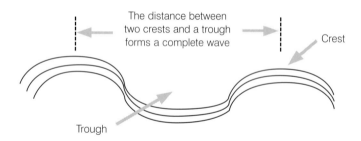

Although finger waving is not used much commercially in salons today, it is a classic skill that all session hairdressers and those working in TV, video and films need to have.

roller setting

Traditional wet sets have long been used in hairdressing to shape and control hair of different lengths using, what are in effect, cylinders of different diameters to help temporarily mould hair into a new form. Roller setting involves taking meshes of hair with a comb before winding the hair around the rollers starting at the hair point, and then securing in place. The objective is to form curls which add lift or volume, hollowness or a particular wave pattern at different places around the head, as part of an overall set look.

To achieve the desired effect, it is important to appreciate the following:

- *The type of cut including length of hair*   The hair should ideally wind around the roller about 2¹/₂ times.
- *The hair texture*   Do you need to use a setting lotion or agent?
- *A visual image of the finished shape*   It is important you set to a definite shape/pattern, one that will create the desired head shape and balance.
- *The size of the roller*   Different diameters will give varying degrees of tightness. The bigger rollers give a large, softer, natural curl movement.
- *The natural fall of the hair*   Set to the natural fall of the hair, taking note of dominant hair lines and the direction in which they fall best.
- *The size of the roller section*   The section should be the same size as the roller used – the section should be neat and precise.
- *The roller direction and root movement*   The hair movement can be directed by careful positioning of the rollers. This needless to say is crucial to the objectives and success of the set. For example, rollers can be directed and wound in alternating, clockwise and anti-clockwise positions or rows to create interesting wave movements. Similarly, rollers can be positioned in such a direction to achieve a movement to one side.
- *Volume control and the angle of wind*   This can be varied according to how much root lift or volume is required.
- *Rolling action*   How smoothly the hair is wound around the roller will influence a quality result. Buckled hair ends or hair that is allowed to bunch will severely affect the finish. Allow the hair to evenly spread out along the length of the roller. If hair starts to fall off the roller, take smaller sections. The key to successful winding is to take clean sections before smoothly winding the hair ends around the roller. Continue to form and stroke the hair around the roller as winding proceeds.
- *Pin placement*   Badly placed pins may mark the hair.
- *Drying time*   Before drying takes place, cover the set with a net. This will help to keep the rollers in position. Ensure that the set is thoroughly dry and cooled down before removing the rollers.
- *Removing rollers*   On long hair remove the bottom rollers at the back of the head first.

At this point proceed to dressing out.

blow-drying

Blow-drying is the process of shaping hair using a variety of brushes or combs in combination with a hand-held dryer. Needless to say it requires practise and patience to develop the correct hand co-ordination, mastering of different drying techniques and achieving the desired result without damaging the hair or causing discomfort to the client.

Blow-drying culture does vary from salon to salon. For many specialist cutting salons, the blow-dry is relatively simple and understated. In these salons, the blow-dry is used to gently ease an almost dry cut into final shape with a minimum amount of effort. Whereas in other salons the blow-dry is a prominent service particularly attracting clients who want their curly hair straightened; extra movement; root lift and volume; a softer, even curlier finish.

What is often dismissed by many as 'just a quick blow-dry' is an unfair comment in view of the amount of time and expertise that goes into the art of blow-styling. Coming from a culture that uses minimal blow-waving, it is enlightening to see a master of the blow-dryer and round brush at work; as they move systematically around the head, often interchanging brushes and leaving hot brushes in the hair to cool before removing. This improves curl formation.

The technique of blow-drying is suitable for achieving a wide range of different finishes. Such finishes will be influenced by:

- *Hair type and texture.*
- *The basic cut and hair length.*   Some haircuts may be more difficult to blow-dry and even retain shape as the lengths may be too long to hold the new shape.
- *The desired effect.*   It is certainly important to start with a visual image of what the finished result will look like.
- *The degree of wetness.*   Pre-shampooed or wet hair allows it to be stretched and remoulded into a new shape.
- *The use of blow-styling aids.*   Styling aids can help to make hair more manageable, give support and substance to the hair as well as offer thermal protection properties (see styling aids).
- *The type of brush or brushes used.*   A brush whether flat or round provides the surface around which heated hair is moulded.
- *The type of hairdryer.*   Choice should be based on a model that is not too heavy, well balanced, easy-to-use controls, heat settings and degree of hotness, airflow speed, nozzle attachments, noise and price. It is certainly advantageous to use a dryer which has two or three speeds and one with a cold air setting.
- *Blow-drying action.*   Methodical sectioning, mastery of the hairdryer and brush in straightening, curving or curling is essential, so is the degree of lift at the roots or conversely root drag is achieved.
- *Root control.*   As in roller setting this is also important in order to create the correct shape and movement.

fashion styling

The growth in the consumer haircare market has seen, over the years, the introduction of new and innovative appliances that enable hair to be quickly, easily and effectively styled. Such appliances include curling irons, heated roller, hot brushes, hot air stylers, dryers with diffusers, crimpers and flat irons. They represent a useful arsenal of fashion styling weaponry with which to 'torture' hair into shape. In spite of this and the knowledge that electrical and thermal abuse contributes to hair deterioration, they are still indispensable for many clients and for the magazine hair session stylist who needs to be able to non-permanently wave, curl, crimp or straighten hair as the foundation of their style and dressing objectives.

In experienced hands, the finally dressed-out set can look more natural than a traditional well roller set. Similarly, so do one of the many waved or curled effects in comparison with a permed look. It is not surprising therefore that what many clients think is a permed look in a fashion magazine photograph is created in the studio using a heat setting method.

This section now looks at the different appliances and appropriate techniques. They include using:

- velcro rollers
- heated rollers
- heated flexible styling rods
- curling irons
- crimping irons
- flat irons

the principle of dry styling

Dry styling works by turning the moisture in hair into steam The steam is then lost through the cuticle or is active in breaking some of the cross linkages within the hair structures. This allows the polypeptide chains forming the hair structure to be moved or remoulded by stretching the hair around a heated roller, styling rod or curling iron. On cooling the cross linkages in hair reform in a new position.

velcro rollers

The desire for a modern quick set in the early 1990s gave rise to a style of roller that could be used on dry hair. Available in various diameters from small to very large, they gave the hairdresser a new styling tool to create smoothness, root volume or natural movement. The beauty of Velcro rollers is that they need no pins because of their self-gripping action. However, for additional security and firmer set, a flat sectioning clip can be applied to the base of the roller section.

The perfect product to accompany a Velcro roller set is a thermo-fixing spray which can be initially sprayed onto the hair prior to setting, or sprayed during setting onto each section. For a uniform curl/wave, the spray must be evenly distributed or just directed onto the roots or ends as required.

On location the set can be let to dry naturally or heat dried using a dryer with a diffuser attachment, or with a portable hood dryer. In a salon put the client under a fixed hood dryer

for about 10–15 minutes. Ensure that hair is thoroughly cool before removing the rollers.

tips

- Comb out hair section to be wound.
- Lightly press the ends of the hair neatly around the roller to ensure that the hair is gripped well.
- To remove a Velcro roller unwind very slowly and carefully, freeing the hair gently as you proceed.
- Avoid causing the client or model discomfort by rushing to remove the roller.

heated rollers

The first heated rollers hit the hair scene back in the mid-1960s. They are still favoured today by many women who desire a softer look, and by the session stylist as a quick means of introducing curl into the hair.

Heated rollers are essentially acrylic cylinders of varying diameters that contained wax. When the roller is put into the electrical unit, the wax heats up and stays hot for about 15–20 minutes after setting. Rollers come in sets of different sizes and quantities enabling a wide variety of looks to be achieved. The early models came with spikes that gripped the hair well although the newer rubber and ribbed surfaces are excellent to use and somewhat kinder on the hair.

advantages

- quick to use
- versatile – can be used to create sort, curly, wavy, bouncy hair
- excellent for improving hair textures, i.e. unstructured curl into stronger curl, or frizzy hair into curly hair
- can be used to create root lift, body lift and volume

disadvantages

- if used excessively, particularly on fine, broken or chemically treated hair, they can cause a deterioration in hair condition

desired effects

Effects depend on:

- basic hair style, its shape, the condition of the hair
- length of hair
- size of roller used
- size and thickness of the section of hair taken
- the angle and direction of setting and tension of hair
- how long the rollers are left in the hair
- whether the hair was hot or cold when the rollers were removed
- whether mousse, blow-dry lotion or fixing spray was used before or during setting the hair
- how the hair is styled after removing the rollers

tips

- Freshly shampooed hair should be partially pre-dried. Roughly dry it off with a hand dryer. Evenly apply setting lotion to the damp hair. Then completely dry the hair before setting.
- Decide on the desired effect and comb the hair into the overall shape to give an idea of the direction of setting and roller positioning.
- Decide on the appropriate size of roller, and size and thickness of sections to be taken.
- Decide on the amount of volume required by the position of the roller relative to the base of each section.
- Leave the rollers in the desired 'setting time' to vary the degree of curl. For example after 5 minutes, the rollers are still warm and a soft curved curl is achieved. After 20 minutes the rollers are cold and a firm curl is achieved.
- Remove the rollers one by one, unwinding them carefully to avoid breaking or tangling the hair.
- Let the curl spring back after removing the roller, wind it back to base and secure with a grip before styling. Ensure hair has cooled down before removing rollers.
- The final look will depend on how the hair is dressed, i.e. technique and what styling products are used.
- It is a good idea to cover each roller with a tissue before using or use perming end papers on the tips of each hair section before winding. This helps to protect the hair from the direct heat.
- Make sure the ends of the hair are neatly wound around the roller, otherwise the ends will become crimped.
- Maintain an equal tension in the hair whilst winding each section.

heated flexible styling rods

Inspired by the principle of rag-rolling hair, heated styling rods (commonly called hot rods, beddie or stylers) are basically cylindrical rods of rubber about 6–8 inches long and about $1/4$ inch diameter with a metal wire running though their centre. They are heated in an electrically heated unit.

advantages

- quick to use, no pins or clips
- extremely flexible and comfortable to wear
- kinder on the hair than heated rollers
- can be used on any type of hair
- can be used to create a variety of effects, e.g. height, volume, loose natural looking curls and waves, spiral curls
- tighter curl than with heated rollers

disadvantages

- sometimes rollers do not get hot enough
- hair can stick to the rubber

desired effects

Effects depend on:

- hairstyle, shape and length of hair
- size of the section taken
- how long they are left in the hair
- how many rods, beddies used
- whether the hair was cold before unwinding
- the winding technique
- whether mousse, blow-dry lotion or fixing spray was used before drying and during winding
- how carefully the hair is managed after removing the rods prior to dressing

tips

- Pre-dry shampooed hair first, dry it off roughly with a hand dryer. Next, evenly apply thermosetting spray from roots to ends of the hair before setting. This not only protects the hair but also aids in giving a firmer curl.
- Divide the hair into random sections of about 25 mm/1 inch wide, comb each section through. The smaller the section the tighter the curls or waves.
- Place the end of the section in the centre of the rod or styler making sure the end of it is neatly tucked in to avoid buckling the end.
- Wind the hair firmly around the rod – maintaining an equal tension on the hair – winding it down to the root.
- To ensure an even tighter curl, spray the section of hair during winding with hair spray.
- To 'lock' the rod or styler in place, simply bend it over in the opposite direction to the roll to form a letter 'C'.
- Processing time will vary according to the texture of hair and the degree of curl required.
- For maximum 'set' leave the rods in for about 15–20 minutes until cold.
- To ensure an extra firm set, the rods can be additionally heated with a hair dryer and resprayed with more hair spray.
- Ensure that the hair is cold before unwinding.
- Take care during unwinding to prevent causing 'pain' to your client or model as the hair sometimes sticks to the rubber surface.
- The final look will depend on how the hair is combed out, i.e. what technique and what styling products are used.

Different effects depending on winding technique

- **Natural loose curl and waves** Twist each section of hair quite loosely from the root to the end before winding it onto the heated rod or styler to produce volume.
- **Spiral curls that give a Pre-Raphaelite look** Twist each section of hair tightly from the root to the end, before winding around the rod. Then, as you wind towards the root, twist the rod in the opposite direction. To get a soft movement off the face, twist hairline sections in an anti-clockwise direction before winding in a clockwise direction into the rod. Maintain a consistent winding action throughout.

curling irons

The modern day electrically heated curling iron has come a long way since 1875 when Marcel Grateau first developed the technique of using thermal irons to wave and curl hair. Over a hundred years later the technique, which takes his name, Marcel waving is still practised, not with stove heated irons but using modern electrically thermostatically controlled models that come in different styles and sizes.

The professional models favoured by hair artists differ from the consumer variety in that they do not have a spring mechanism to open the grooved and movable shell from the barrel. The electrically heated barrel is a cylindrical rod connected to a handle and swivel mechanism into which the power supply enters. The grooved shell in its closed position rests partially around the barrel and is open and closed to accommodate and clamp hair. Clamping is achieved by operating the shell handle with a special hand and finger section.

It is essential to have a number of curling irons with different diameter barrels, ranging from 13 mm to 19 mm.

advantages

- produce a stronger curl than heated rollers or hot rods
- can be used on all hair types and lengths
- an excellent styling tool to visually enhance different hair textures
- can be used to give hair extra volume
- can be used to create different wave and curl effects ranging from:
  - a fractional bend to the hair
  - end curls
  - loose curls
  - tight curls
  - spiral curls
  - waves
  - root lift
  - volume curls on shorter hair

desired effects

Effects depend on:

- basic hairstyle, shape and condition
- length of hair
- density of hair
- texture of hair
- size of the curling iron used
- size and thickness of the section
- the angle of winding onto base
- amount of tension
- the winding technique
- which styling product was used prior to drying, or if hair spray was used during tonging
- direction of tonging

tips

- Dry hair thoroughly after washing. Apply a setting agent or lotion prior to this to help protect the hair and strengthen the curl.
- Before tonging the hair to the desired shape, roughly comb the hair into the required direction.
- During tonging, each section of hair can be sprayed with a fine mist of hairspray to create a firmer 'set' or curl.
- Always use a comb between the tongs and the scalp during winding close to the root.
- Maintain an equal tension in the section during winding.
- Ensure that the end of the hair section is carefully curled otherwise a crimped frizzy end will result.
- Leave tonged curls to cool before dressing out.

four tonging techniques to master

Like setting, tonging is an art that can be mastered, but only with practise. The following techniques will give you the skills to create timeless 'sets' that can be dressed in many different way. The techniques are:

- root tonging
- spiral tonging
- Marcel waving
- short hair tonging

It is important to be familiar and confident with the basic manipulative hand and finger movements used to grip, open, clamp, rotate and open curling tongs. Needless to say these movement should be fluid and need to be practised.

use of flat irons and crimpers

Flat irons or straighteners are extremely useful to 'iron out' kinks, waves and cut from preferably one-length hair. Used on bobs they can give a very smooth, crisp and straight finish with little or no bend.

Crimpers as the name suggests can be used to form a uniform crimped pattern in one-length hair from root to tip. The hair can be left free flowing or dressed.

■ dressing out

The art of dressing out should not be ignored. It is a craft in itself, a craft that will stretch your abilities to control hair, to obtain the correct line, shape and proportion relative to the client's head, face and body, to obtain movement that flows and blends smoothly.

Much of the art of dressing out is traditional, founded on the brushing out of pin-curl and roller sets. The objective is to loosen and break up the rollered hair ensuring that the hair is correctly distributed about the client's or model's head, face and upper body.

Associated with traditional brushing out are the techniques of back-brushing and back-combing. These are techniques used to 'bind' or 'fluff out' hair in order to emphasise shape, add volume and height, where necessary.

A freer and more relaxed method of dressing out hair involves no other tools except your hands: to finger-backcomb hair into shape, to lift, twist, strand or separate sections of hair into position before securing into place with pins and grips or fixing with the aid of hair and fixing spray to finally lock into place.

traditional brushing out

The traditional technique of brushing out is founded on a brushing action which starts at the centre of the forehead and continues through to the centre nape and is performed on both sides of the head. After the hair has been first brushed, start at the ends, then the mid lengths to remove any tangles. Brushing out should be done with foresight and feeling in order to direct hair into the desired shape: a shape that is aesthetically pleasing from all aspects.

Binding or back-brushing are introduced to control and enhance shape in appropriate places, such as volume and height at the crown, or shape to the front hairline and temple region.

binding or fluffing action

To achieve this, take a section of hair, hold it our firmly from the head between the fingers and thumb of one hand. With the comb in the other hand make a series of pushing movements starting a short distance from the roots working upwards along the hair mesh.

tips

- Do not push comb all the way into roots
- Always work from the top of the section
- Use the wider spacing on a cutting/styling comb
- Take random hair sections
- The angle of the hair predetermines the degree of height or flatness
- Smooth only the surface of the hair section by section
- When complete proceed to dressing out

Back-brushing is achieved by using a stiff bristle as above and by rocking the wrist backwards and forwards.

Gentle binding can be used on the ends of set looks to lightly separate the hair, increase volume on the ends and enhance shape or movement.

Binding can be used to build up and give a suitable foundation for further long hair work.

turning the foundations into dressed looks

Having done much of the hard work, your drying or setting foundations can now be turned into a variety of long and short hair looks. Essentially, the key to successful results is to know what 'foundations you need to build' in order to complete and support the final structure. Consequently, the foundation stage is crucial.

Long hair work is something that many salon hairdressers shy away from today, mainly through lack of competence and confidence. However, this need not be so. Like anything, practise makes perfect and with perfection comes the confidence to cope with length and bulk. The trick is to know how to use length and bulk to form different features and give new dimensions of form to the head.

Creating such illusions requires skills to sculpture hair using nothing more than classic long hair techniques, some pins, grips and products to secure and support. Such sculptures often start life from a 'base' on the head, then grow out in all directions. It is from this point that long hair creations begin, such creations involve classic bases and classic techniques of forming a pleat, a chignon, a knot and a twist.

◼ styling and finishing aids

From the hard shellac hair and Brylcream in the 1950s and 1960s to the use of beer as a setting agent and homemade preparations such as sugar and water, soap, egg white and even glue favoured by the punks of the early to mid-1970s, the hair cosmetic industry has come a long way. Today there are a wealth of setting agents, grooming and finishing products to aid professionals and consumers in setting, blow-drying, and dressing out. These products include:

- setting lotions
- blow-dry lotions
- mousse
- sculpturing lotions and glazes
- gels and creams
- oil, waxes and pomades
- serums, glossers, polishes and oil sprays
- hair sprays
- thermofixing lotions

With so much product choice on the market, selection must be based on product performance. There is no better way than to try out the different range and products and select those whose performance you are confident with.

Similarly, testing will give you a chance to experiment and determine how, when and where to use a particular product to suit your design needs.

Styling and finishing aids can be a hairdresser's 'best friend' not only in a salon environment but also on beauty and fashion photographic shoots, where they can be used in different combinations and ways to help create different hair moods and feelings.

product choices

setting lotions

Modern day setting lotions contain plastic resins and polymers dissolved in a mixture of alcohol and water. They coat the hair and aid in improving style retention. Upon the action of heat, alcohol and water evaporate leaving a film of resin on the hair, which helps to 'glue' the hair together. Plasticisers may be added to improve hair flexibility and water-resistant properties, and there may be other ingredients to give the hair body and increased manageability. Setting lotions come in varying strengths as well as those that are specifically formulated for damaged or coloured hair. They are usually sold in single application phials.

Setting lotions are used in roller setting, pin curling, or as a pre-tangling aid.

blow-dry lotions

Blow-dry lotions are similar to setting lotions but with the addition of silicone oils to reduce friction between the brush and the hair cuticle. In addition, many are formulated with thermal protectors and shine enhancers. Blow-dry lotions are sold in single phial applicators and also in multi-application pump-action bottles.

Blow-dry lotions are used in blow drying, finger drying and scrunch drying.

mousses

Mousses exploded onto the hairdressing scene in the 1980s and since then have been a favourite styling aid. They are formulated in a similar way to setting lotions, that is they contain solutions of resins, conditioning agents such as silicone oils and proteins in a pressurised or pump-action container. Mousses are available in different strengths ranging from soft, natural hold to extra strong properties for maximum holding power and root support. Mousses can also be obtained in a range of different colours to give temporary colour to the hair.

Mousses are used in blow drying and scrunch drying to give volume and body and increased manageability. They can also be used as a finishing product on natural, curly or permed hair to give curl definition.

sculpturing lotions and glazes

Sculpturing lotions are of liquid consistency but thicker than setting or blow-dry lotions. They are formulated to behave in a similar way. Sculpturing lotions and glazes are used in scrunch drying and hair sculpturing to give body, volume and curl definition.

gels and creams

Gel covers a multitude of different products of varying degrees of viscosity ranging from spray-type gels to gels of a much thicker consistency that container plasticisers to retain flexibility and give a non-stiff wet-look or those gels that contain plastic resins that when heat activated and dry give hair a stiff quality and feel. Gels are available for different hair types and degrees of hold, ranging from normal to firm. Creams are available which combine styling and conditioning in one product.

Spray gels can be sprayed onto the roots prior to blow-drying to give extra volume, or used on short layered hair to enhance texture. Styling gels in general can be used to sculpture hair into different forms or as a precise styling tool for individual strands, tendrils or wisps of hair.

Some gels are prone to flaking when dry, producing unsightly white deposits on the hair.

oils, waxes and pomades

The development and use of such products in hairdressing has a long history. During Victorian times men used macassar oil to groom their hair. It was this which gave rise to the 'anti-macassar', a cloth used to protect upholstery.

Such products have now given rise to a new generation of 'solid' petroleum jelly-based products that are thickened with waxes such as carnauba, ozokerite, ceresin, paraffin wax and beeswax. To make these solid waxes softer and more pliable, mineral oil and lanolin is added. It is possible to obtain both hard and soft waxes.

Pomades also vary in type, from the ones that are based on petroleum waxes to those that are composed from mineral oil, vegetable oil or silicones. Castor oil is often added to give shine properties. A lighter pomade contains vegetable oil and vegetable wax. This type also provides gloss and hold, and is water soluble. A newer formulation is that of a foaming water soluble pomade which leaves no residue in the hair.

Waxes are of different consistency from soft to hard and they can offer varying degrees of hold, which is useful in dressing out an entire head or specific areas. Waxes are also excellent on Afro hair, not only helping to give it gloss but also smoothness and flatness.

Waxes can be difficult to remove from the hair, in which case use a deep cleansing shampoo.

New pomades are much lighter which makes application easier. They are best applied in small amounts to the end lengths of separate strands of hair. They can be used to slick back hair, decrease fluffiness following a blow dry and calm frizzyness.

serums, glossers, polishes and oil sprays

This range of products are made from oils or silicones which, when applied to hair either in liquid or aerosol, leave a microfine film on the surface of hair. Their action causes the cuticle scales to lie flat, therefore these products are excellent for imparting shine and gloss to hair. In addition they help to make hair feel soft and silky.

They can be used as a defrizzer, cuticle smoother, shine and glosser, curl enhancer. Oil sprays are excellent for delivering a very fine mist. Too much product can make hair look greasy.

hair sprays

The first aerosol hair sprays became available in the late 1940s. These were called hair lacquer and were a mixture of the resin shellac in alcohol. Whilst its hair holding properties were good, the film formed on drying was rather hard and brittle and made the hair stiff. Although firm, rigid hair was desired by many women, the hair had little elasticity to allow dressing out without destroying the set. In addition shellacs are difficult to remove from hair due to their water insoluble properties.

A new type of setting spray followed, based on the polymer PVP which gave hair strength and elasticity, however, in very dry conditions it had a tendency to flake. Humectants were then added to improve their hygroscopic properties, but in more humid climates the hair became tacky after a few hours.

The chemists overcame this problem by developing a more hydrophobic copolymer: PVP/vinyl acetate (PVP/VA). It is widely used today in hair spray formulations together with another formulation containing a copolymer of vinyl acetate and crotonic acid (Resyn 28-1310) to add hardness and flexibility.

The chemist's criteria for evaluating a hair spray are:

- hardness
- visual appearance
- curl retention under different humidities
- moisture pick-up

The hairdresser's criteria for evaluating a spray are:

- fast drying
- doesn't flake
- holding and shaping power
- non stick/tacky
- not too stiff
- not too wet
- use as little as possible
- easy to brush out
- gives shine and gloss

The other main component of aerosol hair sprays before they were banned in the USA was the propellant chloroflurocarbons (CFCs). Because of the alleged damage CFCs have on the ozone layer above the earth they have been replaced by other propellants and hand pump containers, which deliver a liquid 'hair fixing' or 'hair freezing' agent. Like aerosols, fixing sprays are available for different hair types and in varying degrees of 'hold'.

Aerosol hair sprays can be used as a dressing out product to give root lift and volume, to provide overall hold to style, shape and curl definition after scrunch drying, as a light mist to calm flyaway hair and as a setting aid with heated rollers and tongs.

Fixing sprays can be used as a dressing out product that gives hold, control, shine and UV protection depending on formulation. However, fixing sprays do not deliver a fine mist like aerosols and can cause wetting of the hair, particularly if sprayed too close to hair.

thermo fixing lotions

These are heat activated setting lotions that can be used with heated rollers, velcro rollers and curling tongs. When sprayed onto the root area they give extra lift and overall support and strength to a 'dry set'.

product and technique guide

The following charts outline the uses of different products and techniques to achieve different style effects, style features and finishes. These techniques form the basis of transforming many basic cuts into more fashionable and even avant-garde looks.

	Mousse	Gel styling and wet	Glaze or sculpturing lotion	Fixing spray or hair spray	Wax or oil
Scrunching	Apply normal-medium strength mousse to the roots and mid-lengths, ensuring it is evenly distributed. Works best on damp hair. Scrunch either with the head upright or upside down to achieve maximum fullness. Can also be used on dry hair more as a finishing product to enhance natural or permed curl.	Apply the styling gel to the finger tips in small amounts, then work the fingers through the hair to disperse the gel. Scrunch until almost dry.	Can be used as a dressing to the finished scrunched shape, giving a more 'solid' effect. Pour a small amount of glaze into the palm of the hand, massage both hands together to disperse glaze and then distribute onto the hair.	Use as a finishing product on the hair to shape the front and side off the face, giving extra root lift.	After scrunch drying hair naturally, wax or oil can be used on to impart shine and strengthen the ends of the hair to emphasise 'degree' of curl or texture. Use very sparingly using finger tips. Alternatively use a spray oil.
Volumising hair	Use extra hold mousse for that firmer effect, particularly on short to medium length hair.	Apply strong styling gel evenly to the roots. Finger dry using a hair dryer lifting sections of hair, aiming the dryer at the roots. Lightly back-comb using finger or comb to emphasise the shape and create volume.	Apply glaze to middle and ends on towel-dried hair. Dry and style as above. Works well on dry hair as a finishing product to dress the final shape by applying to the ends of the hair.	Use as a finishing product on dry hair to create a quiff at the front or to lift the sides back off the face. Hold the hair in the required direction using a large comb. Spray. Hold until set, then carefully remove the comb.	
Waving	Apply mousse to towel-dried hair in small amounts ensuring it is distributed evenly. Dry hair using a blow-dryer on a slow speed or with a diffuser if naturally wavy. To achieve a wavy effect on straight hair, use a hair dryer and round brush.	Apply the gel to towel-dried hair evenly. Dry the roots and leave the ends to dry naturally.	Once dry use a finishing product to separate out the hair into required shape.	Can be lightly sprayed to hold the hair in the required shape. definite texture that	Great on naturally wavy or curly hair to encourage a more has softness, shine and a 'wetter look'.
Smoothing	Apply a normal hold mousse evenly to towel dried hair. Blow-dry section by section using a large round brush to create smoothness and fullness.			Use a light hairspray. Spray above the hair. Let it settle before running the flat of the hand or brush over the surface of the hair to settle any fly-away ends.	A very small amount of oil can be lightly applied to hair when dry.
Spiking	Apply strong mousse to the ends of the scrunched-dried hair to encourage the ends to stick out.	Apply strong styling gel using the finger tips to the scrunched hair to pick out the 'spikes'.	Use as a finishing product on dried hair as above to create spikiness.	Use a fixing spray on the finished effect by spraying, picking out the spikes when the spray is still wet.	Use on the hair after drying. Best on medium–thick textures. Lightly finger back-comb the hair sections, picking out spikes with the wax on the ends of fingers. This helps to strengthen the ends without making them stiff. Use sparingly.

	Mousse	Gel styling and wet	Glaze or sculpturing lotion	Fixing spray or hair spray	Wax or oil
Wet look		Great for sleeking back or creating a flatness on short to medium length hair. Apply wet look gel to towel-dried hair. Comb through the sculpture into the desired shape. Great on curly or wavy hair to emphasise texture, giving hair shine, wetness without stiffness.	Can be used to sleek back hair into desired shape. Will eventually dry giving a more solid shiny effect than wet gel.		Apply to dry hair evenly – comb through into the desired sleek shape. Great for moulding curly or wavy hair to give a natural look with great shine.
Stranding	For a much stiffer strand, take very thin sections. of long hair, coating each strand with the required amount of mousse down the entire length, using your finger tips. Leave to dry naturally.	For a more supple effect use a wet gel to coat the section of hair. Great for enhancing the natural curl or encouraging a more definite curl, particularly on frizzy, curly hair.	For a much stiff strand, run a small amount of glaze along the entire length of the strand. Leave to dry naturally.		Like wet gel, a light wax or oil is great for separating out fine strands of hair to give greater definition and shape. Best on medium–thick hair textures. Use very sparingly.
Twisting and coiling		Twist long rope-like sections of hair using wet gel before fixing into the required shape. The hair remains pliable with the great wet shiny look.			Twist rope-like sections of hair with a light wax or oil before fixing into the required shape. Best on medium–thick hair textures. Use very sparingly.
Knotting		Use a wet gel before knotting sections of hair along their lengths. Give wetness, pliability and shine.			Sections of hair can be knotted along its length using a light wax or oil to enhance the knotting effect and give the hair shine and structure. Use very sparingly.

■ style effects, style features and finishes

hair: Charles Worthington

▲ Smoothing

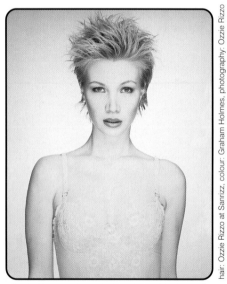

hair: Ozzie Rizzo at Sanrizz, colour: Graham Holmes, photography: Ozzie Rizzo

▲ Spiking

hair: Ozzie Rizzo at Sanrizz, colour: Graham Holmes, photography: Ozzie Rizzo

▲ Flicking

hair: Ian Mistlin, photography: Melissa Helstead

▲ Tonging

hair: Ian Mistlin, make-up: Amanda Cross, photography: Lorna Catel

▲ Setting and dressing

hair: Ian Mistlin for Paul Mitchell Systems, photography: Kim Knott

hair: Ian Mistlin for Paul Mitchell Systems, photography: Kim Knott

▲ Twisting

▲ Stranding

hair: Ian Mistlin, photography: Melissa Helstead

hair: Ian Mistlin, photography: Melissa Helstead

▲ Extending

▲ Tonging

hair: Ian Mistlin

hair: Ian Mistlin

▲ Sculpturing

▲ Coiling

Creating quality images or looks for editorial, advertising or PR purposes requires a whole range of specialised knowledge and skills. Discover these and make your images 'winners'.

There is no better way to advertise your talents, that of your staff, salon or company than by producing striking high quality beauty and fashion photographs. Although it is often said that 'all publicity is good publicity', can you afford to produce and use photographic material that is not up to standard? The answer is no! Besides being costly to produce, your image and reputation rests very heavily on how others receive, perceive and judge this imagery. The question you must consider is, 'what statement does this imagery make about your skills or salon's work standards?' Pictures speak louder than words. In which case, does your visual imagery enhance your ability to attract the right clientele or gain favourable PR in both consumer and trade publications?

There is no denying that photo sessions are excellent for self and team motivation. Consider the thrill when your work or that of your salon appears in print. As with any art form, the more experienced you become the better the results. Better results increase the appetite and desire to do more shoots: shoots that you can use to explore new creative horizons. There is no limit to what you could achieve in time.

However, there are pitfalls along the way which can be easily avoided, making sessions more effective, productive and fun.

Developing your photographic imagery is the section of the book for all hairstylists who wish to uncover the secrets about photographic work. It is an essential companion and overview for those of you who want to:

- evolve ideas and imagery
- successfully organise or plan photographic sessions
- learn what makes a shoot a success
- participate and perform well
- produce better and better results
- progress into doing regular editorial or advertising work

In addition this part of the book will be invaluable for trainee make-up artists or those on fashion styling courses.

7.1 evolving your ideas and imagery

photo session blueprint

The strength and success of a photo session relies very heavily on having a *concept* or *theme*. Call it a blueprint to work to. Whether it be a single image or a collection of related images it is important that you decide on your concept from the beginning. This will help you to clearly brief others involved in the project. Your concept needs to evolve alongside your *marketing strategy*. (More about strategy in a moment.) To help stimulate your conceptual thoughts and mental imagery, look through back-copies of beauty and fashion magazines. Collect interesting ideas for further discussion. Other sources of conceptual inspiration include proposed magazine features available from editorial departments, new films, musicals, special events, dates in the social calendar, looks for life styles, personality traits, historical influences in fashion and beauty, future seasonal fashion and beauty trends or forecasts. There is certainly no shortage of creative inspiration. During this evolution brainstorm your ideas. Make drawings and graphic notes. One technique that I like to use is that of mind mapping.

mind mapping

Mind mapping is a great technique that can be used to develop your creativity and improve the flow of ideas. It is a technique that encourages what Tony Buzan the originator of the technique calls 'radiant thinking'. It can be used to unlock the potential of your brain to imagine and conceive new concepts, looks, compositions and images. The potential is unlimited.

Mind mapping dispenses with traditional note taking or bullet points in favour of structures that are said to resemble spiders' webs. They start from a central point and radiate outwards by way of main and sub branches.

The centre point can represent an idea, theme or design that you wish to develop.

I like to construct mind maps to develop my thinking and conceptual ideas. For instance I have started a mind map to visually represent 'sources of conceptual inspiration'. As you see from the map each main branch terminates in a key source. It is from these that the map will radiate and grow.

The following points may help:

- Use a large sheet of paper.
- Make the map as visual as you like. Use drawings, annotations instead of words.
- Use highlighter pens to illuminate key parts of the map.
- Use coloured pens to *link* together elements of the map that you wish to explore.

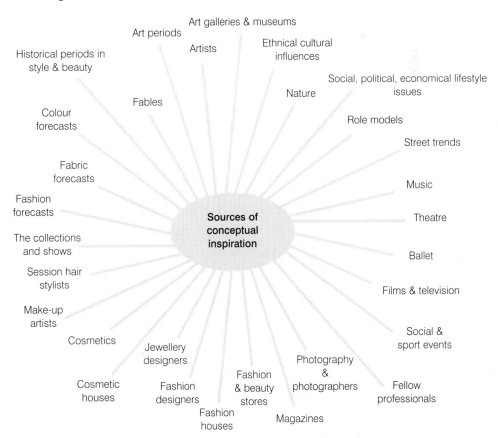

getting creative and food for thought

Getting creative will require you to develop your creative thinking to come up with new ideas, concepts, compositions and creations. It will be mentally challenging and thought provoking. The following schemes summarise key areas of knowledge and information that will make suitable 'food for thought'.

The mind process will require you to

- assess
- analyse
- categorise
- compare
- link
- reflect
- visualise
- evaluate

this essential knowledge and information.

Use these schemes to advance your compositions and creations as you inject new feeling into developing your photographic imagery.

Style preferences	Mood or impression	20th-century style and beauty influences	19th-century style and beauty influences	Historical fashion and beauty inspiration
natural	conservative	art nouveau	Gothic revival	Egyptian
classic	sophisticated	20s	New Rococo	Grecian
dramatic	glamorous	30s	Victorian	Roman
romantic	sensual	40s	Oriental	Byzantium
arty	casual	50s		Romanesque
tomboyish	groomed	60s		Gothic
country	business-like	70s		Renaissance
sporty	formal	80s		Baroque
	informal	90s		French Regency
				Louis XV
				Directoire
				Empire

Head, face and body considerations	Make-up look	Hair look	Material properties of hair to consider	Material properties of skin to consider
height	sun kissed	long straight	type	type
head shape	pale skin	bob	texture	texture
face shape	smokey eyes	graduated bob	density	tone
facial dimension	define brows	long layered	length	pore condition
facial features	false lashes	coupe savage	condition	imperfections
neck proportion	heavy mascara	short layered	colour	pigmentation
shoulder proportions	shaded cheeks	crop		
body shape	strong lips	afro		
body proportions	pale lips	chignon		

Desired hair finish	Desired make-up finish	Cosmetic considerations for hair	Cosmetic considerations for skin	Hair cutting considerations
smooth	matt	shampoo	cleanser	blunt
straight	gloss	conditioner	astringent	graduation
scrunched	iridescent	treatment	toner	layering
volumised	metallic	setting lotion	moisturiser	weave
curly	pearlised	blowdry lotion	exfoliate	chipping
wavy	shimmer	mousse	scrub	channel
frizzy	satin	sculpturing lotion	foundation	thinning
spiky	sheer	gel	cover-up	pointing
matt	dewy	wax	powder	scissor and comb
shiny	luminous	pomade	eye shadow	razoring
wet	shiny	serum	eye liner	twist
		gloss	mascara	undercutting
		oil spray	lipstick	
		hair spray	lip liner	
		fixing spray	blusher	

Style enhancing techniques for hair	Finishing techniques for hair	Hair equipment selection	Make-up technique associated with application	Make-up equipment
semi permanent	natural drying	blow dryer	foundation	sponges
tinting	blow drying	heated rollers	concealing	powder puff
highlighting	scrunch drying	flexi heated rods	powdering	cotton wool
low lighting	trad. roller setting	curling tongs	layering	brushes
bleaching	finger waving	crimping irons	blending	Q-tips
henna	pin curling	flat irons	smudging	eye lash curler
perming	tonging	hot brush	lining	tissues
relaxing	fashion setting	pins	contouring	brush cleaner
straightening	dressing	grips	filling in	
texturising	backcombed	hair nets		
	backbrushed	doughnuts		
		padded rolls		
		combs		
		brushes		

Hairstyle feature or effect	Hair accessories	Jewellery accessories	Garments	Fabric properties
knot	slide	earrings	shirt, top	feel
roll	decorative comb	pearls	jacket	texture
plait	padded band	brooch	dress	lustre
pleat	snood	necklace	trousers	opacity
weave	decorative pin	chains	jeans	weight
twist	tiara	bangles	skirt	drapability
extension	flowers	bracelet	knitwear	print
ornamentation	hat	pendant	suit	colour
hair accessories	scarf	glasses	evening dress	
		watch	bridal gown	
		gloves	swimwear	
		belt	underwear	
		bag	coat	

Colour feeling	Colour families
dramatic	red
pastel	red orange
soft	orange
muted	yellow orange
rich	yellow
elegant	yellow green
delicate	green
vibrant	blue green
	blue
	blue violet
	violet
	red violet
	neutrals

■ landmarks in twentieth-century style

Looking back in time, every era will be remembered for its contribution to history in some way. Similarly when it comes to style landmarks, each era has much to tell with regards to beauty and fashion trends of the day. In many respects trends are a shop window of social, economic and political life at the time. Style tells much about an age. Clothes, make-up and hair all reflect changes in society and in society's perception of beauty.

Society at any time can be made up of a 'cocktail' of trends or looks, some more mainstream and long lasting, others more transitional and fleeting. Hence some trends explode onto the scene, to be copied by those dedicated followers of fashion. In fact many a trend has been seen before only to reappear years later presented in a new way.

The following plans map style trends from the 1920s until today. Use them as a 'shop window' to develop your ideas and imagery.

- Famous flapper look
- Art deco dress
- Short skirts to knee
- Jagged and trailing hemlines
- Cloche hat
- Turbans

- Short shingle cuts
- Eton crop
- Bobs
- Henna
- Peroxide blondes
- Soft curls

- Heavy make-up look
- Pale foundation
- Smudged eyes
- Plucked thin and arched eyebrows
- Red cupid shaped lips

- Long strings of pearls
- Crystal and glass beads
- Ivory and ebony bangles
- Long pendulum earrings
- Art deco 'geometric' lines
- Art deco brooches pinned onto hats, waistbands and necklines
- Chanel look … long ropes of gilt chains
- Modernism influence towards end of decade

- Hollywood inspired
- Extravagant clothes
- Evening dress
- Backs of evening dresses bared to the waist
- Dress lines; slim, long and straight in the early 30s
- Birth of bathing costumes
- Sports clothing
- Nylons hit the scene
- Late 30s skirts become shorter

- Shingle
- Bob
- Pageboy
- Marcel wave
- Henna
- Bleach

- Hollywood inspired
- Heavy 'pan cake' foundation
- Eyeshadow blended over entire eye
- Smokey blue and brown eye colours
- Red lips
- Blusher

- Simple jewellery
- Modernism ... monochromatic colours; heavy chains, tubes, links or discs
- Classic 'egg necklace'
- Gilt coin necklaces
- Heart shaped brooches, gold sovereign buttons, circus inspired jewellery
- Dress clips to draw attention to bodies
- Indian ethnic jewellery
- Flower sprays

- Functional hard wearing clothing
- Classic look for women; tailored suits with square shoulders, nipped at the waist; skirts to knee in the war years; small hats, and functional bags and shoes
- Late 40s Christian Dior unveiled 'The New Look'. A soft silhouette with rounded shoulders, definite waist and flared calf length skirt

- Gently waved 'Veronica Lake' bob
- 'Joan of Arc' cut; a bob with a square short fringe
- Hairpieces, false braids
- Topknots
- Popularity of perms

- Minimal make-up
- Natural eyebrows shaped and darkened
- Red lips
- Towards the end of the decade emphasis switched to eye design
- Use of liner, mascara

- Glittering gems
- Paste jewellery
- Rope of pearls
- Diamante pendants and brooches
- Jewelled buttons
- Hair ornamentation
- Clip earrings for day wear
- Dangling earrings at night

fashion

- Hollywood inspired
- Femininity, sophistication and elegance in the early 50s
- Clothes for every occasion
- Tailored suit and twinsets
- Shortwaisted day dresses
- Cocktail and full length gowns for evening wear
- Softly tailored suits with long skirts of the mid 50s
- Balenciaga famous chemise
- Ready to wear; separates; flat shoes; wrap around dresses
- Tight jumpers
- Cardigans
- Circular skirts
- Beatnik look

hair

- Well-groomed hair; neat
- Chignons, French pleats; softly waved pageboys
- Tied back hair and short fringes
- Shaggy haircuts with nibbled fringes
- Razored short gamine cuts
- Bouffants and beehives
- Dyed hair; peroxide blondes
- Short pincured looks
- French pleats
- Audrey Hepburn look; tiered back hair and short fringe
- Hairspray

make-up

- Hollywood inspired
- Dewy, moist and natural foundations
- Eyes defined with liner and mascara
- Outer ends of brows were plucked and redrawn in an upward sweep
- Colours included violet mascara, blue eyeliner and silver shadow
- Lips painted dark red
- Rouge to emphasise cheekbones

jewellery

- Bold gilt jewellery for the arms and neck
- Paste jewellery
- Plastic beaded necklaces known as poppets
- Enamel flower jewellery
- Rhinestones and fake emeralds
- Big hoops or button earrings

- Mini skirt or dress
- Tight sweaters
- Brightly coloured tights
- White laced boots
- See-through blouses and dresses
- PVC, acrylics and polyester fabrics
- Unisex clothes; velvet jackets, floral skirts and fringe waistcoats
- School girl looks
- Hippie look … Indian caftan dresses; beads, hats and Afghan coats
- Tights

- Long straight hair with fringes
- Geometric precision cuts like the classic bob, graduated bob, isodora
- Ethnic inspired hair of the 'flower power' period
- Short urchin cuts

- Pale skin and foundation
- Eyes heavily defined with black liner and mascara
- Strong eyebrows
- False eyelashes
- Pale lips
- Shaded cheekbones using blusher
- Face-painting was a big craze in the late 60s, so was the use of colour

- Costume jewellery
- Big pins in the shape of spirals, stars or comets
- Moulded plastic, perspex, vinyl and acrylic
- Jet jewellery
- Stones wrapped in curtain ropes
- Pearl beads coloured in lemon, yellow, cream, grey or coffee
- Enamelled shells
- Multicoloured bracelets
- Gobstopper sized earrings
- Marble plastic bangles
- Ethnic inspired jewellery

- Mini evolved into hotpants
- Nostalgic looks reminiscent of the 30s; long flowing romantic skirts, dresses and crocheted shawls (Biba era)
- Flared trousers
- Softly sculptured garments; loosely layered (Kenzo and Miyake)
- Tailored suits (Ralph Lauren)
- Fitness and dance wear
- Fabric Lycra
- Punk and Glam rock inspired looks
- Designer jeans
- T-shirts

- Long layered shaggy 'Coupe Savage' cuts
- Farah; long layered look that flicked back at the sides
- Halo or chic pudding basin cut; bobs were big
- Afros
- Permed and scrunched looks
- Classic graduated cuts like 'Firefly' or 'Wedge'
- Feather cuts
- Punk inspired hair incorporating undercutting and dramatic colouring, using Crazy Colour
- Crimped hair to complement pre Raphaelite clothes

- Face painted inspired by Glam rock scene
- Disco make-up using strong iridescent pigment on the eyes carefully layered and blended
- Browbone highlighted with 'white' streak
- Red; dark, even black, lips
- California look consisting of glowing tanned skin and strong lips
- Glossy pastel lips
- Face contouring to highlight bone structure

- Art nouveau
- Art deco 'flapper' beads
- Mock deco pins and bangles
- Plastic brooches
- Gilt chains with multicoloured stones
- Jewellery worn as body sculpture
- Tribalistic arm jewellery
- Punk influenced jewellery fashioned out of bicycle chains, nuts, bolts, pins

- Designer image and Yuppie look
- Highly decorated garments for evening (Dior, Balmain and Givenchy)
- Sexy image using clingy and stretch fabrics (Thiery Mugler and Azzedine Alara)
- Dress for the professional woman (Versace, Armani and Moschino)
- Power dressing; tailored suits with dominant shoulders
- Fifties style haute couture; bolero jackets, tight waists, short and full skirts
- Preppy look; jeans
- Wealthy street fashions
- Sports clothes and swimwear
- Trainers

- Punk inspired cuts and highlights
- Big hair to complement 'power dressing'
- Groomed layered bobs and graduated cuts
- Softly layered short brushed back styles often referred to as 'Lady Di'
- Glamour and glitz long layered flicked back hair at the sides inspired by *Dallas* tv programme
- Gamine or boyish cuts; often bleached blonde
- Passion for red heads
- Gothic inspired cuts and looks
- Extensions, dreadlocks
- Highlighted hair
- Punk inspired colour

- Those that favoured the Gothic look wore very white foundation; strong eyes; blood red lips
- Natural balanced make-up starting with carefully selected foundation to match skin tones; strongly defined eyes, 'Brooke Shields' bushy eyebrows; well-defined cheekbones
- Corporate look to complement power dressing consisted of natural, matt and sparing use of foundation; strong matt eyeshadow; eyeliner and bright red lips
- Light silicone-based foundations

- Heavy decorated costumes
- Indian inspired jewellery using multicoloured glass and cut stones
- Brightly coloured glass studded, irregular shaped jewellery made from resin
- Gilt jewellery
- Chains of mock pearls
- Fake diamante and emerald
- Paste beads
- Sculptured pieces crafted using different materials
- Designer sunglasses worn in the hair

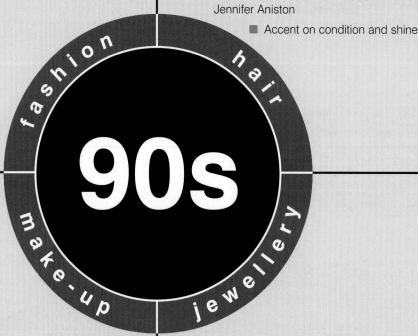

fashion

- A spirit of independence, adventure and individuality entered the fashion arena
- Fashion stores raided past eras for ideas and themes. Themes included: Hollywood glamour of the 1940s; Edwardian 'dandy' look; 1960s 'Mod' look; 1970s hippie chic and glam look; cowboy and Oriental look
- Designer underwear

hair

- Natural flowing hair
- Short heavy layered hair
- Urchin cuts
- 60s inspired beehives with centre parting and back combed crown
- Sensual chignons of tumbling curls and free-falling wisps inspired by 60s idol Brigitte Bardot
- Unkempt or Grunge look reminiscent of hippie era
- Popularity of red heads and dark hair
- French pleats and messy ponytail for work and evening looks
- Curly 'mop tops' popularised by Meg Ryan
  - Medium short layered cuts popularised by Jennifer Aniston
    - Accent on condition and shine

make-up

- Shift towards natural products
- Unmade-up faces associated with the Grunge look in the early 90s
- 60s revival of false eyelashes hit the scene in the early 90s but was short lived
- It was out with powder … in with shine; mid-90s
- Rise of the classic beauty

jewellery

- Less flashy jewellery
- Simple sculptured pieces in silver, pewter, steel and alloys
- Tiaras and crowns for more formal looks

7.2 planning a photo session

marketing strategy

Photographic imagery mainly falls into the following categories:

- basic beauty head shots
- head and shoulder shots
- head, shoulders and three-quarter body shots
- full-length total fashion looks
- avant-garde or strongly art-directed imagery

As your ideas evolve, do *not* lose sight of the following *marketing objectives*:

- What market are you 'playing' to? Is it consumer or trade? If it is consumer, are you aiming for a commercial look that will appeal to a certain age group or type? If it is trade, are you aiming to appeal to other hairdressers, salons and hair-related organisations to promote training?
- Will you be using the pictures for recruitment purposes?
- What do you intend to use the pictures for? Will it be for a window display, sales literature, show cards, posters? If so, have you discussed your needs with a graphic designer?
- Will you be using the pictures to promote a product range?
- Do you want the pictures for advertising purposes? If so, focus on what you are trying to advertise, whether it be a particular cut or style; colour or permed look; haircare and condition.
- Will you be using the pictures for local or national advertising in newspapers or quality glossy magazines? If it is the former, black and white prints may be preferred by the production department.
- Do you want the pictures for editorial purposes? Most magazines work at least three months ahead, so if you are aiming to get editorial coverage, plan your shoot well in advance.
- Are your pictures going to be sent out with a press release? If so the press release and pictures must be in harmony, i.e. they must both tell the same 'story' and reinforce one another.
- Have you researched and taken into consideration forecast fashion trends?
- Do you want to produce timeless looks or high fashion looks that will date more quickly?
- Do you need to produce a collection of 'images' for a competition you are entering?
- Are the pictures for your own self-interest and self-promotion?

✓ tips

- Most of the consumer fashion and beauty magazines are self-sufficient and produce their own photographic imagery. They seldom buy in photographic spreads or collections. However, you may stand a better chance if your pictures reflect the type of magazine.

- Good quality basic beauty shoots are always in demand with beauty editors to support editorial copy or for style portfolio sections.

- Many of the specialist consumer hair and beauty magazines could be a better bet. Talk to the editor about your ideas. If liked they may well use you, provided they can get full or part sponsorship to pay for the shoot.

choosing the team

The success of any photo session depends on team input and effort, including the expertise of the photographer, stylist, make-up artist and hairdresser.

The success of your session will hinge on the individuals you assemble, how well they 'gel' and their ability to deliver the 'goods' on the day.

Before you start talking to photographers, fashion stylists and make-up artists, make sure you are very clear in your mind about your concept or theme.

the photographer

Do you want a photographer who specialises in hair and beauty work or more fashion photography? Most well-known, top photographers have developed a unique personal style. Expect to pay for experience and expertise. Personal recommendations are a good way of getting that first introduction.

Look through magazines, talk to others in the trade, speak to bookers at model agencies about up-and-coming young photographers or assistants. Draw up a short list and arrange an appointment to see their portfolio. This will give you a good indication of their experience, style and technique. Discuss your ideas. See what they have to say. Get their views on lighting, backgrounds, type of model(s), to complement the look and image you are aiming to achieve. It is essential that the photographer is on your wavelength.

Often a photographer will recommend a particular model, make-up artist or fashion stylist that they have already worked with.

Finally, discuss their fees and expenses.

the stylist

The clothes and accessories form a very important part in developing the concept or theme of the shoot. If your budget allows, use a professional fashion stylist to source the right clothes. It's a great idea as it can be a big headache organising the clothes yourself – as well as diluting your energies from what you do best.

Sourcing and organising the right clothes, jewellery and props is essentially about having the right contacts. Professional fashion stylists have, during the course of their career, built up these contacts. They know where to get interesting props, they have built up credibility with PR companies, designers, shops and magazines as well as being up to date with fashion trends.

A good stylist has a sense of colour, style and an eye for detail. They are able to cleverly mix and match combinations of clothes, accessories and jewellery with amazing ease. They should have a good knowledge of forthcoming beauty and fashion trends.

If you are organising the clothes yourself, try local shops and boutiques, they may be willing to let you use their clothes, provided they get a credit. Most places will require a deposit or have a hire charge. It is worth taking out insurance to cover possible damage or loss.

When interviewing a stylist, ask to see their portfolio, discuss your ideas, listen to what ideas and suggestions they have. Ask them what fashion designers they work with. Some stylists have a style book with cuttings, sketches and ideas. Get them to show you this. Play safe and ask to see the clothes prior to the shoot.

✓ tips

- It is inadvisable to rely on a model's own clothes.

- An alternative to clothes is to work with fabrics draped on the body.

the make-up artist

A picture without colour can sometimes look flat, uninteresting and dull. Make-up, besides adding colour, provides depth. It can be used to highlight or camouflage the model's features. Like the clothes, the make-up should help to create the image and be complementary with the overall look.

It is important when choosing a make-up artist to see their individual portfolios. Make sure that they are versatile enough to cope with a wide range of make-ups and have good imagination. Check whether they are experienced in make-up for both colour and black and white photographs.

Discuss your concept or theme. Listen to their views on make-up trends. Discuss choice of colours, shades, make-up effects and whether the make-up should be natural, soft, dramatic, etc.

■ model selection

The success of the photo session heavily depends on the strength of the model and how well they can project. Decide on how many different looks you want from the shoot. Maybe you need more than one model. Too many potentially good photo sessions fall down on the wrong choice of model. Many salons have the habit of using a good looking client or friend. However, often good looks are not enough. It takes more than a pretty girl to put over the image and show off the clothes. It requires bags of personality and attitude.

Once you have a good idea of the theme, begin by ringing around the model agencies, giving them a brief on the type of model you are looking for, such as:

- type of look, e.g. beauty, fashion, moody, romantic, sexy, classic
- hair colour (dark hair can often look very solid in black and white)
- length, texture and type of hair
- bone structure
- height

The next stage is to organise a casting.

holding a casting

Hold the casting preferably with the photographer. The casting will give you the opportunity to see and talk to the models in person as well as going through their portfolios.

You should look at them and their portfolio. Check out:

- head shape and proportion
- shape of face from all angles. Bone structure and other features
- eyes – shape and colour. Do their eyes speak?
- teeth. Are there crooked or discoloured teeth? This may be more noticeable when smiling

- mouth. Do they have a full mouth?
- nose shape
- jawline. Do they have a heavy jawline?
- mouth and lip shape
- ears. Do they stick out? Check ear lobes to see if they are heavily pierced
- body shape and proportions, including neck length, shoulder line, waist and hips
- bust size
- overall height
- skin condition. Do they have a clear complexion, free from wrinkles, spots etc? Is their skin smooth? Do they have dark circles under their eyes?
- hair – type, texture, shape, quality and hairlines. Is their hair condition good? Is it coloured, permed or straightened? Do they have a regrowth?
- overall style – their appearance and general presentation
- posture – how they sit or stand
- personality. Do they project themselves well? Are they friendly? Do they have presence?
- hands. These need to be in good condition with well-manicured nails, particularly if they will be in shot

Ask each model for their Z card (this is an A5 single or double card, usually with one or more of their photographs on, together with their vital statistics and agency name, address and number). As you see each model, make comments on the card so that your final selection is made easier. It is also a good idea to take a Polaroid of each model.

Never book a model without seeing them first. Do not rely on a model's card. The model may have changed her look since the card was produced.

If applicable, ask her to walk. This can say a good deal about her personality.

If it is necessary to cut, colour or perm the model's hair you must check first with the model and their agency. Most agencies are particularly strict on this.

briefing a model

Brief the model personally or through their agency on shoot arrangements including what, if anything, they need to bring. Stress the importance of turning up with freshly washed hair, clean skin, free from styling products or make-up.

If you are planning a very early start, offer to pay their taxi fare or get them picked up. It can be an advantage to get the model's home or mobile telephone number particularly if you are planning a weekend shoot.

■ studio hire

This would normally be organised by the photographer (many have their own). However, it is worth noting that certain studios have a better feel or ambience to work in which is important in terms of 'a good working and creative environment'.

Checks when booking a studio:

- Natural daylight, which can be blacked out if required. Basement studios can be depressing.
- Size. This is important. Intimate working areas have a better feel than vast areas although space may be essential because of the size of your team.
- Comfortable, spacious and well-planned hair and make-up area. This certainly makes for easier preparation of models.
- Facilities to shampoo model's hair. Some studios have installed salon backwash units.
- Heating. Large cold studios are depressing to work in.
- Model changing facilities.
- Toilets. Some studios even have showers.
- Interesting interior design features such as large picture windows, pillars, wooden floors and beams can add interest to shoots even though they may be out of focus. White walls are more versatile.
- Catering facilities.
- Parking. Preferably on site. Having to dash out to feed meters is disruptive and inconvenient. Besides, you stand the risk of being fined!

■ on location

Organising a location shoot will require more detailed planning such as:

- Obtaining location permission to film in historic buildings, by monuments, parks or other public or commercial venues.
- Transport to the location for the team.
- Accommodation overnight or longer whilst on location.
- Location vehicle for hair, make-up and styling preparation.

The advantages of an on-location shoot is that for fashion looks they give added impact and dimension to the shoot and storyline.

The disadvantage in shooting outdoors is that lighting and weather cannot be controlled or predicted.

■ budgeting and cost control

It is important when preparing yearly salon budgets to allocate a sum to cover financing of photo sessions. Depending on your marketing policy, it is worth concentrating on two main photo sessions per year. For instance, spring/summer and autumn/winter collections.

When planning a photo session you need to be aware of what costs are involved. It is quite easy for costs to escalate so it is advisable to agree on individual fees and expenses in advance. Get a written breakdown for each person.

the photographer

Most professional photographers are booked through an agent. The following are typical 'items' you would be expected to pay for. Check out:

■ Photographer's fee. This is usually based on a daily rate and will vary according to experience, popularity and professional standing.

■ Agency fee. Most agents add an agency commission to the photographer's fee.

■ Studio hire for one day.

■ Equipment and lighting hire.

■ Film costs. They will relate to the type of film used; the number of rolls per model; how many different looks; whether you want colour, black and white or both.

■ Polaroid film costs. This, of course, will depend on whether the photographer uses Polaroid.

■ Processing costs. This will relate directly to type of film, how many rolls to produce, contact or negative sheets.

■ Background and prop hire.

■ Electricity and phone costs metered per studio.

■ Courier service to send film during a shoot to a photographic lab for processing.

the stylist

Similarly, stylists are booked through an agent. Expect to pay for:

■ The stylist's time called 'prep' in getting clothes, accessories and props together for the photo session.

■ The stylist's time on the shoot.

■ The stylist's time spent returning any borrowed items or goods.

■ Agency commission of about 20%.

the make-up artist

Base your costing on either a half or whole day rate. Most make-up artists are represented by an agent, who will quote fees plus agency supplement. This is usually 20%.

the model

As soon as you have selected the model(s) phone up their agency. Talk to their booker to place a booking. Agencies, depending on the model's availability for a particular day will give you either: First Provisional. This means that the model is definitely available, or Second Provisional. This means that the model is not definitely available to you and will be subject to cancellation of a first provisional held by another party.

All agency bookings will be subject to agreeing model rates, terms and conditions. Following agreement to the model's fee which is based on a half or whole day rate, and the type of work, you will be asked to complete and return an order of booking form. Model fees will vary greatly according to experience, exposure and status of the model. Do not forget that on top of the model fee agencies add on an agency supplement, usually about 20%.

Only confirm your model booking when you are sure the shoot will go ahead otherwise you may be liable for a cancellation fee.

If you are booking more than one model, plan to stagger their booking times, particularly if you are photographing them separately. Speak to the make-up artist, hairdresser and photographer to successfully co-ordinate hair and make-up preparation thus avoiding unnecessary waiting.

Please note that all services booked through agents will be liable for VAT.

food and drink

Many studios provide refreshment to suit your team's requirements. This usually includes constant coffee, tea and soft drinks throughout the day, a buffet style lunch including sandwiches and fresh fruit.

travel and parking

This may include taxis in getting your team to the studio. For daily location work you will need to cost in the fee to have a location vehicle plus driver.

loss of work for a salon-based hairdresser

If the photo session is conducted during normal working hours you need to consider loss of revenue for that member of staff being out of the salon, as well as their loss of commissable earnings. A weekend may be a good time to shoot. Avoid planning evening photo sessions when time and energy levels will not be on your side.

■ photography and art direction

The photographer will already have a good idea of the type of lighting and background to use from the initial meeting and briefing session. In the studio, lighting is the photographer's basic 'tool' to help create the mood of the pictures. By clever use of different combinations of lights, reflectors, the angle of the reflectors, and distance of the lights from the model, the photographer can define the model's bone structure, highlight or soften areas of the face, hair and other parts of the body.

The photographer will use different combinations of lights, filters, camera technique and types of film to create a mood or style. Shadows can be used to contrast the model against the background. It can be interesting to have certain areas in or out of focus or to create texture.

The majority of hair pictures are beauty shots, that is framing the model's head and shoulders in detail. It is important for both you and the make-up artist to be familiar with the type of lighting and communicate with the photographer before and during the shoot so that all the parties appreciate what techniques are going to produce the best results. Adapt them to suit the concept and the hairstyle.

backgrounds for beauty shots

It is important that the background is kept as simple as possible so that it does not distract from the hair. Highly patterned, fussy backgrounds should be avoided. Good backgrounds are white and grey. The right choice of background should be chosen to suit hair colour, texture and shape.

Plain backgrounds are good for bringing out skin tones.

backgrounds for conceptual shots

These can be designed to fit the theme of the shoot. In these shoots hair is part of the total image, therefore it is important that the hair relates to the background e.g. scenery, setting and props.

Often studios have interesting features such as wooden floors, pillars, venetian blinds, high beams, that make interesting backgrounds even out of focus. Lighting can be cleverly used to add drama.

■ pre-shoot briefing meeting

The success of the forthcoming photo session is going to depend on good communication, team work and team spirit between the individuals you have assembled. Ensure that everyone speaks the same language.

It is important and time well spent to arrange a brief meeting with the team a week prior to the shoot so that you can:

■ explain the concept/theme

■ listen to their ideas and suggestions

■ give everyone a chance to meet each other

■ firm up plans for the actual day

■ reconfirm shoot objectives – what you plan to do with the pictures

This will also give everyone time to prepare and organise:

■ hair accessories if necessary

■ clothes, jewellery, props, shoes

■ background and props

■ model selection

■ lighting, wind machine, etc.

7.3 the shoot

formula for success

Although pre-planning stages are crucial to the build-up to a photo session, in my experience it is often not until the shoot is underway that ideas flow releasing those sudden flashes of creativity and inspiration. This is the period when the best results are often produced.

✓ tips

- Punctuality is essential. Turning up late will not go down well
- A well-balanced team of personalities. No egos or prima donas
- A friendly team, good presence and total participation by everyone
- Collective team effort and positive team spirit
- Effective leadership on the shoot
- Passion and motivation
- Good communication between everyone
- Decor and interior design of the studio
- Comfortable studio temperature
- Easy working conditions
- Good music can help capture and create the right mood
- Healthy food and refreshments during the day goes down well
- Models not having to wait too long for hair or make-up preparation
- Keep the momentum of the shoot flowing constantly
- Exciting concept or theme
- Bags of creativity and innovation
- Strong clothes and accessories
- Good rapport and relationship between the photographer and model(s)
- Give the model confidence and encouragement
- Make the model feel relaxed
- Keep noise and distraction down during shooting
- Alert and observant team members once the model is in front of camera
- Capture the right moment on film
- Praise for team members

model preparation

If you have had previous briefing meetings and a hair rehearsal, you and the team should already have a clear idea of the type and order of looks you are aiming for. Allow about 1–1$\frac{1}{2}$ hours for make-up and a suitable time for hair preparation.

On more fashion styled shoots it is a good idea before any hair or make-up is done to get the model to try on the different outfits. This benefits everyone by firmly establishing clear visual images on how outfits should be styled, accessorised and in what sequence to be photographed. As clothes convey a certain mood and sense of occasion, it is essential that hair and make-up are complementary.

Before starting the model's hair and make-up ask the model to take off any garment of clothing that has to be pulled over the head. The reason is obvious. Similarly, ask the model to loosen or remove her bra to prevent strap marks showing on the shoulders in head and bare shoulder shots.

Depending on how many 'looks' you are going for, plan to co-ordinate the hair and make-up so that:

- make-up, particularly for beauty shots, looks fresh. Start with beauty shots and then proceed onto fashion shoots
- hair is taken through stages of complexity. For example, natural, soft curled look, gelled or hair down, hair up.

It is important that hair does not begin to look overworked, tired, messy or over-loaded with too many products.

It is much easier to take make-up from lighter to darker than the other way round.

In spite of the need for good planning, there still needs to be a degree of flexibility in everyone's approach, including an openness and compromise to sudden flashes of inspiration, which can only arise on the day.

hairstyling on a shoot

On the shoot, your ability or that of another hairdresser to style and transform hair into different looks will depend on how the material is treated. Obviously if a rehearsal was not possible the model's hair will be a new experience. For session hair-stylists this is usually the norm, unless they have worked with a particular model before.

Success will depend on the following qualities:
- ability to interpret a brief
- visualisation
- competence and technique
- product knowledge, selection and application
- creativity and innovation
- experience
- confidence
- composure under pressure
- quickness, but not at the expense of quality
- passion
- alertness once model is in front of camera and if necessary the need to step in quickly to ensure the model's hair constantly looks great

■ in front of camera ... points to watch

After the hair, make-up and styling is completed and a final check is made, the model is ready for photographing. It is now the turn of the photographer to successfully create and capture the imagery on film. Most photographers begin by taking Polaroids of the model on set.

Test Polaroids give an instant picture of the total imagery and are used to check lighting and composition before moving onto film. It is also important for the team to check the Polaroid to see if any minor adjustments need to be made to hair, make-up, clothes, accessories, the model's posture and expression.

Another technique is to ask the photographer to let you view the model through the camera.

Taking Polaroids constantly throughout a photo session can help to storyboard the shoot.

hair
- Overall shape and balance
- Over-complicated – too busy
- Over-worked hair
- Out of condition hair
- 'Cardboard hair'
- Incorrect drying technique
- Incorrect styling technique
- Choice of styling products
- Permanent hair colour looking 'too hard'
- Regrowth
- Perms looking too tight
- Incorrect use of styling products
- Flakes of gel deposits on hair
- Multi textures, i.e. frizz and curl
- Concentrating on one particular area
- Frizzy unstructured curl
- Ends of hair left unfinished
- Lack of direction and movement
- Unfinished hairlines
- Wispy fly-away strands of hair
- Crooked partings unless intentionally part of the style
- Scalp showing
- Fluffy textures
- Holes and gaps showing
- Untidy hair around ears
- Style collapsing
- Hair flicking out unintentionally
- Pins or grips showing, unless part of the look
- Untidy hair breaking on the model's shoulder
- Model's long hair appearing and hanging between her armpits

make-up
- Wrong choice of foundation, either too light or too dark
- Face and neck two tones
- Hands and face two tones
- Streaky foundation
- Shoulders and arms not made up to match the face
- Too much powder
- Eye make-up not blended
- Ears left unmade-up
- Blusher too heavy
- Eyebrows too bushy
- Hard lips
- Shine unless intentional
- Using pearl make-up
- Spots and blemishes noticeable
- Too heavy make-up
- Heavy bags and dark circles under eyes

styling
- Unflattering colours or proportions
- Pierced ears – no studs or earrings
- Earrings hanging badly
- Over-cluttered necklines
- Necklace not hanging right
- Shoulder straps crooked
- Necklines not even
- Necklines not draping well
- Over-accessorised
- Under-accessorised
- Collars not falling properly
- Hems hanging badly
- Buttons missing
- Threads
- Unsightly creases
- Garments that gape and which need pinning at the back
- Dust
- Clothes hanging badly
- Over-styled. Simple clothing may be best

photography
- Loss of hair texture – harsh lighting
- 'Dense', dull, flat hair
- Too harsh light bleaching out skin tones
- Wrong choice of backgrounds
- Harsh shadows
- Bags, wrinkles under eyes } can be bleached out
- Blemishes and spots } with clever lighting technique
- Wrong choice of film
- Poor modelling – expressions and attitude
- Clumsy model shapes such as:
  - awkward arms
  - hand and arms up around the face
  - propping up chin with whole hand – delicate finger better
  - resting the hand on the temple region 'headache look'
  - shoulder hunched up under the ear or chin. This makes it look extra large and also breaks up the line of the jaw
- Lack of contrast between model and background

7.4 fashion styling for make-overs

clothes that suit

After many years working as a session stylist on editorial features, lifestyle and reader make-overs, I have to say that on several occasions the total look was often let down by the clothes and accessories that the model wore. Whilst I appreciate the constraints, magazine features are all too often fashion or trend led as opposed to suitability led. For clothes to work they need to *relate* to the wearer. They need to look good in terms of:

- colour suitability
- shape and line suitability
- fabric compatibility
- fit and scale

In addition, the *style* of the clothes must complement the hair imagery. The converse is also true. Similarly, the *colour* of clothing needs to play a supporting role – and not dominate the image.

how to be a success

To be successful at fashion styling requires a wealth of knowledge. Knowledge about historical periods, sources of inspiration, trends from the catwalk and street, designer influences and designer connections, not to mention technical know-how about the design components of clothing. When it comes to practical fashion styling it is necessary to consider some basic styling principles and concepts to dress bodies in flattering ways.

With the increasing number of salons and individuals becoming more interested in photographic, show and promotional work, there is a need to develop fashion styling expertise in-house, or at least appreciate the knowledge and skills to communicate more effectively with a fashion stylist you engage. Competent fashion styling is essential as it provides the pivot or theme to develop your imagery.

This book has come a long way in the pursuit of helping you achieve this, starting with hair and make-up. The focus now shifts to other props needed to complete the picture and composition. These elements include the clothes, and the accessories. Let's start by first looking at the body.

the body

The so-called perfect figure exists only on the drawing board. The ideal body, as you know, is subject to social changes and fashion influences. Whilst professional models are invariably chosen for their near perfect bodies, particularly those that model lingerie and swimwear, 'real' people have bodies of all shapes and sizes. Body shapes are made up of various combinations of body lines, curves and angles. Bodies are not all ideally proportioned. Consequently bodies come with any combination of figure image problems. Most can be spotted by visually assessing the body. If in doubt ask the model. It is a misconception that a good figure is related to a model's height and weight – being curvy does not mean being fat. It is also possible for a model to be slim and still have a curvy body shape. Many overweight women have straight body silhouettes and even perfect proportions.

Like face, bodies can be classified according to shape. This relates to body structure and surrounding adipose tissue using such names as *wedge, pear, oval, round, hourglass* and *rectangular.*

Each figure type has certain physique characteristics and attributes that need to be maximised. Conversely each figure type has problems that need minimising. Think of it in terms of positives and negatives that require suitable 'style treatment' to enhance facial features, body shape, body proportions and add to the overall attractiveness and beauty. This can be achieved by considering the *design detail* of the clothes you use.

the clothes

For clothes to look good they need to flatter the model's figure and complement her natural colouring. An ill-fitting garment can draw attention to a figure problem. It can make a model look heavier, cause unflattering binding across the shoulders, chest, hips or ballooning of excess fabric in all the wrong places. The key to enhancing the model's figure is to know how to dress her in:

- colours that look good against her skin tones, and with her hair and eye colour
- clothes that complement her natural body shape

- clothes that visually balance her body proportions
- fabrics that complement her bone structure and drape well on her body
- clothes that are scaled to her overall size

You will need to consider each garment or outfit in terms of:

- exterior shape and silhouette
- interior applied details or style lines
- fabric
- colour

It is this design detail which, when correctly applied to the body, can create the illusion of style. The exterior shape or silhouette and interior detail or style lines affect the look of a garment because the eye tends to follow them. Singularly or collectively they can make a model appear taller, shorter, slimmer, fuller or even draw attention away from a figure image problem.

silhouette lines

These are formed in clothing by using *seams, darts, pleats, tucks, gathers, yokes, openings* or any construction technique which helps to control the shape of a fabric or how it hangs on the body. It is this stage which gives the garment its silhouettes.

style lines

Style lines within a garment or outfit are formed by the type of *neckline, collar, lapel, waistline, hemline, pockets, pleats, buttons, sleeves*, and other design decoration. The four basic style lines are horizontal, vertical, diagonal and curved. Each has the effect of drawing the eye in a particular direction. Naturally this can work in your favour or against you. It will depend on where the style lines are in relation to the model's body.

fabrics

There is much similarity between hair as a material and fabric. Both require what is often referred to as 'bespoke tailoring' to produce a quality end product. In terms of how much design it is the experience of the pattern 'cutter' and the right choice of cloth which play an important and collective part in giving a garment its essential shape or silhouette. Depending on how much fabric is used, garments can take on straight, soft or curvy shapes. Consequently when you source clothes or dress your model you should be aware of the visual and tactile properties of fabrics and their effect on the body. The properties you need to consider are *texture, drapability, weight, print* and *lustre*.

colour

Colour without doubt can make or break your model's total look. Not only do you need to appreciate the effect that certain colours have on her facial skin tones but you also need to consider how colour breaks on the body can affect body proportions.

For beauty shoots, the colours of clothes worn near to the face need to be carefully selected for colour suitability and colour harmony. The aim should be to select colours that complement her natural colouring and colour direction. Put another way, it will require you to appreciate the relationship between the colour properties of the clothing and the model's colour profile in terms of the degree of:

- warmth or coolness
- lightness or darkness
- brightness or softness
- contrast

accessories

Accessories are those key pieces worn as adornments or as ornaments that can change a person's look. They can add impact to a basic wardrobe outfit and give the wearer added style appeal. Accessories can alter the mood of your outfit and change it from day to evening wear. Clever accessorising can turn the versatile black dress into a classy number, although poor quality accessories and poor accessorising can be most damaging to a person's image. For this reason, accessories can make or break a total look.

Creative accessorising is an art and a skill. It requires artistry to know what is the best shape, colour and texture as well as how to mix materials and style pieces to create an element of reality, fantasy or a focal point. For example, earrings and glasses to draw attention to the face; necklaces to décolletage and hair ornamentation to the head and face. Selection and styling of jewellery on the face and body requires considering complementary shape and lines to flatter, and the shape, line and proportion of the face and neck. Likewise, the styling of hats and hair accessories must not only take into consideration style appropriateness but also style suitability and in particular, the most flattering shape and proportion to suit different face shapes and overall face and body symmetry and scale.

styling objectives

So much for the props with which you will complete a model's look. What about your objectives? This will depend on 'the image' you are trying to put together and, of course, the model's needs. Your overall aim is to create an image that has feeling, is creative, has impact and yet looks visually balanced. As a guideline consider the following objectives:

1 Styling the model in colours that complement her natural colouring

2 Dressing the model in garments or outfits with style lines that complement her natural body shape

3 Visually changing width and length proportions on the body to create a more pleasing body form

4 Ensuring that fabric is compatible for the model's bone structure

5 Using focal points to accent or divert attention to or away from a specific part of the body

6 Getting the scale of the clothes, accessories and jewellery right

To help you achieve these objectives, consider some basic styling principles and concepts which I am sure you are now familiar with – *line, proportion, balance, symmetry, repetition* and *scale*.

◼ style principles and concepts

In a fashion styling context you will need to apply these principles if you are to master the 'art of dressing illusions'.

line illusion

The four basic types of style lines are vertical, horizontal, diagonal and curved. Each can be used to create different illusions on the body. Style lines may be created shoulder detail, waistbands, hemlines, pleats, seams, rows of buttons, lapels and any other applied detail to a garment.

Vertical lines draw the eye up and down the body and create the illusion of height and slimness. Hence they can be used to make a model look taller and thinner.

Horizontal lines draw the eye across the body. They emphasise width and shortness.

◼ Use vertical lines on the parts of the body that you want to lengthen and narrow.

◼ Use horizontal lines on the parts of the body that you want to widen or shorten.

However, vertical lines can be widening if they are placed too far apart.

Study the following examples:

Model A.
Vertical style lines are created by:
◼ the jacket opening
◼ jacket buttons
◼ shirt panel
◼ shirt buttons
◼ skirt pleat
◼ skirt silhouette

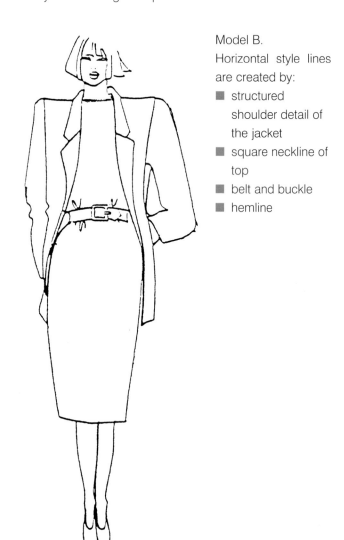

Model B.
Horizontal style lines are created by:
◼ structured shoulder detail of the jacket
◼ square neckline of top
◼ belt and buckle
◼ hemline

Converging lines are formed when diagonal lines come towards each other. Diverging lines spread apart.

■ Use converging lines on the parts of the body you want to look smaller and diverging lines on the part of the body you want to look wider.

■ When lines converge they focus attention towards the point where they meet.

Curved lines can make a figure look rounder and fuller. Slightly curved lines are more flattering on the body.

contrast illusion

All too often you see a person wear an outfit made up of two completely contrasting colours, with little or no real understanding of how they look and what it does for their figure. They are not aware of the illusions created by introducing contrasts of colour or colour breaks on their body. This is more pronounced the darker the colour. Very light colours, including white, will make a body appear larger, while dark colours, including black, have a slimming effect.

Study the following illustrations and see how you can use these illusions to enhance your model's figure.

▲ Contrast illusions

repetition

Repetition as the word suggests, involves the principle of repeating related *lines, angles, curves, textures* and *colours*, to create a harmonious effect. This will be of particular relevance as you decide on:

- the best shape or silhouette of outfits/garments to suit their contours
- fabrics that suit their body type
- the most suitable style detail
- colours that look best
- the shape, line and scale of jewellery
- the most compatible cut or style to suit their face shape

The answers focus on the need to create consistency and a visual experience that is pleasing to the eye by:

- repeating a person's body shape in the silhouette of an outfit or garment
- repeating the body line by choosing a garment with the same style lines, for example on straight bodies, straight lines; on curved bodies, curved lines
- matching fabric types to body type for example straight bodies, crisp, taut fabrics; curvy bodies, more fluid fabrics
- relating style detail of accessories such as earrings to 'lines in the face'
- relating style line and detail of a cut to that of the client's face, i.e. soft features to a soft style
- matching textures, for example smooth slightly textured fabric with sleek straight hair; a more highly textured fabric to complement curly, permed or frizzy hair

Style features:
- angular face shape
- geometric haircut
- angular buttons, jewellery, belt buckle
- straight style lines to complement body line
- smooth, crisp fabric

Style features:
- softer facial features
- unstructured style, softly curled
- rounded earrings and buttons
- unstructured jacket
- textured fabric of jacket and skirt

colour styling
fashion styling objective 1

'To style the model in colours that complement and are in harmony with her natural colouring'

The colour of clothes are critical for enhancing your model's attractiveness. The best colours are complementary to the model's natural colouring.

You are probably thinking this is very restricting. However, it is important to note that your model can wear almost every colour on the colour wheel as long as it is the best *hue, value, intensity* and *undertone* for her and particularly those colours worn closest to the face.

▼ The physical effects of colour need to be considered when styling.

Body size	Value	Hue	Intensity
To enlarge	High values Tints Light tones High contrast	Warm colours High intensity	Bright True colours
To reduce	Low values Dark tones Shades Little or no contrast	Cool colours	Dull Greyed colours Low intensity

In addition, it is also important to appreciate the 'power' of colour as a silent communicator of associated and symbolic messages.

When it comes to colour styling, the key isn't just about selecting colours to flatter, it's also knowing how to put together winning combinations.

The secret to creative colour co-ordination is to get your eye tuned into colour, so that you can create different colour themes, work with fashion colours and even break the rules.

Imagine you are an artist. You are given a palette made up of the following colour groups or families.

Your creativity will depend on your ability to work with colour.

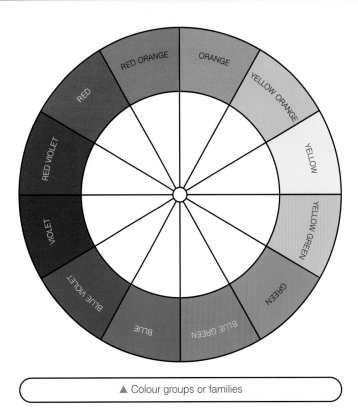

▲ Colour groups or families

assessing the model's colour profile

First you need to assess your model's colour profile and identify her colour direction.

The most widely known and used system for describing a person's colour direction is based on a seasonal classification. For example:

- A *'winter'* describes a person who is of overall cool and striking colouring. They look best wearing blue-based dramatic or vibrant colours. Winters need contrast.
- A *'summer'* describes a person who is of overall cool, light and soft colouring. They look best wearing blue-based medium to light more pastel colours in a soft contrast.
- An *'autumn'* describes a person who is of overall warm, rich and natural colouring. They look best wearing elegant, rich and natural colours with golden tones.
- A *'spring'* describes a person who is of overall warm, vibrant and more delicate colouring. They look best wearing colours that are delicate, medium to light and warm with an underlying gold tone. Springs often need contrast.

▼ Colour and words used to describe a colour or a person's colouring

Words	Colour\Colouring
Dramatic	Deep, vivid and bright, providing a sharp contrast
Pastel	Light and soft
Matt	Soft and muted
Rich	Deep, intense and strong
Elegant	Rich, deep, muted and have little contrast
Delicate	Light, bright and clear
Vibrant	Vivid, bright and clear

There is a tremendous variation of colours found within each season as illustrated below.

Each season is made up of certain colour patterns. These can be further described in terms of the six dominant tonal characteristics or colour directions – deep, light, bright, muted, warm and cool.

colour palettes

The following palettes represent a selection of colours that are compatible for each season and respective dominant colour direction.

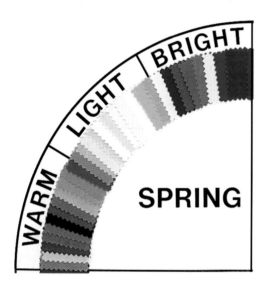

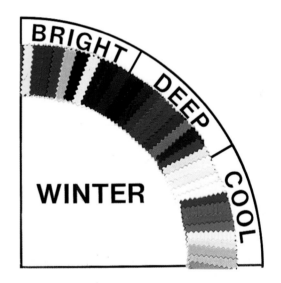

In order to help you co-ordinate colour successfully and put together exciting colour schemes, I have split the palettes into the following colour components:

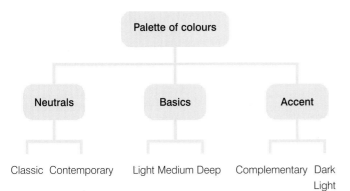

Palette of colours
- Neutrals
  - Classic Contemporary
- Basics
  - Light Medium Deep
- Accent
  - Complementary Dark Light

a palette's colour components

A typical palette is made up of the following colour components: neutral, basic and accent colours.

neutrals

Neutrals are colours that go with everything and form the back-bone to a scheme.

Classic neutrals include white, blacks, navies, greys, beiges and browns.

Contemporary neutrals are found by the mixing of three or more colours together, turning them into a nondescript colour. Colours include pine green, forest green, olive green, mauve and burgundy.

basics

Basics are colours based on a person's dominant or second-ary tonal characteristics including hues of light, medium and deeper values.

The *softer lighter basic tones* of red, red/yellow have a close relationship to a person's skin tone. Colours include *pinks*, *corals*, *apricots* and *peach* colours

The *medium to deeper basic tones* have more energy than neutrals and can play a supporting role to a model's natural colouring. Colours include *reds*, *blues* and *greens*.

accents or dramatics

Accent or accessory colours can be used to add drama, contrast or plain umpf to a model's look.

Dramatics can be used to add excitement and give tension. They are contrast colours relying on the principles of colour relationships to create cold–warm or warm–cold contrasts or light–dark or dark–light contrasts. The former effect is created by styling a combination around complementary or opposite colours on the colour wheel to those of a model's skin tone.

Skin, and to a lesser extent hair and eye colour, can be contrasted by first deciding on whether the client's skin tones are of the red, yellow-red or yellow type and then selecting its opposite. Blue, blue-green and green colours emphasise skin tones. Colours include *blue*, *periwinkle blue*, *blue green*, *teal*, *turquoise green* and *aquamarine*.

How far you go with creating a light–dark contrast will depend on the level of contrast your model exhibits.

colour co-ordinating

neutrals

Neutrals are colours that go with everything. In terms of colour styling neutrals are especially good for articles of clothing such as suits, trousers, jackets and coats as well as accessories such as shoes, hats, bags and hosiery.

working with neutrals

- try layering neutrals of the same colour family but of different intensity
- for a sharp look combine black and white together
- for a slightly softer look navy or grey looks good with white
- combine those softer shades such as soft ivory, oyster whites, beiges, tans and browns in varying combinations
- for a more creative feel combine a darker neutral with a lighter basic
- to make a neutral come alive add an accessory in a brighter accent colour

colour combinations

- for a one colour or monochromatic look, style your model in neutrals head to toe. It can give the illusion of height but introduce texture, detail and accessories as well to provide elegance
- combine a neutral with two *analogous* colours to form an interesting three-colour combination

basics

Basics are those family of colours that form a major part of a palette and can be used in interesting and varied ways as jackets, blouses, skirts, T-shirts, trousers, knitwear, dresses and lingerie.

working with basics

- combine one of the lighter basics with a darker neutral. This creates a softer effect than wearing white
- lighter basics or more skin tone colours can give a more delicate and feminine image
- the lighter basics such as ices, pinks, aquas, pastels have a softer, more gentle effect on the skin. These look good in combinations with neutrals or medium to deep basics depending on the model's level of contrast
- darker basics make great alternatives to neutrals, especially in suits and jackets, to give a more creative look, especially when co-ordinated with lighter basics
- the deeper basics such as deep purple, pine green, emerald green and dark reds, are excellent for sophisticated evening wear

colour combinations

- compose a *monochromatic* look by combining the same colour but in lighter and darker values
- compose an analogous colour combination using three closely related colours. If combining more than two basic colours, the colours will look best if they are the same intensity
- in a two-colour or more combination use the darker colour in a larger proportion and the brighter colour in much smaller amounts
- consider a three-colour or *triadic combination* using hues of the same value and intensity

accents or dramatics

Accents are those colours that can add a little drama to a neutral colour scheme. Similarly, they can be worn as an accessory colour to intensify a fashion look. Accent accessories can include a scarf, belt, handkerchief, glasses, a hair accessory or a piece of jewellery.

working with accents

- never over-do accent colour
- when styling a model wearing different coloured separates, top and bottom halves of the body, always introduce the same colour of the bottom into the upper half of the body as an accent
- accents are useful for creating focal points and grabbing attention
- contrast harmony is achieved by wearing a basic or neutral colour with a complementary colour in the ratio of 60:40
- a colour blend of accents worn as a blouse or scarf can add impact to a look

playing safe with colour

It is important to appreciate that there are some colours that exhibit *'in-between'* characteristics. They are classified as universal colours by virtue of the fact that they are neither warm nor cool. For this reason they are *'safe'* colours and can be worn successfully by everyone.

They are:

- turquoise
- coral pink
- greyed navy
- watermelon red
- medium violet
- periwinkle
- soft white
- medium true grey
- medium warm turquoise
- teal
- taupe
- buff

■ dressing your model
fashion styling objective 2

'To create a harmonious relationship between the model's body shape and the silhouette of a garment, outfit or combination of garments, by repeating the body's natural silhouette in the clothes worn'.

This is achieved by dressing the model in garments whose silhouettes are the same as their natural body shape or silhouette. This means that any combination of clothing pieces can be worn as long as the overall silhouette looks like a natural extension.

body shapes

inverted triangle
This body shape dictates the need to maintain the balance between broad straight shoulders and a narrower bottom half. This can be achieved by wearing garment bottoms that are narrower than those worn on the top half of the body.

rectangle
This body shape dictates the need to wear clothes with a sufficiently structured and straight shoulder line that ensures the shoulders do not extend beyond the hips, nor do skirts taper or flare.

The vertical line must be also maintained by straight vertical side seams or a continuous shoulder to hem line.

Vertical style lines within the garment will enhance the look.

triangle
This body shape dictates the need to ensure that the garment worn on the lower half of the body is wider or fuller than that worn on the top so as to maintain the body's narrower shoulders.

oval/rounded
This body shape dictates the need to wear longer loose fitting jackets, dresses or tops that have side seams that follow the curved line of the wide waist. The line of these tops will be better in a simpler unstructured garment from the shoulder. Use rounded shoulder pads if necessary to balance top and bottom halves.

hour glass
This body shape dictates that the well-defined waist is maintained by wearing outfits that emphasise this area, combined with straight or square shoulder line and flares over the hips.

figure eight
This body shape dictates the need to emphasise the waistline supported by curved shoulders and hips, finishing in a tapered hemline.

fashion styling objective 3

'To visually change width or length proportions on the body in order to create a more pleasing body form'.

This will require you to effectively change a model's natural silhouette by visually creating an entirely new fashion form using techniques to rebalance width proportions on their body. This may mean narrowing or widening the shoulders, waist or hips, by using appropriate line treatment.

'To visually rebalance a particular body length using clothing and the most appropriate style line or colour combination to optically lengthen or shorten, thereby creating flattering and pleasing proportions'.

The illusion of proportions can be created by positioning horizontal style lines that are incorporated within different garment designs at different positions along the body or by using colour illusions to create proportional contrast. Naturally how this is done and where to place a 'horizontal line' will depend on the model's needs and the type of garment or garments that are to be worn.

Another fashion styling technique we shall adopt is based on the concept of aesthetic proportions to create enough difference for interest but not so much variation that it creates imbalance.

It works on the principle that it is more pleasing to the eye to create unequal proportions on the body such as one-third, two-thirds or three-fifths than to divide the body equally in two.

'To achieve either a 2:3 or 3:5 proportional relationship when choosing the best style lengths for your model to wear'.

These fashion styling ratios provide the basis of making any top and bottom combination work for each client's unique length proportions and associated figure problems.

The following sketches are based on the 'proportional model' in which the total length proportions of an ideally balanced body is equal to eight head lengths and that the ratio between:

- ■ top of head to waist and waist to floor is 3:5
- ■ chin to waist and waist to knee is 2:3
- ■ chin to waist and waist to floor is 2:5

The ratio of 3:5:8 known as the Golden Mean creates eye-pleasing proportions. The Golden Mean works on the principle that proportion is most pleasing when all areas of a design are not exactly the same, but when there is an eye-satisfying relationship between the unequal parts.

Garment parts of little or no difference create little interest as do very unequal proportions. Gentle unequal proportions create interest and pleasing looks.

The following diagram illustrates this.

Model A   The jacket and skirt are of equal proportions and cut the body in half.

Model B   The short jacket to the waist and skirt to the knee form an interesting 2:3 ratio.

Model C   A pleasing ratio of 3:5 is created through colour co-ordinating the hosiery, skirt, top and hair.

mapping figure image problems

vertical line treatment

- short neck
- dominant shoulders
- full or low bust
- heavy arms
- short waist
- wide waist
- wide hips
- protruding abdomen
- protruding bottom
- large thighs
- large calves
- short legs

horizontal line treatment

- long neck
- round sloping shoulders
- small bust
- thin arms
- long waisted
- flat bottom
- thin legs

fashion styling objective 4

'To consider fabric compatibility'

The draping properties of a fabric will affect how good your model's figure looks.

Crisper fabrics, those that are more lightly woven, fall in straight lines and can make a figure look bulky and add extra volume.

Loosely woven fabrics, those that fall into soft folds and known for their soft draping properties, can be less rewarding for a fuller figure.

Texture of fabric not only adds softness to the line of a garment but it also adds volume or bulk. Therefore care must be taken to ensure that too much texture does not create excessive volume to those parts of the model's body that need to be minimised. Consequently, heavy tweeds, knits, wide corduroy, quilted fabrics and velvets can make a fuller figure appear larger. Fabrics such as fine jersey knits or lycra which cling to body contours reveal every curve and bump.

Aim to create a better visual balance between the model's upper and lower body by varying the amount of volume.

Consider the surface quality of the fabric. For instance, compare the difference between matt and shiny fabrics. The latter reflect even the most minor figure curve. This has to do with the way that light is reflected more effectively from a smooth surface. Shiny fabrics like satin, taffeta, brocade, sequins or metallics add width.

When deciding on *print suitability* it is important to take into consideration:

- the space between the shapes. It is the space that makes the difference to how a model's figure is flattered. The greater the space the bigger the body appears
- the size of print to complement the model's bone structure
- that the print balances with the line of the garment

☑ tips

- Prints can be mixed successfully if they are colour co-ordinated
- The stronger the model's colouring the bolder the print
- Only place prints on the parts the body you wish to draw attention to.

---

fashion styling objective 5

'To use focal points to accent or divert attention to or away from a specific part of the body'

If I used a luminous highlighter pen on the heading it would draw attention to it. Similarly on the body, it is possible to highlight a viewer's attention to a specific spot. Conversely, a focal point can also be used to shift attention away from a non-flattering region of the body.

This can be achieved by skilfully using colour, shape, line, repetition, texture, print or accessories to capture attention or act as a diversion mechanism. Focal points can also be created using jewellery, belts, scarves, shawls, buttons, draping or other design detail on a garment. They can also be used to add interest.

☑ tips

- Straighter body
  - Little or no texture. Use volume if necessary to balance figure proportions.

- Softly curved body
  - Consider softly woven fabrics that fall into soft to straight lines without creating too much fullness in the wrong places.

- Curvey or fuller figure
  - Looks better in soft, flat fabrics.

▲ texture tips

■ the illusions of style

The visuals on the following pages illustrate this point. Observe how the focus of attention is subtly shifted even on the same outfit.

▲ Colour

- Different colours in tops, buttons and belts present a fluid movement of the eye.
- Colours add visual impact.

▲ Line

- Vertical lines draw the eye up and down and make a body look taller and thinner.
- Horizontal lines pull the eye from side to side and make the body look wider.

▲ Shape

- The cut or line of a garment should balance with the natural body line.

▲ Repetition

- Repetition creates a harmonious effect and a visual experience that is pleasing to the eye.

▲ Texture

- Texture adds softness to the line of the garment.
- Texture also adds volume.
- Texture can be used to create visual interest.

▲ Print

- Prints can be used to draw attention.
- Prints can be worn to emphasise figure assets.

fashion styling objective 6

'To get the scale of clothes, accessories and jewellery right'

How many times have you looked at fashion photographs and thought how much bigger the person appears in comparison to their true size, while in others how elegant and slim they seem even though they may be on the larger size.

This has as much to do with the way garments are sized as it has to do with scaling.

Refer back to the earlier section in Part 2, Section 2.3 and refresh your memory on the principles relating to 'the perception of scale' to appreciate how one object appears in proportion to another. This principle can be used to minimise body size and body features by surrounding a feature with more space to optically change its size or surrounding a feature with a larger item to optically diminish its size.

The trick is to choose garments or accessories that satisfy the following criteria: scale, proportion and fit.

As a general guide height is also an important factor in determining the scale of clothes.

For women, height can be broken down into:

- short – 5'3" or under
- medium – 5'4"–5'5"
- tall – 5'6" or over

Short requires small-scale designs, medium requires average scale designs and tall requires over-scaled designs.

However, it would be more precise to say that people need clothes 'proportioned in their scale'.

Many a small person has made the mistake of buying a dress that is too big for them and opted to have it altered without realising the effect this has on the remaining dress proportions. To look truly elegant and flattering the total dress would need to be scaled down.

Equally a taller person who needs to look for a larger or over-scaled garment must consider its total proportions to balance with, say, her larger torso, larger legs and arms or wider shoulders.

Measuring the wrist will give you a fairly accurate indication of the right scale of clothes and accessories for the model's body frame.

Wrist measurement	Frame classification
Less than 5½" (14cm)	small
5½–6" (14–15cm)	medium
greater than 6" (15cm)	large

Use the same principle to appreciate the correct scale of your hairstyle to complement their face and head size.

If they have a small face, a very full large hairstyle will make their face look even smaller. Equally, for a person with a large body a very short compact style would make them appear even larger.

This also applies to the size of facial jewellery such as earrings and glasses, paying careful attention to ensuring that they are neither too small nor too big for the face.

8 it's a wrap

This final section contains a portfolio of photographic images showing the looks, concepts and themes created by artists drawn from the world of hair and make-up, together with their views on some challenging questions.

working with fashion

gallery of images

insight … tips from contributing artists

twenty ways to improve your creativity, artistry and
  imagery

final words

working with fashion

This book has come a long way in the pursuit of composing and creating some aspect of a client or model's total look. How accomplished you are will largely depend on changing attitudes and habits, increasing confidence and style awareness. Everyone has the potential. However, it is often knowing what aesthetically suits your client best; how to creatively adapt beauty and fashion trends and how to successfully integrate the elements of style – colour, make-up, hair, accessories and clothes – within your compositions.

Take for instance clothes. They should reflect the client's personality and mood, be appropriate but most essentially flatter the figure. Colour of clothes needs to play a supporting role and complement natural colouring. As with all the most stylish modes of dressing it can be the accessories that can make or break the effect – none more so than hair. Stylish hair is a must. The key qualities being condition, cut, colour and finish.

If hair is your forte clients need enlightening on how to get the best out of this very versatile material. Show them how to customise their look by integrating a suitable hair accessory particularly for a special occasion. There's plenty of scope from the wide range of hair accessories on the market.

To add the finishing touches, well applied make-up can provide the icing on the cake. Although many clients may shy away from make-up, being able to advise them on product selection and application is an extra skill for you and provides an extra service for clients.

Clients seek your services with one thing in common, they want to feel good, look their very best and be fashionable. As advisors, designers and artists you need to understand and work with fashion to create your imagery. The secret to successful creations lies in your ability to interpret it.

Fashion very much reflects current trends. Trends that often start on the street; in the clubs, in haute couture houses as collections; on the catwalks around the world and fashions that eventually find their way into the shops, boutiques and even salons in some diluted form.

Fashion has the habit of repeating itself. Areas of the body emphasised one year, are hidden and forgotten the next. The same goes for beauty, one season it may be the eyes that are dominant, the next season it may be the lips.

Fashion draws on the past. Trends evolve from trends that went before. From ethnic, religion and historic influences as well as influences drawn from past and present role models, from film stars of stage and screen to music and catwalk idols of today. Sometimes these trends achieve popularity with the masses, other times they fade into the archives perhaps never to be seen again or to re-emerge revamped in another form. The fashion calendar falls into two main seasons: spring/summer and autumn/winter. The fashion calendar year is made up of designer ready-to-wear collections, fashion fairs and trade shows.

Fashion is about change that follows seasonal cycles and couture collections in the major fashion capitals: Paris, Milan, London and New York. The couture collections are the closest thing to Mecca in the fashion world. Everyone who is anyone connected with the industry, including buyers and press, makes this pilgrimage. They are the platform for new and established talents. They are the conclusion to months and months of designing, planning and producing, when designers let the world know what they have been up to; what are the latest silhouettes, proportions, colours, textures and prints. But while all eyes are on the fashion houses, they are also on the models that grace the catwalks, with their own sense of individual style. However, let us not forget the immense contribution the celebrated session hairstylists and make-up artists give to the collections. The collections for them are also a time of inspiration and innovation, as they twist, coil, curl, dress and accessorise hair into creations to complement the particular fashion theme or paint faces in new colourways. The collections are a time of energy, adrenaline, creativity, excitement and artistry. They are a rich source of visual imagery, none more so than the stunning images served up by John Galliano of Dior and Alexander McQueen of Givenchy. These two British designers have taken Paris and the fashion world by storm. They have taken fashion and given us pure theatre on the catwalks. The message is that fashion is exciting and fun. It gives all a means to express individuality. It allows designers the platform to mix imagination, ingenuity, technique and artistry. The buzz word in fashion in the nineties is individuality. Who knows what it will be next year or in years to come. However, what we do know about fashion is there will always be another day and a new twist, a new look, a new theme and a gallery of images to choose from.

gallery of images

It is with a gallery of images that I end this journey. The gallery contains images composed and created by individuals drawn from the world of hair and make-up, who I believe see the head, face and body as their vehicle for artistic licence and artistic expression. For them the head, face and body is their canvas and hair, make-up, clothes and accessories their art medium.

Let us not forget the artistry of the photographer who without them these images would not be possible.

Visit the gallery and explore how each have stretched their creativity and talents to new limits.

As you cast your eyes over each image absorb how each artist has worked magic and moulded hair into a particular form. Observe how line, shape, texture and colour interplay. Take note of the make-up and fashion styling and in particular how each model has been 'decorated and adorned'.

millennium girl

[Sanrizz]

Hair and make-up will
be the strongest
accessories for the
Millennium Girl, along
with bold jewellery.
Fashion will be
minimalistic

Hair: Ozzie Rizzo
Colour: Graham Holmes
Photography: Ozzie Rizzo

award collection

[Guy Kremer]

Contemporary reworking
of decadence with a
touch of romance. The
key elements of the
collection are curls,
volume, accessories and
femininity

Hair: Guy Kremer

sophisticate

[Ishoka]

Contemporary,
commercial classics
formed by working with
both natural and
chemically treated
afro hair

Hair: Kathryn Longmuir
Make-up: Karen Lockyer and
Cheryl Pelps Gardner
Clothes: Peta Hunt
Photography: Nick Cole

the collection blue

[Cheynes]

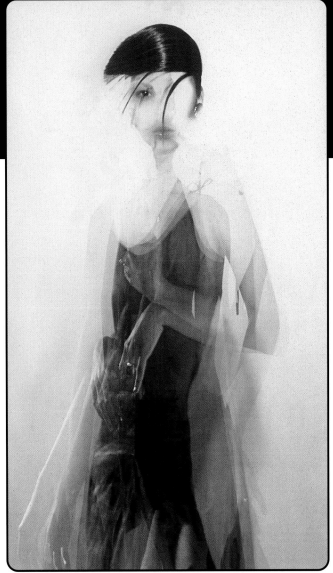

Edinburgh street life and
a Café Bar called Blue
provided the inspiration
for these simplistic,
stylish and chic looks
that harmonise
sleekness, shiny
definition with a cut
against gravity

Hair: Jennifer Cheyne

urban couture

[D & J Ambrose]

The Urban Couture
Collection is Modern with
a capital M. It's high
fashion … high tech hair
that's living, breathing
and very now for those
movers and shakers that
want to be ahead of time

Hair: Daren Ambrose
Make-up: Jane Wilson
Styling: Laura Platman
Photography: Ronny Eshel

the mondrian collection

[Klownz]

Inspired by the artist, Mondrian, the emphasis
is on classic, uncomplicated and commercial
hair with a contemporary twist

Hair: Derek Preston
Make-up: Christina
Clothes: Cannon
Photography: Hiedi Niemala

the mondrian collection

[continued]

dolly mixtures

[Staffords]

An assortment of
fun, frivolous and
fashionable images

Hair: Mark Smith
Make-up: Sarah Riley
Styling: Sarah Yapp
Photography: Dean Chalky

grown up grunge

[The natural hair company]

Grunge and a new
generation

Hair: Martine Finnegan
Make-up: Pascal Marin
Fashion styling: Rachel Fanconi
Photography: Simon Bottomley

the paris collection

[Andrew Jose]

The Paris Collection is a photographic collection of styles inspired by the work of Grace Jones and the concept artist Jean Paul Goude. Strong lines, contours, light and dark are essential characteristics of the collection

Hair: Andrew Jose
Photography: Tim Brett Day

spring/summer collection

[Vidal Sassoon]

Inspired by the organic form and functionality of liberated architects, interior designers and the shapes of everyday objects the collection represents a refreshing interpretation of design 'classics' to set the mood for the millennium. The overall feel is precision and versatile hair. Colour adds an essential dimension

Hair: Tim Hartley and Mark Hayes
Make-up: Leslie Chilkes
Colour: Annie Humpries
Photography: Christian Hartman

avant garde collection

[Mark Hill]

Inspired by images of aliens and tribal warriors this fantasy collection fuses together the elements earth, air, fire and water to produce an extravagance of beauty

Hair: Mark Hill
Make-up: Suzy Kennett
Photography: Malcolm Willison

spirit of adventure

[Ian Mistlin]

Sea, sun and sand
provided the perfect
backdrop for a beautiful
body, hair and make-up

Hair and make-up: Ian Mistlin
Photography: Jim Wilson
(Courtesy of Lambs Navy Rum)

metamorphosis

[Ian Mistlin]

A collection of conceptual
images inspired by the book
Gulliver's Travels and tree
nymph folklore

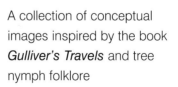

Hair and styling: Ian Mistlin
Photography: Dave Antony

white at night collection

[Ian Mistlin]

These images evolved through my
bridal work and desire to compose
and create a dramatic style
statement. The essential features
of the collection are sculptural
shapes, strong lines and high
contrast

Hair, make-up and styling: Ian Mistlin
Photography: Amanda Jobson

insight ... tips from contributing artists

I would like to thank all the contributing artists for supplying me with such inspiring imagery and in addition for sharing their views, advice and tips in response to the following challenging questions:

■ question 1

What advice would you give to those hairdressers who want to develop their photographic imagery?

❝'Always have everything planned out before going into a studio.' **Ozzie Rizzo, Sanrizz**

'Make sure all elements of the photographic shoot are coherent. Keep it simple and remember that less is often more.' **Guy Kremer**

'Get to know a local photographer and experiment on images or have a go at the photography yourself.' **Kathryn Longmuir, Ishoka**

'Plan in advance what you want to achieve and use the pictures for. Work with the best professionals you can afford, i.e., models, make-up artists and photographers.' **Jennifer Cheyne**

'Keep in control.' **Daren Ambrose**

'Seek advice from designers on colour and textile predictions. Never try and duplicate or adapt an image that you have seen before.' **Derek Preston, Klownz**

'Find a good photographer and develop a relationship through sharing of views and ideas.' **Mark Smith, Staffords**

'Study what is going on around you. Stay committed. It can be a very hard and dedicated journey to develop "your edge". Gather the best team you can afford and grow your vision together.' **Mark Hill**

'Think about the image you want to project . . . how you can achieve this within your budget . . . where you can place them and why you are doing them.' **Martine Finnegan, The Natural Hair Company**

'Get eye contact . . . get the best that you can afford in everything.' **Anon**

'Research ideas and experiment with photographers using different lighting etc.' **Anon** ❞

■ question 2

What makes a photographic image a winner?

❝'Good hair . . . make-up . . . photography . . . concept and a great model.' **Ozzie Rizzo, Sanrizz**

'A coherent theme, a well-balanced picture and a clear mood. Don't go too extreme – a timeless image works year after year.' **Guy Kremer**

'Research the theme of the images as much as possible before the shoot. Practise hair looks to perfection.' **Kathryn Longmuir, Ishoka**

'There is no one single element. It must be very tasteful and make a statement.' **Jennifer Cheyne**

'Producing an innovative yet individual feel.' **Daren Ambrose**

'A shape and image that shows creativity. It's a marriage of clothes, make-up and obviously hair. It has to be your own fresh and original ideas.' **Derek Preston, Klownz**

'Lots of hard work, preparation, good styling and a good make-up artist. On the question of photography, it is an art form and like art it is in the eye of the beholder. If you like a photo . . . then it's a winner.'   **Mark Smith, Staffords**

'When everything works in tandem with other looks that have consumer value and appeal.'   **Mark Hill**

'Working closely with your team from the initial casting onwards on developing your theme and ideas.'
Martine Finnegan

'Taste comes into it but the more professionals you surround yourself with, and in particular good models, the stronger the image.'   **Anon** 99

question 3

What tips can you give to those hairdressers who wish to develop their creativity and artistry?

66 'Initially through training and then lots of practice to develop your skills and eye.'   **Ozzie Rizzo, Sanrizz**

'Follow what is happening in the fashion world in design, art, theatre, even politics. Let yourself be inspired. Do not be afraid of experimenting.'   **Guy Kremer**

'To be aware of what is happening in the world of fashion and hair. Experiment with ideas and evolve them.'
Kathryn Longmuir, Ishoka

'Passion, awareness and experimentation. Never give up.'   **Jennifer Cheyne**

'Don't suppress yourself . . . break the rules.'
Daren Ambrose

'Encourage your staff to create story boards for each season, through sourcing forthcoming fashions, colour trends and predictions.'   **Derek Preston, Klownz**

'Learn from your peers. Go to shows, seminars and courses. Read fashion magazines. Push the boat out and take chances on haircuts. Believe progress is everything and is only achieved when rules are broken.'
Mark Smith, Staffords

'It is imperative that you learn all the basics first – then you learn how to break the rules implementing your own artistic licence. Take advantage of the many hair shows. The ultimate training would be to shadow your hero for a day.'
Mark Hill

'Listen to the experts. Speak to other hairdressers or your manufacturer. Get a PR in the industry that has a myriad of contacts.'   **Martine Finnegan**

'Listen to everyone. Observe all you can. Make your own choices.'   **Anon**

'Attend as many seminars and shows as you can to see what is being done on the circuit, then practise and experiment in your own time using different techniques and products.'   **Anon** 99

question 4

From what sources do you get your inspiration?

66 'Looking through magazines and of course having a beautiful model.'   **Ozzie Rizzo, Sanrizz**

'I find inspiration everywhere, but mainly from fashion designer shows, street people, art, including photography, film and theatre, fabrics, drapes and textures. I also find Italian Vogue a great inspiration and very much an indicator of what is coming into fashion.'   **Guy Kremer**

'Magazines, media and other hairdressers.'
Kathryn Longmuir, Ishoka

'Many different sources, including fashion designers, magazines and speaking to people.'   **Jennifer Cheyne**

'Music and architecture surrounding me always inspire, but fundamentally creativity comes from within.'
Daren Ambrose

'Life'. **Derek Preston**

'An inspiration can come from anywhere. It can come from clubs, magazines, the catwalk, from an old film. Always keep an open mind. Go with your instincts.'
Mark Smith, Staffords

You have to try and think ahead and think what can I do next. I use my library of books as a resource when I am thinking of a new collection.' **Mark Hill**

'From magazines . . . mostly international consumer titles. Endless sources from natural shapes, i.e., tidal movement.' **Martine Finnegan, The Natural Hair Company**

'Everything and anything.'   **Anon**

'Magazines, mainly fashion. Also peers in the industry.'
Anon 99

question 5

How do you stay motivated?

66 'Being in tune with the fashion world. Talking and sharing ideas with your staff. Teamwork is one way to stay motivated.' **Ozzie Rizzo, Sanrizz**

'I surround myself with innovative young people to keep in touch with what's hot on the street. I'm always striving for perfection and excellence, seeking new ideas from my environment. But most of all, I am always prepared to learn.' **Guy Kremer**

'Keeping in touch with what is happening and attending as many events as possible, such as seminars. Always looking for new direction.' **Kathryn Longmuir, Ishoka**

'People motivate me and I am surrounded by them nearly all the time.' **Jennifer Cheyne**

'Always giving 100%, and hoping to get it back. This motivates me.' **Daren Ambrose**

'By always wanting to better myself. You are constantly learning whether it be from adults or children. Age is irrelevant.' **Derek Preston, Klownz**

'Where I work there is such a love for our industry that I cannot help be motivated. Surround yourself with like minded people. It helps to be in a salon where the enthusiasm and motivation is the same or greater than yours. Strive to be better than your colleagues.'
Mark Smith, Staffords

'I love educating and enjoy seeing my team develop their skills. It excites and motivates me to see my team motivated and being involved with a new team of people in shows and seminars.' **Mark Hill**

'My team ensures that I stay motivated. My team inspire me constantly, whether in our weekly artistic team meetings or by just watching their clients leave the salon.'
Martine Finnegan, The Natural Hair Company

'Constant and never-ending improvement.' **Anon**

'We attend seminars to see what is being done and to reassure ourselves that we are on the right track with fashion.' **Anon** 99

twenty ways to improve your creativity, artistry and imagery

1 Ensure you have a strong technical foundation and understanding of cutting, styling, dressing, colouring, perming and make-up application

2 Work on constantly improving your foundation skills

3 Keep in touch and take refresher courses

4 Be willing to learn from others

5 Practise, practise, practise: practise makes perfect

6 Have patience. It will come eventually

7 Have perseverance. Don't give up too easily. Stick at it

8 Recognise and rid yourself of cultural and emotional blocks

9 Work on developing your confidence. That means believing in yourself and your abilities

10 Explore. Seek and you will find

11 Experiment. Be willing to try new ideas

12 Suspend judgement. Don't kill off an idea too soon. It may well work if you persevere

13 You may need to put principles aside and break the rules in order to discover new ways, new concepts, and new looks

14 Do not follow the crowd. Put your own stamp of individualism into what you do

15 Stand back and appraise your performance

16 Set your own standards of perfection

17 Learn to communicate your ideas

18 Set yourself challenges and goals

19 Broaden your interests into complementary areas such as the arts, fashion, media, music and photography

20 Keep yourself physically fit

Have fun

final words

The book carries the following important messages:

- It is never too late to change and seek personal and career development

- Unlocking potential is the key to personal and business growth

- Providing training and development opportunities in the workplace is a must

- Encouraging a learning culture is essential

- Learning is central to sustaining competitive advantage in the marketplace

- In changing times we need to look at curricula across a wide range of aesthetic disciplines

- National Vocational Standards are but a stepping stone

- Learning processes must be designed so as to develop technical understanding, technique and artistry

- Management must encourage creativity not stifle or suppress it

- Every customer or client must be treated as an entity not a commodity; that age, lifestyle and personality must be part of their personal style equation

- As advisors and designers in whichever capacity it is wrong to consider any one area or feature of the head, face or body in isolation. Instead it is important to appreciate the total look and to understand how the different elements of style can be integrated successfully

- Customers or clients do not want to be cloned or positioned in neat restricting categories

- As advisors and designers it is impossible to instil confidence in customers or clients unless you are confident in your ability

- There are no short cuts to being successful. Success will require determination, dedication and continuous improvement

- As advisers, designers and creators you need constant creativity and innovation

Index